Revolutionary QuickTime Pro

Bradley Ford
Andy Grogan
Frank Lowney
Manuel Minut
Jonathan Puckey
Barb Roeder
Jurgen Schaub
Francesco Schiavon

friendsof

DESIGNER TO DESIGNER™

Revolutionary QuickTime Pro

First published March 2002

Trademark Acknowledgments

friends of ED has endeavored to provide trademark information about all the companies and products mentioned in this book by the appropriate use of capitals. However, friends of ED cannot guarantee the accuracy of this information.

Published by friends of ED
30-32 Lincoln Road, Olton, Birmingham. B27 6PA. UK.

Printed in USA

ISBN: 1-903450-52-7

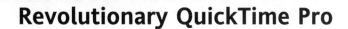

Revolutionary QuickTime Pro

Credits

Authors
Bradley Ford
Andy Grogan
Frank Lowney
Manuel Minut
Jonathan Puckey
Barb Roeder
Jurgen Schaub
Francesco Schiavon

Additional Material
Bert Moss
Alex White

Technical Reviewers
Gabrielle Smith
George Birbilis
Francesco Schiavon
Alex White

Indexer
Fiona Murray

Proof Reader
Jason Cuthbert

CD Creation
Corné van Dooren

Commissioning Editor
Lumbotharan Thevathasan

Lead Editor
Jon Bounds

Editors
Phill Jackson
Victoria Blackburn

Author Agent
Chris Matterface

Project Manager
Jenni Harvey

Graphic Editors
Chantal Hepworth
Deb Murray

Cover Design
Deb Murray

Managing Editor
Sonia Mullineux

Frank Lowney

Dr. Frank Lowney is currently Director of Electronic Instructional Services as well as Professor of Educational Foundations in the School of Education at Georgia College & State University. He resides in Gray, Georgia where he and his wife Olga pursue a variety of interests including antiques, gardening, computer graphics and multimedia.

Frank and his staff work with faculty, staff and students as well as external agencies to develop, maintain and find ever more innovative uses for a room full of computers dedicated to the production and deployment of both standard and experimental educational applications.

Bradley Ford

Bradley Ford is a professional guitarist with a Master of Music from Yale University. He has pushed, poked, prodded, and otherwise tortured QuickTime for the better part of four years as a teacher, technical writer, interactive media developer, and programmer. While passionate about his music, Brad has come to appreciate the value of not starving, and will soon join Apple's QuickTime engineering team. Brad wishes to thank his wife, Martha, and his little guy, Milo, for not strangling him mid-keystroke as he muttered endlessly, "Deadline...must...keep...typing..."

Andy Grogan   www.netgate.co.uk

Born in England, Andy Grogan was trained in graphic design in Amsterdam and took to computers because typesetting in lead "took too long". He now works as a freelancer for various companies as a designer and illustrator, and publishes his travel CDs through his own company, Netgate Publishing Ltd. He has travelled extensively making QTVR panoramas and has recently returned from a QTVR tour of Cuba. Check out his work at www.netgate.co.uk.

Francesco Schiavon

Tall? Nah. Joyful? Oftentimes. Love for QuickTime? Oh, yes! This guy teaches interactive production at VFS where his focus is on anything that has to do with QuickTime. He was nominated as "Educator of the year" by the Canadian New Media Awards 2000.

Apart from teaching full time at VFS, Francesco can be found as a speaker in a number of conferences and a ton of mailing lists all pretending to interactive media and QuickTime. The little time Francesco has available, he spends it offering consulting for companies like Apple Computer, Totally Hip Software, Blastradius, etc.

Barb Roeder   www.barb-wired.net

Barb Roeder is the founder of BarbWired LLC, a technology consulting firm serving the creative professional community. She translates the technical jargon of digital media creation into real world solutions for her clients, who range from video producers to streaming media start-ups, distance learning companies to technology developers. Research of new technologies and training in video compression and delivery methods is her forte. Connect with her at www.barb-wired.net.

Jonathan Puckey

Jonathan Puckey lives in Amsterdam, The Netherlands. He works as an interaction designer at Amsterdam based Capcave, doing interactive video and design work for clients such as U2.com, Lucent Technologies and The Dutch National Lottery.

When not working on commercial projects, he spends his time experimenting on sites such as Quicktimers.com and Paraphonic.com. His personal work mainly focuses on ways of expanding the possibilities of audio and video through user interaction.

Jurgen Schaub

Rescued from the wilds of Africa as a boy, Jurgen travelled the world with his pet lemur before settling in Vancouver, where this second heir to the throne of Leicester spends his time teaching tuna to hula and figuring out how to get his carpet to import a QuickTime file properly.

Sometime before the carpet thing, he co-founded BOPJET, the first consumer-accessible QuickTime Streaming provider (now a part of digital.forest). This is his first attempt at something like non-fiction. Chapter 10 is mostly his fault.

Bad Batz Maru props to Hil, Grats, Alex, Nick Martin, j.mo, sko, and the Weezer.

Manuel Minut

digital content creator

When first started editing he thought it was cool, then he discovered non-linear editing and found it mind-blowing. He likes to edit on fast-paced music, "playing with the beat and images". After more than 20 music videos, on-air promos, a series of five small documentaries for the BBC, next step he took was into interactive media. He joined CreativeCOW's Team as a forum leader. He is trying to implement a new concept, urban design into two new projects: gitanmedia.com and digitallmedia.com.

Contact: manuelminut@yahoo.com

Dedicated to my parents, my girlfriend Roxana and my friends.

Revolutionary QuickTime Pro

Table of Contents

8   Creating Images for QuickTime Virtual Reality   177

Table of Contents

I Introduction

"Hey, wanna be in movies?" Whether you want to send a home movie of your pet cat to someone across the world, create an interactive presentation to impress the boss, or even cut real, digital video, produced films, QuickTime could be just the tool you need.

QuickTime has come a long way since its auspicious debut on December 2, 1991. The video playback window was no larger than a postage stamp, frame rates were low, and the video quality required a little imagination on the part of the viewer. But QuickTime 1 (affectionately codenamed Project Warhol at Apple) was an absolute technological breakthrough. The original QuickTime engineers had the foresight to build QuickTime as system-level software, independent of third-party add-on cards. This meant that, despite all its shortcomings, QuickTime was the first pure software solution capable of playing video on a computer screen – no longer would users need to first tether the machine to a laserdisc player, or add in a dedicated hardware card. And, of course, video capture and playback quality improved immeasurably as computers became faster.

These days, QuickTime is much more than a desktop video player: true interaction is possible. You can explore real or imagined 3D worlds and even create immersive web sites that differ from anything else on the Internet. And, because of QuickTime's unparalleled open architecture, there are wide and varied tools to help your creative juices flow in just the right direction, many of which are free or very modestly priced.

There are literally millions of QuickTime installations on Macs (where it's standard) and PCs around the globe. Most people will have the QuickTime Player installed and may not even realize it. Couple this with Apple's forever expanding technology and their commitment to backwards compatibility – content created for QuickTime 1 will play perfectly in the all new version 6 – and you have an amazingly powerful tool on your hands.

But despite all this a lot of people think QuickTime is just the movie player. This book is about to help you blow this whole world apart, with little more than a copy of QuickTime Professional and some inspiration we'll explain what you can create – and how.

The first 3 chapters will talk about the reasons that QuickTime *is* so powerful, moving on to a tour through the QuickTime landscape looking at linear movies and then QVTR – the virtual reality feature added in QT4 – and that's where the interactivity really begins! Chapter 4 is a full overview of the interactive capabilities of QuickTime and it has a tutorial on how to script quickly and easily with Totally Hip Software's LiveStage Pro – a trial version of which is included on your CD.

Then it's time to be less selfish and think about your audience, the next section of the book exposes the details that you'll need to know about compression and delivery in order to get your projects out there in the best quality possible. The whole creation process from materials capture to final delivery is then expanded upon, including a real-world case study.

In closing there is greater detail about what tools you'll need and how to go about producing your QuickTime projects.

Layout conventions

We want this book to be as clear and easy to use as possible, so we've introduced a number of layout styles that we've used throughout.

- We'll use different styles to emphasize things that appear on the screen, KEYSTROKES OR SHORTCUTS and also hyperlinks.

- If we introduce a new **important term** then these will be in bold.

> *If there's something you shouldn't miss, it will be highlighted it like this! When you see the bubble, pay attention!*

■ When we want you to click on a menu, and then through subsequent sub-menus we will indicate to like so: File > Import This would translate to:

■ If there's a practical exercise for you to follow then it'll be headed.

Like this, in a shade of gray

1. Then the steps that you have to follow will be numbered.

2. Follow them through, checking the screenshots and diagrams for more hints.

   Further explanation of the steps may appear indented like so.

3. When you get to the end, you can stop.

On the CD

On the CD-ROM packed inside this book you'll find all of the support materials that you need to complete the examples within the chapters – even if you haven't got round to creating any source files for yourself. There are also some further examples of QuickTime projects supplied by the authors to help you see the potential you're about to unleash. As an added bonus there is a fully functional trial version of Totally Hip's LiveStage Professional, Live Slideshow, and Hip Flics.

Support – we're here to help

All DVision books from friends of ED aim to be easy to follow and error-free. However, if you do run into problems, don't hesitate to get in touch – our support is fast, friendly and free.

You can reach us at support@friendsofed.com, and even if our dedicated support team are unable to solve your problem immediately, your queriess will be passed onto the people who put the book together, the editors and authors. We'd love to hear from you, even if it's just to request future books, ask about DVision, or tell us how much you loved *Revolutionary QuickTime Pro*!

> *To tell us a bit about yourself and make comments about the book, why not fill out the reply card at the back and send it to us!*

You can also check out our web site for news, more books, downloads and, of course, our packed message boards! Point your browser at Dvision.info.

1 Welcome to QuickTime

This book has been written for those who are interested in authoring dynamic media and have heard that QuickTime offers a rich palette with which to do that. This book will help the reader understand whether and how QuickTime can fulfill their authoring aspirations. As a decision support book, it will help you answer this kind of question:

- Does QuickTime offer a palette that will enable me to communicate what I want to my chosen audience? Is it the best palette available to me?

This book is a first resort for those current and aspiring authors who wish to expand their palette beyond the media that they are currently using. It's important that we cover the entire QuickTime spectrum, illustrating the wealth of options available. Other, more specifically focused, QuickTime resources will follow this one in your deeper investigation of this subject, but don't worry we'll tell you where they are to be found.

To cite a few examples, this book is for people who work in or are preparing to work in TV, film, rich media on the internet, CD-ROM, people who are computer fanatics, students, journalists, graphic designers, musicians, educators, authors and storytellers, and PR professionals. Indeed, anyone who is interested in communicating in ways that go beyond the printed word.

Understanding what QuickTime can do is not like reading the manual for a computer application because QuickTime is not an application, it is an architecture that enables the creation of a wide variety of media, the applications with which to create that media and applications that can integrate QuickTime media with other data types such as a movie in a word processor file, e-mail message or even a spreadsheet. It's far more than just passively watching movies.

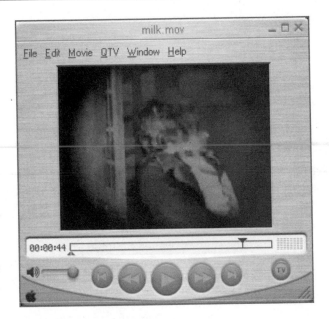

Understanding the QuickTime architecture will allow us to not only understand the current status of QuickTime but assess its future as well. This is where we should begin.

QuickTime as a multimedia architecture

QuickTime is an enabling architecture. It enables programmers and content authors to quickly and easily invoke a wide variety of multimedia events on Macintosh, Windows and other computers using vehicles as diverse as web browsers, word processors and other applications, PDF documents, the QuickTime Player and presentations built with multimedia runtime development systems such as Microsoft PowerPoint, Macromedia Director and Tribeworks iShell.

QuickTime media is found in vast quantities on CD-ROM disks and the Web and underlies an impressive number of works on film, TV, and DVD. QuickTime is ubiquitous without being intrusive, a quality that has been honed throughout its ten year history and one that is very attractive to people who take design seriously. The means with which to play QuickTime media and develop QuickTime applications are freely available on the web and bundled with CDs and other media. Even some basic QuickTime authoring tools are free or available at very low cost such as the QuickTime Player Pro upgrade at $29.95. This is a big part of the reason that QuickTime is everywhere. It is for the most part free and it is very, very good at displaying and integrating time-based media. The latest versions of QuickTime can display movies and slideshows, can integrate with Macromedia Flash and Director projects, and even have their own immersive imaging format, QTVR, which can provide a stunning 3D effect.

The things that have enabled QuickTime to evolve to its current form are likely the same things that will take it well into the future. The QuickTime architecture is modular, extensible, open, and standards compliant with an amazing track record of backward compatibility. QuickTime movies developed in 1991, the first year that QuickTime was available, will play just as well, or better, in QuickTime 6 as they did in QuickTime 1.0. Very likely the same will apply for QuickTime 12, if and when it becomes available. The QuickTime Player can display almost any format of image, and you can even adjust their appearance from within the program.

Understanding QuickTime and how QuickTime media might serve your communications needs can be done rather effectively by looking at these attributes in detail and taking note of their implications for the work that you plan to do.

Architectural traits of QuickTime

Once the architecture is reasonably well understood, the chapters in this book will illuminate how all of these extensive and varied powers relate to one another and to the potential that you can tap into.

Modularity

The modularity of the QuickTime architecture permits growth in many different directions while at the same time assuring the coherence and interoperability of all those pieces, however numerous and different from one another they might be.

The most noticeable of these modular attributes is the track-based nature of QuickTime media. Beginning with just a few track types (video and audio), QuickTime now boasts more than a dozen track types. In addition to audio and video, there are text tracks, Flash tracks, tween tracks, VR tracks, skin tracks and many more. Tracks can contain any number of media samples and they are able to communicate with one another such that they can operate independently or in concert as needed.

Revolutionary QuickTime Pro

Think of QuickTime as a container of containers (tracks) that are used to arrange various bits of media along a timeline sequentially, concurrently or in an overlapping manner. The visibility, action ability and behavior of these tracks can vary in infinite ways over time.

Another example of modularity is the way that components such as video and audio codecs, video effects, transitions, and filters can be added to QuickTime both by Apple and by third parties. Simply add a properly constructed component and it's available to all QuickTime-aware applications, the QuickTime Player, and the QuickTime Plug-in or QuickTime ActiveX Control for web browsers. QuickTime is a pretty big download (as are RealPlayer and Windows MediaPlayer) but the component system means that the user can just select the minimal installation for a faster installation and download any other components as necessary. There is less to keep the web user from your project.

Extensibility and openness

Modularity is one of the things that make QuickTime so easily extended. Using publicly available documentation from the Apple web site, any third party can develop a new modular component that will integrate with the QuickTime architecture in a seamless fashion without requiring the modification of any other QuickTime components or the underlying architecture of QuickTime. Areas of QuickTime extensibility recently developed by Apple are:

- New Media Types: Cubic VR www.apple.com/quicktime/products/qt/overview/qtvr.html

- New codecs: MPEG-4 www.apple.com/pr/library/2002/feb/12qt6.html

- New Effects & Transitions: Movie Plug-in Pack 2.1.1 www.apple.com/imovie

Of course, anyone can extend QuickTime in the same ways using the same documentation and recent third party examples include:

- New Media Types: MNG www.tarkvara.org/mng

- New codecs: ZyGoVideo www.zygovideo.com

- New Effects & Transitions: Buena Effects pack 1,2 & 3 www.buena.com

Because the QuickTime APIs (Application Programming Interfaces) are publicly accessible and open to all comers, we're assured of wide availability of authoring and playback environments - all competing for your attention and patronage. Anyone with the interest and programming expertise (C++, Java and even RealBASIC) can go to http://developer.apple.com/quicktime/ for all of the documentation, sample code and many of the programming tools one needs to understand how to develop a QuickTime component, a QuickTime authoring tool, or a QuickTime-savvy application.

To get a feel for how this manifests itself in today's software market, please take a look at the following three lists (QuickTime components, QuickTime authoring applications and QuickTime-savvy applications).

Components

These are usually freely available to audiences through Apple's component download system or, less conveniently, from the vendor directly. Authoring to the capabilities of these components usually requires a fee-based version of the component but virtually all of the playback components are free.

- **QDesign Music Codec** enables audio files to be compressed to levels beyond 100:1 while maintaining good quality sound. The basic version is included with QuickTime distribution, thus encoding is possible with QuickTime Pro, but there is also a fee-based pro version that produces even better results, it is of course free to playback. www.qdesign.com

- **Sorenson Video 3 Codec** delivers twice the compression speed as Sorenson Video 2 and up to three times the speed when using Variable Bit Rate (VBR), again it is free to playback and basic encoding is possible with QT Pro. www.sorenson.com

- **On2**'s full-screen, full-motion, TV-quality codec. www.on2.com/vp3_quicktime.php3

See www.apple.com/quicktime/products/qt/components.html for further details and the most recent additions to Apple's QuickTime component download program.

Authoring applications

QuickTime authoring applications output QuickTime files that can be played with the QuickTime Player, Plug-in and ActiveX Control or used in QuickTime-savvy applications. They can also be used in conjunction with other media as in the case of Director files. Thus, Director, Flash and Authorware are included in this class because it can contain QuickTime movies and is an application typically used by professional content authors rather than amateur content authors. Flash can be contained in a QuickTime file so there is full-circle reciprocity between Flash and QuickTime.

There are many free and inexpensive authoring environments in addition to Apple's own QuickTime Pro (see: www.apple.com/quicktime/products/qt/overview/). Appendix A contains a list of Web links to a large number of these.

QuickTime-savvy applications

These applications output files that may contain QuickTime media as well as other data types (a QuickTime video in a spreadsheet worksheet, for example) and are typically created by non-professional content authors rather than professional content authors.

So, imagine a QuickTime streaming video right in the middle of a page in a Word document, a QuickTime movie as an animated graph in an Excel file, a PowerPoint presentation with embedded video and a VR movie in an e-mail message. Your QuickTime content will play in all of these venues as well as on the Web and from CD.

All of this openness has brought forth a plethora of tools and components with which to create compelling QuickTime media. The palette is rich and the canvas is wide. The CD that comes with this book, for example, uses a Director created Shockwave file running QuickTime movies.

Standards-compliance

As of this writing, QuickTime supports more than 200 media types (see: www.apple.com/quicktime/specifications.html) and they all use formats that are well understood by other standards-compliant software. The kinds of media you want to work with can come from a variety of sources because the standards are public and open.

You can go from Photoshop to a QuickTime application and back without translators and importers or other intermediaries. You're not wedded to a system that's in the hands of just one entity that can withdraw or raise the ante for support of that format. From streaming, to interactivity, to virtual reality, to linear video, your work can be transcoded, exported, and repurposed as needed. With standards-compliant software, you'll never be stuck. It's to QuickTime's advantage that it's not in itself a standard but can be used with as many standards as people care to introduce.

Convergence

These many fine attributes (modular, extensible, open and standards compliant) are all well and good but what really amplifies their advantages stratospherically is the convergence that is made possible by QuickTime's integrative architecture.

Hundreds of media types, organized with any number of tracks of a dozen or so track types along a timeline yields an infinitely variable mosaic of well organized media. Coupled with that, these tracks can communicate with one another and some of them (for example sprite tracks) can be scripted to control all of the other tracks and their contained media samples in a QuickTime movie. These last two attributes (track intercommunication and track scriptability) combine to make QuickTime media highly programmable.

Programmability is what makes interactivity possible and interactivity is what truly differentiates digital media from film and television. Without interactivity, digital media is simply a less-than-perfect imitation of radio, TV, and film, especially where bandwidth is constrained such as on the Web. All other things being equal, that's not very compelling.

But that's not all! Movies can communicate with one another, with external databases and other things such as telling a web site to load a new page in a frameset at a particular time in a movie. QuickTime even enables authors to skin their media as they choose so the entire audience experience is under your authorial control.

QuickTime is where all of these wonderful digital media attributes converge to generate and offer unprecedented power and flexibility to the demanding communicator. QuickTime can stand on its own in the QuickTime player or it can be integrated with all sorts of other data types. It plays just about everywhere.

Summary

Is this still true?

The opportunity to experience QuickTime media is free and hundreds of millions of people have either downloaded QuickTime, gotten it from a CD, or found it pre-installed on their computer. The venues available to QuickTime are vast. You could just as well find QuickTime media in a word processor, spreadsheet or database document as on the Web or on a CD. There is a great potential audience for compelling QuickTime media.

Authoring QuickTime doesn't require wizardry, but neither is it shallow. With an abundance of highly intuitive tools, a long history among developers and content authors who have built up an impressive store of knowledge that's openly available to all who are interested, as well as a large and generous community of colleagues, one can achieve a high level of skill in many aspects of QuickTime authoring. Apple's documentation is extremely thorough and easy to understand. Unless you're very narrowly specialized, QuickTime's architecture capabilities will usually exceed your needs.

How far has WMT come?

As an architecture, QuickTime enables the integration and convergence of almost all important forms of visual and auditory digital media. Most importantly, the QuickTime architecture enables that media to interact with the audience and thereby set itself apart from and ahead of the media that preceded it.

The QuickTime world is expanding even as we speak, both in terms of what can be done with it and the number of people who can access its media. During the course of the book we'll discover just what QuickTime can do for your projects – and it's a lot more than passively watching movies!

2 Linear Media: Slide shows to Feature Length Movies

Over the years, QuickTime has matured into a mini-platform, capable of hosting interactive games, describing virtual reality worlds, and performing database-communication. But let's not forget why QuickTime was invented – to fill a gaping void in the Macintosh operating system. The Macintosh of 1990-91 had fantastic graphic capabilities, a robust mechanism for handling events (such as mouse-clicks and key presses), and a simple, logical, graphical user interface, but it had no paradigm for handling **time-based** media. At its core, QuickTime is all about time, and coping with disparate media types to make them all play in sync. QuickTime's unprecedented longevity –10 years is like 100 in software-years – is a testament to its fundamentally sound core. Let's look at the way QuickTime organizes linear media, and then we'll hone in on a few track types specific to time-based content.

Redefining the movie

Throughout this discussion, it will help if we keep in mind the distinction made in the previous chapter between QuickTime as an architecture and QuickTime as a player. The QuickTime Player isn't QuickTime. It's the familiar public face of QuickTime, but it's just one of many applications that tap into QuickTime's capabilities. So what *is* QuickTime? It's a bunch of low-level system calls (or functions) that move bits of data around. The fundamental data structure manipulated by QuickTime is the movie.

QuickTime's definition of a movie has nothing to do with popcorn or $8 seats – a QuickTime movie is like a card catalog drawer at a library. It's an abstraction, an organizer for other data. The index cards in a QuickTime movie are called tracks. Index cards in a library are useless without the books they reference – their only value is in showing us where to find the information we want. QuickTime tracks operate in the same way. A QuickTime video track holds no actual frames of video it just holds a reference to real data, which may be contained within the QuickTime file, or somewhere else (be it hard disk, CD-ROM, or a far-off streaming server). Cards in a card catalog tell you about one piece of information; they don't stop midway through the card and start describing a different book. QuickTime tracks describe one type of media apiece, and they don't change. An audio track doesn't stop halfway through the movie and magically turn into an image sequence. A QuickTime movie can, of course, house more than one track of the same media type (for example two video tracks and three audio tracks), but each one remains the same type of track throughout. In addition, each QuickTime track must contain a common set of information, just as each card catalog must reference an author, title, and call number. For instance, every QuickTime movie track has:

- Time information (track duration)

- Spatial information (width, height, position in the movie frame)

- Media information (a description of the type of data the track references)

- Volume information (sound level)

- An edit list (list of references to actual media and the order they are to be played).

Besides acting as a wrapper for tracks, the movie itself has some global characteristics, including movie duration, time scale, current time, and preferred volume. The movie's time coordinate system, of which time scale is a component, gives all of its tracks a common time reference. For instance, if I'm a QuickTime movie, and I have a video track that was recorded at 24 frames per second and an audio track that was recorded at 44,100 samples per second, I'm able to use my master timescale to map my current movie time to corresponding points in my individual tracks. If I tell you that I'm paused at a time unit of four, I've given you no meaningful information, since you don't know what my time base is. If, however, I tell you that I'm paused at a time unit of four, and each one of my movie time units is equal to half a second, you can deduce that I'm paused two seconds into the movie, since you now know I have a time base of two (two time units per second – a second is the "absolute" measure of time in QuickTime). My video track is now at frame number 48 (2 X 24), and my audio track is at sample number 88,200 (2 X 44,100). QuickTime is remarkably flexible – it can cope with a wide range of time bases, as defined by the movie. You may be asking, "How do I determine what the time base of my movie should be?" The good news is, unless you're a programmer, this level of complexity is shielded from you. QuickTime determines the necessary granularity for you on a movie-by-movie basis. Why is any of this important to us as media authors? Let's try to make some sense of this information by looking at two short cases.

Video clips and time manipulation

Let's say you're working with a video clip of a 50-metre dash, in which a runner pulls up lame. The scene lasts five seconds, but you have the replay shown from a different camera angle, so your movie lasts a total of ten seconds. You decide you want to see it in super slow motion, so you use your QuickTime-savvy video program to set the speed of the movie to 30% of its original speed. QuickTime magically plays the movie at the designated slower speed. But under the covers, QuickTime has translated your request by setting its duration to 33.33 seconds (10 / 0.3), and adjusting its time coordinate system to reflect the longer duration. If the video track was playing at a frame rate of 30 frames per second, it now plays at nine frames per second, and the edit from the first camera to the second camera now takes place at 16.66 seconds. This is an elementary example. Think of the number of timing calculations and adjustments QuickTime makes in a complex edit with multiple tracks of differing lengths and timescales!

Multi-track sound mixer

Let's say you're working with a sound mixer built on QuickTime, and you're setting the levels on a movie consisting of three different audio tracks. As you move the volume faders up or down, the program sets the individual volume levels of the affected tracks (for the sake of simplicity, we'll say min. is one and max. is ten). The program has a master fader that affects the overall volume of the movie. Underneath the hood, QuickTime keeps tabs on the levels in each track and in the movie as a whole. You set Tracks 1 and 2 to ten (maximum), and Track 3 to five (halfway), but if the overall movie volume is only set to five, you'll hear tracks 1 and 2 at 50% loudness, and track 3 at 25%. The movie's global volume setting scales the volume of each track down as necessary. QuickTime's movie abstraction and track-based structure lend it great flexibility in manipulating linear media.

Now let's talk about some specific track types you'll commonly encounter in working with linear content.

Video tracks

The video track type is certainly the most well known and commonly encountered. QuickTime's core (also called the Movie Toolbox) is only concerned with timing. It doesn't implicitly know how to encode or decode DV video, or MPEG-1 video, or any other format for that matter. But it can run through a list of installed QuickTime components and figure out if any of them know how to handle a given piece of video data. If one of the components says, "Yes, I recognize it, it's DV, and I know how to play it", QuickTime gladly delegates responsibility to the component, and then concerns itself solely with timing and synchronization. QuickTime's flexible management of components provides for continual extension by Apple and third parties. New functionality may be added in small bite-size pieces without necessitating a long download of a whole new QuickTime Player.

QuickTime can play any video at any resolution your hardware can handle, as long as it has a component that understands the video format. In this regard, QuickTime's playback performance is limited only by your computer hardware. Third parties are free to write their own video codecs to take advantage of proprietary hardware acceleration, if QuickTime's software-only decoding lacks sufficient performance for their needs (for instance, the Media100 video codecs, which require decoder PCI cards for optimum performance). So, as far as QuickTime is concerned, a video track is a video track is a video track, be it a 6 frame-per-second, 180 x 120 pixel, Cinepak encoded video circa 1994, or a 24 frame-per second, 1080 x 720 pixel uncompressed HD progressive-scan video circa 2004. If QuickTime has information about a video track's frame rate and image resolution (the image's width and height), it will attempt to play all the frames, and if your computer hardware can't keep up, QuickTime will accommodate by dropping frames, but keeping the time consistent. QuickTime developers can rest assured that, regardless of platform or playback capabilities, their linear content will always play back at the speed it was intended.

Working with video tracks in the QuickTime player

A great way to learn about video tracks is to open up any QuickTime movie using QuickTime Player Pro, and choose Get Movie Properties from the Movie menu. The movie properties dialog that appears offers a wealth of information about the different tracks in a movie by allowing you to view and manipulate properties on a track-by-track basis (similar to the Layers palette in Adobe Photoshop). This simple box has great potential, let's investigate.

1. Insert the CD-ROM accompanying this book into your computer's CD/DVD drive, and navigate to the Chapter2/video demo folder.

2. Double-click bach998.mov to launch it with QuickTime Player Pro, press the SPACEBAR to watch a little of it, then pause it by hitting the SPACEBAR again. Press the right-arrow on your keyboard and the video steps forward by one frame. Press the left-arrow and it steps back a frame. Now choose Get Movie Properties from the Movie menu.

3. Click the pop-up menu on the left side. This is the track list pop-up menu. It lets you investigate the movie's global information, or individual tracks. We see that this movie contains two tracks – a Video Track and a Sound Track. As we make our selection in the left pop-up menu, the right pop-up menu will change to reflect the options available for whatever track we choose. Select the Video Track.

4. Select Files from the right pop-up. This gives a list of other movie files referenced by this video track. Our movie is self-contained, so it doesn't refer to any external movies, but it's not uncommon to see a long list of file names here if you have created a reference movie from several different movie files.

5. Select Format from the right pop-up menu. This tells us the track's format (Sorenson 3), size (240 x 180), and color depth (Millions of Colors).

6. Select Frame Rate from the right pop-up menu. This tells you how many video frames QuickTime will try to play per second.

7. Select General from the right pop-up menu. This tells you, among other things, the track's duration and the amount of time between the start of the movie, and the start of this track (in other words, the track offset).

8. Select Size from the right pop-up menu. This gives you some spatial information about the track, namely its width and height in pixels. Remember, a track's spatial characteristics may differ from the movie's spatial characteristics. This particular movie is 240 x 180 pixels, as is the video track.

9. Now go to the Window menu and select Get Movie Info. This brings up a Movie Info dialog that summarizes most of what we just saw by browsing through several different pop-ups. In addition, it shows you the total data size of the movie and the data-rate of all the tracks summed together. You should use the Movie Info dialog when you want

a quick run-down of a movie's read-only characteristics. If you need more detailed information on a track-by-track basis, or you want to change some of the movie's characteristics, you should use the Movie Properties dialog.

Now we'll edit the movie by adding a video track and changing its spatial layout.

10. Drag logo.jpg from the same folder as bach998.mov onto the QuickTime Player icon (or choose File > Import in QuickTime Player to open it). It will open in a new player window. QuickTime allows us to generate a video track from a still image (more information on this powerful feature in the following Still Images section).

11. With the logo.jpg movie in the forefront, choose Select All from the Edit menu, then Copy. This copies the image's contents to the clipboard.

12. Now click on the bach998.mov movie, and push the left-most rewind button in its player controls to return the movie to the start. Choose Edit > Select All again, but **don't** select Paste. The Paste command would add the image to the beginning of the movie as a new track and push all our existing tracks over to the right by one frame. We don't want to do that. Instead select Add Scaled from the Edit menu, to add it as a new video track with the same duration as our selection, which happens to be the whole movie.

13. Re-open the movie properties dialog for bach998.mov if you closed it, and click the left-hand pop-up menu. Notice that we now have a Video Track 1 and Video Track 2. QuickTime adds a sequential number to the end of a track name when a new track of the same type is added. This can become confusing as the track numbers grow. Select Video Track 2, and then in the right-hand pop-up, select General. Now click the Change Name button, type in The Logo, and click OK. QuickTime lets us rename our tracks with meaningful titles.

14. Now select Size from the right-hand pop-up menu. We want to position the logo on the bottom right of the video window, so we'll click Adjust in the Properties dialog. A red box with re-sizeable handles appears around the logo.

15. Click on the movie window again, and drag the logo to the bottom right corner, then go back to the Properties dialog and click the Done button to signal that you're finished changing the track's layout.

If you wish, experiment with making the logo larger or smaller, or push the other buttons in the Size dialog to rotate or invert it.

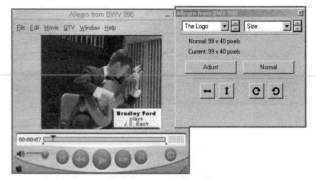

16. Choose File > Save As to save your new movie to your hard drive. Make sure to specify that the movie be saved self-contained rather than Normally (allowing dependencies). If you choose Normally, you'll create a QuickTime movie that refers to the video frames and the image on the CD. The new QT movie file will be very small in size, but you won't be able to play it in the future without having your CD in the drive. Saving self-contained copies all the necessary data from the original movie (including the video and image) into your new movie. You should usually save movies self-contained, unless you're working with very large movie files and disk space and copy time are a factor.

You've just edited your first QuickTime movie! Congratulations.

Still image formats

We tend to think of still images as being very dissimilar to video, but in truth there is only one difference between the two: time. Video is a sequence of still images displayed at a given frame rate. Since QuickTime is all about time, it stands to reason that QuickTime can import still images and bestow on them an element of time. QuickTime handles a myriad of still image formats, the most popular being JPEG, PSD (Photoshop), GIFF, TIFF, PICT, PNG, and BMP (Windows Bitmaps). When QuickTime imports a still image, it imports it as a *video* track, and thereafter, makes no distinction between it and "genuine" video tracks, as evidenced in our last tutorial. QuickTime's remarkable flexibility in dealing with image formats makes it an attractive piece in any content creator's toolkit. Besides importing images and giving them duration, QuickTime can go the other way, exporting any paused frame of video to a still image in any of the formats it understands. For a complete listing of the file formats QuickTime can import and export, visit www.apple.com/quicktime/specifications.html.

Creating a simple slide show

In this short tutorial, we'll demonstrate two techniques for creating simple slide shows in QuickTime Player Pro. Inexpensive niche applications such as Totally Hip's LiveSlideShow are better suited for this particular task, allowing you to add nice transitions between your still frames. Nevertheless, this tutorial will teach you some valuable concepts about how QuickTime imparts a time element to an otherwise static medium.

1. Insert the CD-ROM accompanying this book into your computer's CD/DVD drive, and navigate to `Chapter2/still image demo/`. For this demo, we've prepared four images with a common filename and sequential order: `humpty1.gif` through `humpty4.gif`.

2. Launch QuickTime Player Pro and select Open Image Sequence from the File menu. Navigate to `Chapter2/still image demo/` and select any one of the four `humptyX.gif` images.

    QuickTime Player will automatically include all pictures in the sequence, beginning with the lowest-numbered picture.

3. Next QuickTime Player asks you to give your slide show a frame rate. If you choose the default 15 frames per second, the images will fly by so fast you won't be able to read them, so we'll choose 3 seconds per frame.

4. QuickTime Player imports the images and shows them in a new window. Press the right-arrow key on your keyboard, and notice that each step is equal to three seconds. You can play your slide show at 3 seconds per frame, or step through it one picture at a time, as you would in a PowerPoint-style presentation.

5. Our sequence is missing one phrase. We'll add one more frame with a longer duration at the end. Click the right-most arrow on the QuickTime Player controller to advance the movie to the end.

6. Choose File > Open Image Sequence menu again, this time choosing `the_last_humpty.gif`, and give it the longest possible duration (10 seconds per frame). The image opens in a new window.

7. Now we'll copy and paste it into the other movie. With Untitled 2 movie in the forefront, choose Select All from the Edit menu, then Copy. Click on the Untitled 1 movie and choose Paste from the Edit menu.

8. Choose File > Save to save your new slide show to your hard drive. Make sure to save self-contained as we did in the previous tutorial, otherwise your new movie will not play if the CD is not in the CD-ROM drive.

Sound tracks

QuickTime's Sound Track type refers to Digital Audio – that is, sound originating in the real world that has been recorded as distinct samples into a computer. Sound is quite a different beast from video. Our eyes are analog devices, as are our ears, but our ears are a lot more difficult to trick than our eyes. Take film, for instance: motion picture projectors move along at 24 frames per second, which is fast enough to fool our eyes into believing we are seeing continuous motion on the screen. But what about audio? We hear sound continuously as vibrations in the air that our ears translate into electrical pulses. There's no such thing as "frames per second" in audio. Or is there? As it turns out, computers must sample incoming sound around 44,100 times per second in order to faithfully recreate the shape of sound waves and "fool" our ears into thinking we're hearing a continuous wave form. (If you're interested in reading more about the complexities of recreating sound in the digital domain, I recommend *Modern Recording Techniques* by Huber & Runstein). QuickTime simplifies our lives by hiding much of the complexity associated with capturing and playing back all those thousands of samples per second, while still retaining perfect synchronization with other movie media elements.

Although we commonly think of QuickTime movies as having a visual element, they can also consist of sound and nothing else. In fact, many developers of video games and multimedia software take advantage of QuickTime for its audio capabilities alone. If I'm a video game developer and I need to play various explosion sounds at different times to go along with my visuals, I can either tap into QuickTime, or I can spend a month researching the audio formats I need, and debugging my new and untested code (a scenario called "reinventing the wheel"). As an added incentive to choosing the first option, QuickTime supports virtually **all** standard audio file formats available. If I tell QuickTime to play `big_explosion.wav`, followed by `smaller_explosion.mp3` in my game, it will happily accommodate, despite the fact that WAV files and MP3 files are formatted quite differently. QuickTime supports uncompressed audio and a number of standard compressed formats, such as MP3, MACE, IMA 4:1, and some proprietary compressed formats, such as QDesign Music and Qualcomm PureVoice. With the release of version 6, QuickTime supports some exciting new audio standards, namely CELP (an MPEG-4 low-bandwidth codec for speech compression at 2400 – 4800 bits per second), and AAC (Advanced Audio Coding), an improvement to the MP3 codec that achieves roughly the same quality with a 30% lower file size.

Newcomers to QuickTime sometimes have trouble wrapping their brains around the idea that a QuickTime movie can have 10 or more sound tracks, yet we hear everything coming out of two speakers. QuickTime has a built-in mixer, a component called the Sound Manager. No matter what you do to your audio tracks' individual levels, equalization, and panning, the Sound Manager internally mixes their output down to a stereo signal before feeding it to the speakers. An audio track may be monaural (mono) or stereo, with sampling rates up to 48 kHz, and bit depths up to 16 bits. QuickTime can save volume and panning information in any save-enabled movie (movies may also be authored as "save-disabled"), so the next time the movie is opened, it retains the previous volume and panning changes. Let's illustrate some of these points with a quick demo.

QuickTime sound track tutorial

1. Insert the CD-ROM accompanying this book into your computer's CD/DVD-drive and navigate to the Chapter2/sound demo folder.

2. Open up bach_andante.mp3 using QuickTime Player Pro by dragging and dropping the file onto QuickTime Player's icon, or opening up QuickTime Player, selecting File > Open, and navigating to the file.

The first thing we'll do is save a reference movie to this MP3 file on our hard drive. We must take this preliminary step because the media is burned onto a read-only CD, and as such, cannot be edited directly. Our reference movie file will "point" to the read-only media and contain the edited playback information itself.

3. Choose Save As from the File menu, and save it as bach_andante.mov on your hard drive. Make sure Save normally (allowing dependencies) is checked in the bottom portion of the dialog. We're creating a QuickTime reference movie as a "wrapper" to the .mp3 audio data, thus the change in extension to .mov in our saved file.

4. Choose Get Movie Properties from the Movie menu, and then choose Sound Track from the left pop-up menu in the Movie Properties dialog and Volume in the right pop-up.

5. In the bach_andante.mov movie controller area, click on the equalizer bars to the right of the movie's timeline to reveal balance, bass, and treble controls.

6. Click the play button to play the sound. As it plays, move the balance block all the way to the right to pan all the sound out the right speaker. Experiment a bit with these three controls, and notice that as you move the balance, bass, and treble in the player, the corresponding controls update themselves in the Movie Properties dialog.

The volume slider in the QuickTime Player's controls maxes out at 100%, while the volume slider in the movie properties dialog is only at the mid-way mark. QuickTime allows you to "overdrive" your volume level by as much as 200%. This can come in handy for sounds that were recorded too softly into the computer.

7. The solo guitar track we're previewing is quite soft, so we'll go ahead and push up the volume slider to 125% in the Movie Properties dialog.

8. Select Save from the File menu and quit QuickTime Player. Now go into your file system and reopen bach_andante.mov. Notice that the volume and panning information have been retained.

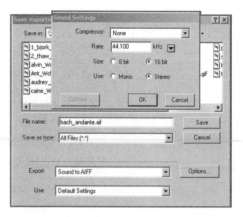

Experiment! Open up a sound file of your own with QuickTime Player Pro and try exporting it to various other sound formats. Select Export from the File menu, and then explore the available Options in the Export dialog for each available export format (such as Movie to QuickTime Movie, Movie to AIFF, or Movie to WAV). For example, selecting Movie to AIFF and clicking the Options button lets you specify such parameters as sampling rate, bit-depth, and number of channels (Mono or Stereo). Take note of the aural coloration of each codec, and the resulting file size. We'll discuss codec choices in-depth in Chapter 7.

Music tracks (MIDI)

QuickTime's Music track deals with a different type of sound information. The name is somewhat misleading – a better name would be Synthesized Music Track. Unlike QuickTime's sound track, a music track holds no audio samples. Instead, it attempts to capture a musical performance with such information as instrument category and type (for example, Strings > Cello), pitch (the note middle-C), velocity (a number representing the force with which a note is played), and duration (how long the note lasts). This type of information is typically stored in a standard format called MIDI (Musical Instruments Digital Interface). When a musician hooks up his MIDI-controller to a synthesizer module or a sequencer (a computer program that "records" and edits MIDI performances), the notes he plays are transmitted as MIDI data and interpreted by the module and/or program. QuickTime can play back MIDI using its own set of synthesized and sampled sounds that Apple licensed from Roland, an industry leader in MIDI products. Roland's sounds conform to the "General MIDI" (GM) standard, which requires that various instrument sounds be located in consistent "banks" (piano sounds are always in the first bank, followed by Chromatic Percussion).

MIDI is a powerful and efficient format for limited bandwidth delivery, such as a modem connection. If virtually all of your bandwidth must be devoted to video, but you still would like to include music with your movie, a music track is a perfect solution. Here's an example: Bach's *A Minor Fugue* for violin lasts about five minutes. As a digital audio file consisting of uncompressed CD-quality samples, this file occupies roughly 50 megabytes. The MIDI equivalent is a mere 16 kilobytes (or 0.03% the file size). MIDI also provides a great deal of flexibility to media authors. Once a performance has been saved in MIDI format, it can be easily manipulated – for instance, all notes can be shifted five steps higher for instant transposition to a new key.

Having said that, MIDI isn't perfect. A MIDI performance is only as good as the sounds available to play it back, and no synthesized violin is ever going to come close to the sound on an Itzhak Perlman recording. In all honesty, QuickTime's default MIDI banks sound predictably generic and clunky; however, QuickTime Music Architecture (QTMA) does allow users to expand the palette of sounds available to the playback engine. As of QuickTime 5, musicians can save their own sampled sounds in DLS (Downloadable Sound – the standard used in MPEG-4) or SF2 (SoundFont 2) format. A detailed discussion of these formats falls beyond the scope of this book, but more information is available at www.midi.org/about-midi/dls/dlsspec.htm, **and** www.soundfont.com/tutorials/quicktime1.html.

QuickTime music track tutorial

1. Navigate to the `Chapter2/midi demo` folder on the CD-ROM accompanying this book.

2. Open `bach_fugue_am.mid` using QuickTime Player Pro. (Incidentally, this MIDI file was obtained royalty-free from www.partnersinrhyme.com).

3. Select Get Movie Properties from the Movie menu. Select Music Track from the pop-up menu on the left of the Movie Properties dialog box, and then select Instruments from the pop-up on the right.

    The author of this MIDI file has set all six MIDI instrument channels to "Acoustic Nylon Guitar".

4. Play a little bit of the file and listen to the guitar sound.

5. Double-click the first Acoustic Nylon Guitar channel, and up pops the Instrument dialog. Begging Bach's pardon, let's change the instrument to something a little more fun. Set the Category pop-up to Sound Effects and the Instrument pop-up to Bird Tweet. The Keyboard at the bottom of the dialog lets you preview the sound you've chosen before committing to it. Click OK.

6. Replay the movie and bask in the dulcet chirps.

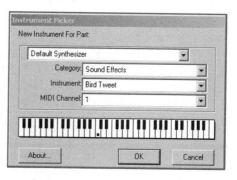

7. Select Export from the File menu, and export Music To AIFF, saving the new file as `bach_fugue_am.aif`. Though the notes in the Music Track are synthesized, QuickTime can output them as digital audio, which can then be burned to an audio CD, if so desired.

For an excruciatingly complete discussion of the QuickTime Music Architecture, see http://developer.apple.com/techpubs/quicktime/qtdevdocs/RM/tp_rm_qtma.htm.

Real-time rendering

In addition to playing a variety of media types in tight synchronization, QuickTime provides a means for visually manipulating various tracks. Any track type that pushes pixels around on the screen (video tracks, sprite tracks, Flash tracks, text tracks, etc.) is a candidate for real-time rendering, and a potential "source" for a QuickTime effect (more on that in a minute). We'll discuss QuickTime's powerful rendering capabilities in the following two sections: graphics modes, and QuickTime Effects Tracks.

Graphics modes

Visual tracks can be layered on top of one another in a QuickTime movie. A layer's graphics mode, or drawing mode, determines how it will interact with layers stacked behind it, and whether or not any portion of an obscured layer will show through. To illustrate some of the interesting effects achieved by changing a track's graphics mode, we'll look at a movie on the CD-ROM in the folder Chapter2/graphics modes demo.

First open up the two PSD files in the directory (if you don't have Adobe Photoshop, open them with the QuickTime Player), then use QuickTime Player to open graphics_modes.mov. This movie contains the two PSD files as two video tracks, stacked directly on top of one another. Video Track 1 is set as layer 0, and Video Track 2 is set as layer 1, so we see all of Video Track 1 and none of Video Track 2 by default (layers with smaller numbers are considered further forward). Open up the Movie Properties dialog (as in previous demos), choose Video Track 1 in the left-hand pop-up, and then select Graphics Mode in the right pop-up. Change the track's graphics mode to each type in the following list, as we explain each mode's function.

- **Copy**: Tells the top layer to copy all of its pixels onto the layer behind it, completely obscuring the second layer's image.

- **Dither Copy**: Usually the same as Copy. If the image's color depth is higher than the current monitor's resolution (a millions-of-colors image displayed on a thousands-of-colors display), QuickTime "dithers" (reduces) the top image's color resolution to the appropriate depth before copying its pixels onto the layer behind it.

- **Blend**: Blends pixels in the two layers by the amount specified in the user-specified color channel. For instance, if you choose gray as the proportional color, the two layers will show up in equal proportions. White will mask out the second layer entirely, and black will mask out the top layer entirely. Try changing the color in the Movie Properties window to achieve different levels of blending.

- **Transparent**: Lets you designate a color as the color to make transparent. If any pixels on the top layer match the color you pick, they will 'disappear', revealing the second track. Pick pure yellow in our movie, and watch what happens.

The next four modes pertain only to images with an alpha channel (a channel that defines degrees of opacity). Using Adobe Photoshop, we created a crazy alpha channel for the image in Track 1 (see figure) to illustrate the functionality of the four alpha modes.

- **Straight Alpha**: Blends the pixels in the top layer with those in the layer underneath, using the alpha channel to control the proportions of blending. Where the alpha channel is totally transparent (black), the top layer disappears. Where the alpha channel is totally white (opaque), the second layer is totally obscured.

Photoshop's Channel palette, showing Video Track 1's alpha channel. Black = 100% transparent, White = 100% opaque.

- **Alpha Premultiplied With White**: Same as Straight Alpha, except that each pixel is blended with a white background first. This can sometimes reduce jaggedness of lines (see for yourself!).

- **Alpha Premultiplied With Black**: Same as Straight Alpha, except that each pixel is blended with a black background first, in effect increasing the sharpness or jaggedness, and altering the overall color.

- **Straight Alpha Blend**: Same as Straight Alpha, except that you can specify a color to blend with the existing alpha channel, and, in effect, darken areas of the alpha channel. Choosing pure white will give you the same look as Straight Alpha. Any other color will make your top image more transparent.

- **Composition (dither copy)**: The entire top track's image is drawn off-screen first, then copied onscreen using Dither Copy (as described above). This mode is useful for tracks that have lots of different images in them (like sprite tracks).

QuickTime effects tracks

We've already seen that a graphics mode acts directly on the track in which it is set. QuickTime Effects, however, manipulate the look of one or more tracks by copying media from them and forming a new track on top of them. Effects Tracks show up in QuickTime Player's Movie Properties dialog as plain old Video Tracks. QuickTime internally distinguishes them as effects tracks, but never lets on to the end-user. A description of each effect's look would prove long-winded and inadequate – a picture is *definitely* worth a thousand words. So to illustrate the look achieved by various QuickTime effects in the following sub-sections, we'll download a small, free application called Effects Teaser from http://developer.apple.com/quicktime/quicktimeintro/tools.

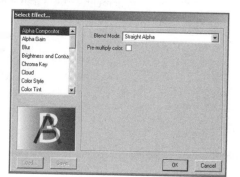

Effects Teaser is a Windows/Macintosh application that shows a preview of every QuickTime effect listed in the table below. Our use of this utility is necessitated by QuickTime Player Pro's lack of support for adding QuickTime effects directly. Effects tracks can be added to movies programmatically, or using commercial software packages, such as Totally Hip's LiveStage Pro (www.totallyhip.com), or Adobe's GoLive (www.adobe.com/products/golive/main.html). QuickTime effects come in three flavors: Zero-Source (codec effects), One-Source (filters), and Two-Source (transitions).

- **Zero-Source Effects** are freestanding effects that require no other tracks. They can be composited onto other visual tracks if desired. Apple has released three zero-source effects to date (see below).

- **One-Source Effects** are filters (similar to Adobe Photoshop or After Effects filters). They act upon one visual track to change its look. For example, a movie with a single video track could have a "Film-Noise" filter applied to it to make it look like old, damaged film. The result would be a movie with two video tracks. One is the original, and the other is an effects track modifying the original's media. A filter need not be applied to an entire track; it can be selectively applied to parts of a track if desired. Apple has released 14 QT filters (see below), and third parties have written many more. Note that if you simply want to apply a single filter across an entire track, you can export from QuickTime Player Pro as a QuickTime Movie, choosing Options, followed by clicking the video settings button, and then the filter button. This will, however, render the filter into the video track, causing each frame to be recompressed.

- **Two-Source Effects** are better known as transitions. A transition acts on two other visual tracks, creating a temporal link between them. Transitions are the bread-and-butter of mainstream video editing applications from Apple's free iMovie all the way up to Avid's high-end Media Composer. The Society of Motion Picture and Television Engineers (SMPTE), an organization devoted to promoting video standards, has defined 34 Wipe effects, 26 Iris effects, 39 Radial effects, and 34 Matrix effects. Apple has implemented these transitions and nine more of its own as of QuickTime version 5 (see chart opposite).

Zero-Source Effects

| Cloud | Fire | Ripple |

One-Source Effects (Filters)

Alpha Gain	Blur	Brightness & Contrast
Color Style (Solarize)	ColorSync (Mac only)	Color Tint (Sepia, etc.)
Edge Detection	Emboss	Film Noise
General Convolution	HSL Balance	Lens Flare
RGB Balance	Sharpen	

Two-Source Effects (Transitions)

Alpha Compositor	Chroma Key	Cross Fade
Explode	Gradient Wipe	Implode
Push	Slide	SMPTE Iris Effects
SMPTE Matrix Effects	SMPTE Radial Effects	SMPTE Wipe Effects
Traveling Matte	Zoom	

Apple's QuickTime Effects in all their flavors are well documented (with QuickTime movie examples) at: http://developer.apple.com/techpubs/quicktime/qtdevdocs/REF/refEffects.3d.htm#pgfId=324.

A word of caution on QuickTime effects

QuickTime's real-time rendering capabilities are formidable, but limited by your computer's processing power. Exercise caution when applying multiple graphics modes, effects, filters, and transitions to your movies, as they may cause dropped frames and general sluggishness. Some video codecs demand more processor time to decode than others, Sorenson Video 2 or 3 are prime examples. Performing a real-time cross-fade dissolve between two Sorenson video tracks will probably not adversely affect movie playback performance on a modern machine, but performing a cross-fade, plus applying an alpha graphics-mode, plus rendering a ripple effect on top of the two Sorenson tracks is pushing your luck. The old, familiar maxim "Test early, test often" should govern your use or non-use of real-time effects.

Timecode tracks

One of my all-time favorite movie lines is Ben Stiller's "You're in MY world now, Grandma!" from 'Happy Gilmore'. This line is quite apropos to QuickTime's handling of video and audio as they leave the world of linear tape and enter QT's self-contained little reality. In previous sections, we've tried to drive home the fact that QuickTime implicitly handles time. When video or audio is captured to the QuickTime format, it must inform QuickTime about its timescale, its desired frame rate, and its duration. This information alone is enough for QuickTime to perform all of its editing functions on the media. But QuickTime handles time in its **own** way, discarding the video and audio's original time as it appeared on the tape. This is usually not a problem for smaller projects, but for professional, large-scale work this limitation can prove a hindrance.

For instance, let's say you're the editor for a big Hollywood production, and you use a QuickTime-based program to do your work. Every day new tapes of footage arrive, which you must "digitize" into the computer, then preview and make rough edits. You don't have enough hard drive space to keep the whole project online, so every week you must delete the video files from the previous week. At some point you're going to need to bring the sections back online to refine your edits and show the results to the director. Your program needs a way of keeping track of the original time of the video as it exists on the tape; otherwise, you'll have to go back, redigitize the parts you need, and redo your edits. For this and similar scenarios, QuickTime's implicit handling of time is not enough, QuickTime needs some additional "glue", a link to the reality of the linear tape world. Timecode Tracks are QuickTime's answer.

Linear timecode

All professional and most prosumer tape formats support timecode. The two most popular and prevalent standards are SMPTE timecode and DV timecode. SMPTE timecode is used in pro analog tape formats, such as Beta and S-VHS. DV timecode is recorded digitally onto tape in DV, DVCAM, and DVC-Pro equipment. An excellent paper discussing the differences between the formats can be found at www.mindspring.com/~d-v-c/Timecode.htm. Though the formats store timecode differently, they perform essentially the same function – they assign a unique, sequential time to every single frame of video on a tape, in 24-hour format:

```
HH:MM:SS:FF  [Hours]:[Minutes]:[Seconds]:[Frames]
```

A tape need not start at time 00:00:00:00. The camera or deck operator may manually set the start time.

A QuickTime timecode case study

Apple's own professional editor, Final Cut Pro, gains a great deal of power from QuickTime's Timecode Track. When Final Cut Pro captures DV media, it writes it to a QuickTime file with a Video Track, an Audio Track, and a Timecode Track. The timecode track is tied to the video track, allowing it to retain its original tape time, as well as a QuickTime time. For instance, if the video clip is 25 frames per second, and 30 seconds long, QuickTime counts the first frame as 00:00:00:01, and the last frame as 00:00:30:00. The timecode track knows that the real time (on tape) of frame 1 is actually 12:02:15:15 and the real time of the last frame is 12:02:45:14.

Final Cut Pro remembers the real start and end times of each clip that you capture, even after you delete the media. This can come in very handy if you need to return to a two-year old project in which all the video files have long-since been erased. When you open up your project file, Final Cut Pro informs you of all the missing media files, and then allows you to re-import them with a single command. It then uses the saved timecode numbers from the QuickTime timecode tracks to rewind the source tapes to the correct points and batch import all of the specified media to hard drive, resurrecting your project.

Text tracks

One of QuickTime's most powerful and underutilized features is its superb handling of text. For years video editors have been adding titles, credits, subtitles, and closed captioning to their video content by rendering it directly onto each video frame, obscuring the action behind it, and adding complexity (and bandwidth) to their content. This is a necessary evil in TV or film, where the screen has a limited viewing area, all of which is intended for displaying images, not metadata such as text. But with QuickTime, we're not limited to the borders of the video frame. Content creators can author text tracks of virtually any size, and display them beside, below, above, or composited on top of other tracks. Plain text is remarkably small in file size (each letter occupies a paltry 8 bytes) and undemanding for QuickTime to composite, making it an economical choice for bandwidth-limited delivery. QuickTime gives you a great deal of control over the look of your text (font, face, size, color, justification, anti-aliasing), and, as an added bonus, QuickTime calculates the rendering of your text at run-time, so if your movie is resized, it scales cleanly and crisply (unlike rasterized images which tend to pixelate when scaled). Text tracks have long been a selling point for QuickTime among educators, researchers, and content creators sensitive to hearing-impaired audiences. They provide a lightweight, nimble tool for closed-captioning, a logical choice for karaoke-type kiosk applications, and a flexible alternative to video for text-based credits.

Unlike flattened, rendered text in still image and video formats, text in text tracks can be edited in a simple text-editor. If you've ever created a film and rendered all your end-credits as video frames, you know what a royal pain they are to redo. Each time you discover a misspelling will cost you a long re-render. Editing QuickTime text tracks entails a simple change in a text editor, followed by a five-second re-import into your movie. In addition, text tracks give your movie an instant third dimension – metadata. QuickTime can *search* the text added to a movie and jump to the point in the timeline where it occurs, which can make working with long-form video a great deal less arduous.

Text tutorial

As with still images, QuickTime allows you to add a time element to an otherwise static medium. Using the QuickTime Player's Movie Properties window, you can see the exact current time of a playing movie and copy the time into a text file to mark the starting point of a new text sample, like this:

```
[00:00:00.00] This is the start of the movie.
[00:00:15.00] This is 15 seconds into the movie.
```

QuickTime uses special formatting tags called QT text descriptors to express the size, font, justification, color, and time-scale of text. A complete listing of valid QT text descriptors is found at: www.apple.com/quicktime/products/tutorials/textdescriptors.html. In the interest of brevity, we'll use a pre-written text file that you can use a model for your own text tracks.

1. Navigate to the Chapter2/text demo/ folder on the CD-ROM accompanying this book.

2. Open bach998.mov in QuickTime Player Pro (this should look familiar), and then open its Movie Properties window. Select Time from the right-hand pop-up, and then click back on the movie window again. Note that each time you push the right arrow key on your keyboard, the movie moves forward by one frame and the Current Time (in the Movie Properties dialog) moves forward by a count of .02 until it reaches .30.

Thus QuickTime Player is counting 30 time units per second and counting each frame as two time units (or 1/15th of a second).

3. Double-click `bach.txt` to see the guts of a QuickTime text track. This file describes the font of the text (Geneva), the face (plain), size (9-point), time-scale (the same as our video track), the dimensions of the track (240 x 40), justification (left), text color (white – in 16-bit Red, Green, and Blue values), color of the background (black), the time-stamps (absolute, not relative), and language (English, with a code of 0). A timestamp appears in straight brackets directly above text that occurs at any given time. Notice that there is also a final timestamp indicating the end of the movie at `[00:01:31.19]`.

4. Now we'll tie the text track to our movie. In QuickTime Player Pro, choose Import from the File menu, and select `bach.txt`. QT Pro makes a new movie from your text file. Choose Select All from the Edit menu, followed by Copy.

5. Click to select the guitar movie, and make sure it is rewound to the very beginning, or else the durations won't line up. Now choose Add from the Edit menu. Note that we don't have to choose Add Scaled because our text track already is the correct duration.

6. As a final step, we'll move our text track above the video frame. Go to the movie properties dialog for our guitar movie, choose Text Track from the left-hand pop-up, and Size from the right.

7. Click the Adjust button, and then click back on the guitar movie window to drag the text track up above the video track. You can also use your arrow keys to do fine adjustments.

> *Hint: it will be easier to adjust the placement of the track if you advance the movie to a point where you can see the guitarist instead of blackness.*

8. When the track sits nicely atop the guitarist's head, click Done in the movie properties dialog.

Save your movie changes from the File menu, if you so desire. Sit back, relax, and watch your masterpiece.

Advanced QuickTime text

Beyond the rudimentary placement of text markers at precise times in our movies, QuickTime allows us to achieve some nice effects with our text tracks. These effects are achieved using QT Descriptors, just as we used in our tutorial. Here is a list of some noteworthy effects at our disposal:

- **{anti-alias:onOrOff}**: Anti-aliasing pleasantly smoothes the edges of text at the expense of increased CPU load.

- **{keyedText:onOrOff}**: Keyed text does not draw a background color. Instead it renders text in the specified {textColor} on top of the layer directly below it. Keyed text is a good choice when you need to display text on top of video or an image. NOTE: before using keyedText to draw text on top of your video, ask yourself if it really needs to be there, as this compositing draws processor power and sometimes clutters the video display. You are not limited to the video frame in a QuickTime movie, and sometimes it makes better sense to offset the text area to a different region of the movie frame.

- **{doNotDisplay:onOrOff}**: If set to on, doNotDisplay will cause your text track to not render to the screen. This is useful if you don't want to display text, but you still want text associated with certain times in the movie. Hidden text is still searchable in the QuickTime Player using the Find command from the Edit menu.

- **{scrolling:onOrOff}**: If turned on, scrolling allows you to easily put scrolling text credits into your movie without rendering them into the video track using a video editing application. There are a host of other descriptors associated with scrolling that give you fine control over scrolling direction, and timing (see http://www.apple.com/quicktime/tutorials/textdescriptors.html) for a complete list.

SMIL

SMIL, or Synchronized Multimedia Integration Language, is a subset of another language called XML, drawn up by a subgroup of the World Wide Web Consortium (www.w3.org). W3C also standardized and codified the syntax for HTML, the language in which web pages are written; so it should come as no surprise that SMIL and HTML look very similar. Both Apple and Real Networks participated in writing the version 1.0 SMIL specification, first published in June of 1998 at www.w3.org/TR/REC-smil. Consequently, both QuickTime and Real Player added SMIL support shortly thereafter.

SMIL is a simple, plain text language suitable for organizing different media elements in a time-based presentation with hyperlinks. Think of it as HTML with time. It's a very good way to automate the generation of media content in a web-based application. It also provides a simple way to spatially position different pieces of media. It's not good for dynamic visual layout (for example, animating a piece of media over time), interactivity (anything beyond a simple hypertext link is pushing it), and interoperability (Real's and Apple's implementations are largely incompatible with one another). Peter Hoddie, the Apple delegate who helped define the specification (now an emeritus QuickTime team member) has provided an excellent overview of the SMIL format in PowerPoint presentation format at www.hoddie.net/dvexpo/smil_dvexpo.htm.

One might ask, "Why bother with SMIL when QuickTime can already do everything SMIL can and more?" Though the QuickTime architecture is **much** more flexible than SMIL, it provides no easy way to automate multimedia presentations on the fly the way that SMIL does. SMIL shines in an environment where various movie elements must be thrown together in real-time, in response to a user's requests. Conventional QuickTime movie-authoring applications are written in a low-level programming language such as C or C++, and they must be compiled to run on Windows or Macintosh. Since SMIL is just text, it can be generated from any machine or platform, for instance a Sun Solaris Web Server, then served up to a Windows or Macintosh client running QuickTime software that can import and interpret SMIL.

SMIL in use

Let's look at a scenario in which SMIL would be a good choice. What if you administer all the video and multimedia content for an international news agency's website, and your boss asks you to tailor each visitor's video newscast to his or her geographical area and demographic? SMIL is the perfect solution. Your website already collects demographic information from visitors – you know each one's city, language, age, sex, and favorite hobbies. Your only task then is to write an application for your web server that can match user information with a database of available multimedia, write out a text SMIL file, and embed it as a QuickTime movie into the user's customized start page. You decide that all visitors will see the same video clip and news jingle at the beginning, followed by a 10 second still image giving the current weather conditions for the user's area. This is to be followed by a five-minute video clip of breaking headline news in the user's language (supposing you have several different broadcasts to choose from). After that, the user will see three different Flash animations, advertisements targeted to his or her demographic. Clicking on any of these ads will open up a new browser window and point it to the advertiser's site. Throughout the newscast, a box underneath the video area prints close-captioned text for the hearing-impaired.

You already have the necessary media assets in a database. SMIL allows you to instantaneously organize them into a presentation using a simple text file. It also trivializes the process of changing any of the media elements at a later date, such as altering the web links provided by the advertisers.

SMIL basics

SMIL is a huge topic. A detailed discussion of the language, its syntax, and all of its features would easily fill this entire book. But don't let it frighten you. Writing SMIL does require a little code writing, but it's no more difficult than HTML, and can usually be learned in about a day. We won't delve any deeper into the nooks and crannies of the language here; instead we'll refer you to a wealth of SMIL resources and tutorials at Apple's QuickTime SMIL start-page: www.apple.com/quicktime/authoring/qtsmil.html. And, for the daring, we included a sample SMIL file on the accompanying CD-ROM. Navigate to the Chapter2/smil demo folder and open qtsmil.smil with your favorite text editor if you wish to see a working example of SMIL in action. The file contains HTML-style comments, enclosed in brackets with a leading exclamation mark, like so:

```
<!-- This is a comment, it is ignored by QuickTime's SMIL
➥importer, and only exists for humans to look at. -->
```

These comments should give you a good idea of what's happening in each section of the file. After you're done perusing the code, open it up with QuickTime Player and observe the results. Also note that all the media referenced resides in the same directory as the SMIL file. The links to various media elements are "relative" links. We authored it this way to make the project self-contained, but we just as easily could have used "absolute" links and referenced QuickTime content residing on a remote http web server, or rtsp-streaming server.

QuickTime-specific SMIL considerations

QuickTime's SMIL implementation covers about 85% of the SMIL 1.0 specification. Apple has also extended SMIL with some QuickTime-specific tags. You can access the QuickTime extensions to SMIL by adding the qt namespace to the beginning of your SMIL text file like so:

```
<smilxmlns:qt="http://www.apple.com/quicktime/resources/smilextensi
➥ons">
```

This line tells QuickTime's SMIL importer that you'll be using the letters qt throughout your SMIL file whenever you want to perform QuickTime-specific functions on your media. Note that if you try to open this SMIL file in Real Player, it will not know how to interpret the qt tags, and will spit back an error message. QuickTime's qt-namespace extensions add a great deal of valuable functionality to SMIL. For instance, you can use the QuickTime graphics modes (explained previously in the Real-Time Rendering section of this chapter) to provide transparency to a video or image element, like so:

```
<img src="foo.jpg" qt:composite-mode="transparent-color;black"/>
```

This line specifies that QuickTime should interpret all black pixels in foo.jpg as being see through or transparent. A complete listing of qt-namespace extensions and examples of each are available at: www.apple.com/quicktime/authoring/qtsmil2.html.

For a working example of QuickTime SMIL in use, open up QuickTime Player, click the TV button on the controller, and then select Video Music Network. This Sony Music QuickTime TV Music Channel is composed using SMIL.

SMIL hijacking

In an ideal world, all SMIL files would be interchangeable among all SMIL-enabled media players. Alas, it's not an ideal world, and SMIL authored for one player seldom works in another. This is a perilous situation. Let's say you author a SMIL file for QuickTime with a default extension of .smi or .sml or .smil, and create a simple link to it from a web page. A user visiting your site might have both Real Player and QuickTime Player installed on his computer, and whichever player was installed last probably has appropriated the SMIL extension for itself. You, the SMIL author, have no guarantee that your audience's computer will launch the right player to view your content.

Once again, the QuickTime engineers save the day by offering a means of forcing QuickTime-specific SMIL to be viewed with the QuickTime Player or plug-in.

The simplest fix is to author your SMIL as you normally would, then add a single line of text to the beginning of the file:

```
SMILtext
<smil xmlns:qt=" ....etc.
```

Save it with a .qt extension rather than .smil. The .qt extension is unambiguous; if QuickTime is installed, it will try to open the SMIL presentation.

Movie tracks

Earlier in this chapter, we told you that every QuickTime track has a specified, known type (video, audio, text, etc.) that never changes during the course of the movie. Well, we fibbed a little. The exception to the rule is the Movie Track, which was introduced with QuickTime 4.1 to solve some problems specific to long-form and streaming content, like SMIL. Before the appearance of movie tracks, QuickTime suffered from a fundamental architectural limitation: every time QuickTime opened up a movie file, it would walk through all the tracks contained in the file and identify the type of media in them. This works fine for movies that are stored locally, but not for remote and potentially changing media.

A movie track is a generic placeholder for movie data, a catchall track that can hold any QuickTime movie content. In effect, when QuickTime opens a QuickTime file with one or more movie tracks, each movie track says, "Just call me a Movie Track, for now. You don't really need to know what I am until such-and-such a time in the movie. Wake me up about 15 seconds before that time, and then I'll tell you what kind of media I am, and how long I last!" A movie track allows a QuickTime movie to append itself on the fly – no instantiation of media occurs until the last possible second before the particular element is needed. This provides three enormous benefits to QuickTime's architecture.

- **Complex movies are more responsive and nimble**. Instead of loading media into computer memory immediately, QuickTime can wait until it needs a particular chunk of media. If the viewer closes the movie before a particular element is needed, it never gets loaded.

- **False hit-counts are minimized**. This is largely a concern for advertisers. Suppose I am a large web advertising company, and you are a QuickTime content author. As your web-based QuickTime movie plays, various clickable JPEG image advertisements appear and disappear in the movie frame. These ads are loaded from a database of my clients' products. I need to ensure that your QuickTime movie doesn't request an image from my database until it's actually presented to the viewer, since my clients pay me (and indirectly, you) based on per-view ad counts. Without movie tracks, QuickTime would request all the images at the beginning of the movie, regardless of whether the viewer actually watched the entire presentation.

- **Media can change at run-time**. Movie tracks allow individual elements in your movie to change between the time the movie is started and the time they are requested.

Movie tracks in use

Armed with your new knowledge about the benefits of movie tracks, you might be curious to know how to make them. The short answer is: unless you are authoring interactive media (as a programmer, or using a professional commercial package such as Totally Hip's LiveStage Pro), you don't do anything. The use of movie tracks in interactive QuickTime movies will be discussed in Chapter 5 (see Movie-in-a-Movie). In a simple linear media presentation, QuickTime generates movie tracks for you when the situation arises. Each media element in a SMIL presentation, for instance, shows up as an individual movie track. You can verify this by opening up a SMIL file with QuickTime Player Pro, then selecting Get Movie Properties from the Movie menu, and browsing through the track list. You will find a single video track with a solid background color, and a number of Movie Tracks. QuickTime also creates movie tracks when it imports plain-text MP3 play lists (.m3u files).

Content presentation – thinking outside the video frame

As content creators we must be sensitive to our audience's total viewing experience. In an ideal world, content would be king, and delivery mechanism would be totally transparent to the end-user. Television is an apt example of this delivery model. A typical TV viewer makes choices based on a show's content, the time it airs, and possibly on the quality of the channel's reception. Answer truthfully, have you ever based your TV viewing choices on the color of your television set or the usability of your remote control? As preposterous as this analogy sounds, this is **exactly** what happens in the world of computer video. Delivery medium is often equally important as the content itself. I recall painstakingly authoring a piece of video for Internet consumption, only to receive such feedback as, "Why on earth did you choose Player X? Its interface is cluttered; it bogs down my entire system, and it doesn't run on my mother's Mac!" It is indeed a deflating experience to realize that your content's packaging has undermined your content's message.

Computer video is a decidedly different market from television. Real, Apple, and Microsoft compete for market share with proprietary technologies and video formats. Some viewers feel passionately about their media player of choice, and will shun content that is encoded in a different format. Others have no choice – their computers at work have one media player installed, and they're not at liberty to install another. This is a frustrating reality for us as content creators. We must ask ourselves, "Which player's interface is the least annoying? Which will detract **least** from my content's message?" Each format has its merits, but Apple has shown greater willingness to give QuickTime developers control over the look of the player and their content, a concession the competition has not been willing to make.

Real Networks produces their Real Player, encoding tools for the Real formats, and not much else. In order to be profitable, they must cater to advertisers. This strategy is evident in their marketing, and in their player's user interface. They prefer to have Real media content presented inside the Real Player where they can serve up advertisements and channel choices directly from the interface.

Microsoft makes most of its money through licensing agreements. Their Windows Media technology is, for the most part, a vehicle to add value to the Windows platform, and a bid to dominate the streaming market. Interactivity and maintenance of cross-platform feature parity is neither high on their priority list, nor in their company's best interest. As a result, their player looks and functions differently, depending upon the operating system on which it is running.

Apple, on the other hand, still considers itself a hardware company – they like to sell Macintosh computers. But with a narrow 5% Desktop PC market share, they know that QuickTime must maintain strong Windows compatibility in order to remain viable. Apple sees QuickTime as an enabling technology and a vehicle to sell hardware. Since Apple does not expect QuickTime to bring in direct revenue through advertising or licensing, it has given content creators a great amount of leeway in customizing the player's look. One such way is skinning.

Pros and cons of skinning the player

Skinning the player provides some important benefits to end-users and developers: It gives a measure of control back to the consumer. If I dislike a player's default look, or simply resent being force-fed advertisements and channel choices every time I fire up my preferred media player, I have the option of changing the look to one of those readily available on the web. Third-party developers get free publicity for their designs and receive automatic exposure as they publish their new skins to the web. Large corporations gain the benefit of branding their media player with a corporate logo or company slogan.

But player skinning also presents some tricky technical and proprietary content issues. If I am Pepsi, I probably dislike the fact that anyone can download and install a Coca-Cola branded skin as their default look and feel. There always exists the potential for my Pepsi-media content to be hijacked by a competitor's skin. Video content also poses a technical dilemma for media authors.

Skinning works fabulously for audio content, because the only visual element requiring skinning is the controller. In essence, it does not matter how big or oddly shaped the skin is, since the content (audio) requires no screen real estate itself. Video, on the other hand, can vary in width and height. A slideshow video targeted to modem users, for instance, might be authored and encoded at 240 x 180 pixels in size, while a wide-screen MPEG-2 video clip for DVD might be prepared at 740 x 480 anamorphic pixels (stretched horizontally to accommodate wide-screen TV's). The programmers who write the media player software take these size discrepancies into account, and program their player window to shrink or expand in response to the content being played. A third-party skin developer, however, must prepare his player's background and buttons with fixed-size images. The technical problem then, is that a fixed-area playback rectangle cannot possibly accommodate all video sizes. Microsoft's Windows Media Player handles the problem by scaling the video up or down to the area allotted by the custom-skin. This frequently means that content is viewed at a size and quality level for which it was not intended.

Skinning the media

Apple's QuickTime engineers have devised a much more elegant solution to the problems presented above, a process called media skinning. With the release of QuickTime 5.02, media authors add to their palette a new track type, the skin track, which may be used to skin *individual* movies rather than the player as a whole. The skin is embedded in the movie along with the content, so media authors can rest assured it will travel everywhere their content travels.

Apple's per-movie approach to skinning should come as no surprise to long-time QuickTime developers. Since version 3, the QuickTime architecture has supported turning off the default QuickTime player and plug-in controller on a per-movie basis. After setting a movie's controller to None, developers can create a custom movie controller using a Flash track, or a unique and powerful interactive QuickTime technology called sprites (Flash, sprites, and sprite tracks are discussed in detail in Chapter 4).

When QuickTime's default controller is turned off, all that remains of the stock Apple QuickTime Player design is a draggable, brushed-metal window frame atop the video containing the movie title. If embedded in an HTML page with its controller set to false, a QuickTime movie is stripped of all its Apple design.

As a simple demonstration, open up any QuickTime movie using a registered copy of QuickTime Player Pro. Choose Get Movie Properties from the Movie menu. Select Controller from the right pop-up menu in the resulting dialog box, and then choose None Movie Controller. Substituting the default control buttons with custom controls of your own (again, using a Flash or sprite track), you can approximate the "skinned" look offered by other media players, such as WinAmp.

But wait, there's more! QuickTime's new skin track goes two steps further, ridding your content of any bounding box, and letting you, the author, define your content's visible and draggable areas. Your skin can be non-rectangular, and even porous, if you like. You can punch holes through your content's visible area by defining a window mask graphic for the skin track. For instance, you can define your movie's backdrop as a briefcase, with beveled edges and a handle on top. You can make the space between the top of the briefcase and the handle transparent, and define the draggable portion of your movie as just the handle area. The end-result is visually stunning, and can greatly enhance the effectiveness of your linear media. The process for skinning a QuickTime movie is best explained with a quick and dirty, no-frills tutorial. In this demonstration, we'll remove the bounding box from a movie that displays a video track of a boy inside a picture of an Apple Cinema Display monitor (see the above figure).

Skinning a movie

1. Insert the book's CD-ROM into your computer's CD/DVD drive, and navigate to `Chapter2/skin demo/`.

2. Using Adobe Photoshop, open up `studiobck.psd` (if you do not own Photoshop, you can open it using QuickTime Player). This image has three layers. The background layer is the Studio Display with a blank dark screen.

3. The second layer, winmask, is transparent except for the area of the Studio Display, which we have painted solid black. This layer defines the visible portion of our movie's window. The black portion will be visible; the transparent portion will disappear in the resulting skin. Export this layer (with all other layers turned off) as a PICT file, and named it `winmask.pct`.

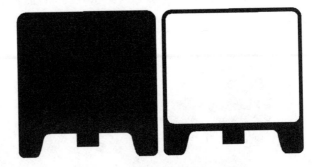

4. The third and topmost layer, dragmask, looks similar to the winmask layer. Its black portion defines the window dragging area. Remember that a skinned QuickTime movie loses its default draggable window frame, so we must define an area of the movie that a user may click to reposition the window. Define the outer edge of the screen and the monitor's feet as the draggable region, and Export this layer as another PICT file, named `dragmask.pct`.

The demo folder also contains the movie `milo.mov`, which contains two video tracks – one for the boy, and one for the monitor (open it with QuickTime Player to see for yourself). With `milo.mov`, `dragmask.pct`, and `winmask.pct` in the same directory, we're ready to look at the text file `skinned.xml` (use your favorite text editor to open it). QuickTime has a built-in XML parser that can read this file and interpret it as instructions for constructing a skinned movie. This XML file defines which picture should be used as the window mask, and which one should be used as the drag mask.

5. Copy `skinned.xml` to another file called `skinned.mov`. It's a text file as well, but will probably carry a QuickTime icon and will open with the QuickTime Player by default. Double-click on this file to open it with the QuickTime Player and you will see the results.

6. Select Save As from the File menu and check Make self-contained, then save the movie to a new file, named `finished.mov`. This movie is now self-contained and ready to distribute.

The finished skinned movie hovers elegantly on screen

Batch skinning

The preceding six steps should not prove too painful if your deliverable is a single QuickTime movie, but if you have thousands of existing movies to skin, you're likely to be reaching for the aspirin bottle right about now. Take heart. The XML Import > Save Self-Contained procedure is one of three methods available. You can write an AppleScript to batch process a folder full of movies with a single mouse click, or, if you know the C programming language, you can accomplish the same task at the QuickTime API level (see http://developer.apple.com/techpubs/quicktime/qtdevdocs/PDF/quicktime502.pdf for details). Go ahead and put the aspirin bottle back – hopefully you won't need it.

Media skin problems

Media skins are a great tool, but you should be aware of some potential showstoppers. Media skins only work when your content is viewed in the QuickTime Player (version 5 and higher). Remember that QuickTime is an architecture, not just a player, and that your media can be viewed in other host applications that support QuickTime, such as a web browser. When your skinned movie is embedded in an HTML page, viewers will see the whole movie, including the area you masked out in your `winmask.pct` file.

With great power comes great responsibility, and media skins are no exception to the rule. Apple has given media authors a tool to create truly unique-looking content, but there is a potential for abuse. By overriding the default player, you override the default buttons as well. Your skin should make your content more attractive, not cripple it. Therefore, it's incumbent upon you, the author, to provide custom buttons of your own (such as play, stop, volume control, and most importantly, a close window box or button – see Chapter 5 for details). See Chapter 4 for an overview of techniques available to do this. If you don't provide your users with interface controls, the only way they'll be able to play your media is using the keyboard shortcuts available in QuickTime Player (such as spacebar for play/pause, and cmd/ctrl + up arrow or down arrow for volume up or down). Don't assume that your audience will be QuickTime savvy – if your content is worthy of its own media skin, it is worthy of its own controls.

MPEG-4 and the future of QuickTime

Standards are a very, very good thing. They help a lot of people get things done efficiently. Take traffic laws, for instance. I would personally love it if all drivers would just pull off to the side of the freeway and let me race by whenever they saw me coming. I would also not mind being able to make a left turn without waiting in line at a traffic light. But I adhere to regulations, like most everyone else does, because I don't want to die before I reach my destination, and I assume that most rational drivers on the road want the same thing. I sacrifice a few minutes a day in traffic in the name of personal safety.

Technology is no different. Just think what a nightmare it would be for all of us if the television broadcast industry couldn't agree on the type of signal to broadcast. We would probably have to choose between buying an NBC-compatible TV, or a CBS-compatible TV, or an ABC-compatible TV. What if telephone companies couldn't agree on a common audio compression and decompression scheme? What if there were no agreed upon frequency ranges for FM and AM radio? What if early Internet-adopters hadn't agreed upon HTML as a common language for communicating ideas? The Internet might never have developed beyond a niche market.

Standards in technology are especially important to the computer industry, because they provide a vehicle to drive technology outside the desktop box, and into people's everyday lives. The JPEG image compression scheme's ubiquity on the World Wide Web helped it find its way into digital still cameras. The unprecedented popularity of the MP3 audio format has propelled it into small, handheld Walkman devices. The IEEE-1394 Firewire connector built into almost all DV cameras provides a simple, standard means to import video to the desktop computer, and has contributed mightily to the DV format's success.

In short, the only bad thing about standards is that there are so many to choose from!

MPEG's place in the world of standards

MPEG (Motion Picture Experts Group) is a group of scientists, researchers, and industry professionals who convene regularly to create standards for video and audio. These standards typically take a few years to iron out, and they go through several drafts before they are finalized. Large, influential companies like to push their technologies and intellectual property into MPEG standards because of MPEG's historically successful adoption in various markets. Here's a very brief summary of some of the important work they've done:

- MPEG-1, finished in June of 1996, established a video and audio standard for achieving near VHS quality at around 1.5 megabits per second. Its intended deployment was VCD (Video CD, a very popular set-top format in Asia).

- MPEG-1, Layer 3, also known as MP3, was also part of the June, 1996 document. It achieved near CD-quality audio at 128 kilobits per second. Its intended deployment was low bandwidth markets such as the Internet.

- MPEG-2, finalized in its entirety in October of 2000, defined a high-quality video codec at around 5 – 8 megabits per second. It formed the basis for Digital Television set-top boxes and DVD.

MPEG-4 and QuickTime

MPEG's latest offering, MPEG-4, is its most ambitious yet, promising to standardize video, audio, and interactivity into a common format for fixed and mobile web markets. Portions of the specification have been frozen since 1998, though the last draft of the international standard only went final in March 2001. Much talk has been made of MPEG-4 over the last five years, with many companies hurrying "MPEG-4 compatible" products to market before the standard was finalized. Consequently, a lot of misinformation has circulated around technologies industries, making it difficult for the working content-author to separate fact from fiction. MPEG-4 is not, contrary to popular belief, a strictly low-bandwidth video format. It was indeed envisioned for Internet delivery, but it's also dramatically more **scalable** than its predecessors, MPEG-1 and MPEG-2. This means that MPEG-4 as a video format provides a wide spectrum of usability, from sub-modem data rates up to fast, wide corporate Intranet and television networks. MPEG-4, for instance, can achieve roughly DVD-video quality at about 20 - 40% lower data rates than MPEG-2. MPEG-4 is the first international standard to attempt a common means of providing interactivity. When MPEG began writing its specification, it chose QuickTime's file format as a starting point to imitate.

It should come as no surprise, then, that Apple is throwing its full weight behind the MPEG-4 standard. Apple co-founded the International Streaming Media Alliance (www.isma.tv) along with such heavy hitters as Sun, Cisco, IBM, and Philips. They formed the organization with the goal of accelerating industry adoption of video and audio standards. With the release of QuickTime version 6, Apple became the first of the big three media player providers to support the whole MPEG-4 video, audio, and file format specifications. This means that every copy of QuickTime 6 is capable of encoding and decoding standard MPEG-4 streams and reading and writing .mp4 files. QuickTime's future success is inexorably linked to the success of MPEG-4. In essence, Apple hopes to undermine the ongoing streaming-media wars by beating Microsoft and Real to the emerging Internet video and audio standard, while Microsoft and Real continue to push their proprietary codecs and try to win enough market share to become the de facto standard. Apple's approach is daring and somewhat risky, but the potential dividends are enormous. Think of the utility of having instant access to high-quality video and audio and real-time video conferencing on your cell phone, or Palm Pilot, or built in to your car. Large-scale wireless and stationary network providers most decidedly want this to happen... but they won't gamble on a proprietary format. This is precisely why the closed, competing Real, Windows Media, and QuickTime formats have had trouble breaking out of the desktop computer.

Apple is in an extremely enviable position with its early, complete adoption of MPEG-4. Besides being the first mainstream playback technology provider to support MPEG-4, they have the most mature media editing and authoring framework in place. Chances are good that if MPEG-4 takes off (as it invariably should), QuickTime will become the tool of choice for authoring MPEG-4 content. If QuickTime is already essential in your workflow, then you gain the added benefit of automatic support for MPEG-4. Any tool capable of authoring or exporting a QuickTime movie is automatically capable of authoring MPEG-4 content (for future PDA's, cell phones, set-top boxes, etc.). Hopefully, in a few years, we'll be able to achieve the goal of authoring once, encoding once, and deploying everywhere.

Summary

Even without offering any choices to the viewer, there are a multitude of choices to be made by the author of QuickTime media. The numerous ways even still image formats can be presented within the basic QuickTime player offer a wealth of design opportunities to you as a developer. Later in the book we're going to learn exactly how to best utilize all of the different tracks, but first there is a whole world of interaction to delve into, first the pseudo-3D world of immersive imaging.

3 QuickTime Virtual Reality

The first time I was in San Francisco I visited the Palace of Fine Art and I had an incredible feeling of déjà vu. I had never been to San Francisco and yet I was looking at something I was sure I had visited before. This puzzled me for a while until I realized that the building was the subject of a panorama that Apple had used to demonstrate its new **QuickTime Virtual Reality (QTVR)** medium. From that moment on I was sold on the possibilities that this new media type had to offer. It was certainly a revolutionary change as to how we look at and perceive images, and is referred to by Apple as **immersive imaging**. I had downloaded the panorama from the Internet while I was working in Europe. At that time, even though I was very impressed with the feeling of interactivity, I was concerned that it might have a high gimmick value and would soon be forgotten. Since its introduction QTVR has not yet had a spectacular impact on multimedia. However, it is a product that is finding more and more niches and I have a feeling it will soon reach a critical mass. Even today, when I demonstrate my own QTVR movies I can tell from the expressions on my client's faces whether they've experienced this form of immersive imaging before, and there are still many that have not. However I expect that soon, QTVR, or other VR media types will become accepted and valuable communication tools.

What is QuickTime Virtual Reality?

QTVR is a "movie" that allows the user to explore photorealistic virtual worlds in an interactive way, with the keyboard or a mouse, for example. This world can be made up of photographs made in the real world, or images rendered in a computer or made by an artist. The virtual world can be viewed by looking out and around, as in a panorama, or looking in at and about a virtual object, it is so successful because the metaphor of QTVR maps very tightly to our concept of real world space. One of the problems with QTVR is that although it is reasonably easy to make, it can be quite daunting to see all of the procedures set out in a row, so it is discussed fully in this chapter and in Chapter 8 we'll delve further into the capture and creation process. The tools for creating these virtual worlds can be downloaded free from the Internet and are discussed in Chapter 10. Once you have made your first panorama, CubicVR or object movie, it will be relatively easy from then on to create a powerful and exciting media experience that can be delivered on many media forms and for many platforms.

Lets take a look at the members of the QTVR family.

QTVR Panoramas

QTVR Panoramas are in essence a panoramic photograph or picture that is wrapped around the viewer's field of view to create the illusion of being surrounded. A number of images are stitched together and projected onto a cylinder or cube, or some other geometrical object surrounding space, which is then displayed through a window on a Macintosh or Windows computer. Because of this stitching and projection, QuickTime can pan smoothly through the images as the viewer drags left or right, rather than clicking from one photograph or image to the next. The viewer sees one continuous image, like a cylinder or cube, rather than a series of views.

A panoramic movie therefore has three aspects that can be controlled by the creator or the user. Firstly it has a field of view, which is the window through which the user looks at the panorama, the height and width of which can be set by the creator of the movie. Secondly it has a pan angle, which can be from 0° up to 360°. A pan angle of 0° means the user cannot turn the panorama (defeating the purpose of the panorama) while a pan angle of 180° means the user can turn the panorama half way round. Lastly there is the tilt angle. A tilt angle of 0° points the viewer straight at the horizon. Increasing the tilt angle points the view up while a negative tilt angle points the view down.

The images can be created by photography or using a 3D drawing program or any other kind of image creation software. If the panorama is to be created with photographs, then these are first loaded into the computer and "stitched" using software, that is, they're joined together to give one single large image. This is not as easy as it sounds. Try taking several photos in a circle, and then place the photos next to each other to form a long strip, as shown in the following example (in this case there aren't enough photos to create a full 360° panorama):

You will notice that, although some parts of an image might join up with another, quite often there are points in the distance or in the foreground that do not connect up. The software can actually distort the images, via a process called **morphing** them, to give a homogenous and convincing whole. You can see the difference in this new version.

The image itself seems to be distorted but the QuickTime VR engine compensates for this, creating a smooth consecutive whole. At playback, the user doesn't experience the images as segments:

but as one view that is continuous:

There are several software packages available on the market that can stitch images into one panoramic strip (QuickTime VR Authoring Studio, PhotoVista, and VRToolbox) and these are discussed in detail in Chapter 10. A good example of this is an image I took while standing near the Palais de Chaillot in Paris.

The image is taken at a tilt because I wanted the user to first look down at the water and then up at the Eiffel tower. When viewed as a whole it seems excessively distorted but when viewed as a VR movie it is displayed as a continuous panorama. The image created by the "stitcher" is a PICT file that can then be turned into a QTVR movie using software that is freely available on the Internet.

Spinning around

The resulting QTVR movie is referred to as a **node**, or a single **panorama**. When a QTVR movie is played using the QuickTime player, the control menu has several functions that can be operated by the user.

There is a reverse button furthest left, which allows the user to go back to the previous node. This control, which restores the previous pan angle, tilt angle, and field of view, is enabled only for **multi-node** movies; that is, a QTVR movie with more than one panorama. A node can be another viewpoint in another movie or a different viewpoint in the same movie. There is a zoom out button, with a minus sign. This control causes the field of view of the displayed panorama to increase, thereby making the panorama appear to move back from the viewer. Having zoomed out to infinity and beyond there is also, thankfully, a zoom in button which allows the user to zoom back in, and correspondingly represented by a plus sign.

The SHIFT key can also be used to zoom in and the CTRL key can be used to zoom out. The creator of the movie can preset the extent to which the user can zoom in and zoom out. If the user zooms out too far, it has the outcome of flattening the movie, loosing the cylindrical or surrounding effect of the movie. If the user zooms in too far, then the user will be confronted with a single pixel. The amount the user can zoom in and zoom out also depends on the resolution of the original image material and the compression used in making the movie, we'll talk more about this later.

There is a **hotspot** display button, furthest right here, which allows the user to highlight the hotspots. Hotspots are by default invisible to the user and are usually only detected when the cursor changes as the mouse passes over it. This is advisable because the hotspots would only spoil the image, but sometimes it's impossible to find the hotspot you need to click on to get to the next node or interactivity. By clicking this button the hotspots reveal their presence. In QuickTime 5 a single click toggles hotspots on; another click toggles hotspots off. This is a difference from previous hotspot buttons, which displayed hotspots only while the mouse button was held down.

The developer of the QTVR isn't confined to the standard navigation system, but has several options at his command to add extra user interactivity to his movie. This is done with the help of **calls** or the previously mentioned hotspots. Up to 255 of these hotspots can be created to add additional control to the author and the user outside of the standard QuickTime navigation tools.

Moving on

One of the most important features of this added interactivity is the ability to add links to other nodes or panoramas. Although the panorama is in itself a great multimedia object, it comes into its own when two or more nodes are linked up to each other to create a tour of a virtual area. These links can link up to another panorama, an object movie, a web address, or an external source. It is also possible to perform basic positioning, animation and orientation control. For example, by clicking on a hotspot it is possible for the user to pan to a specific view in the panorama.

It's even possible when using calls from an application to intercept and override QTVR's mouse tracking and default hotspot behaviors. In this way it's possible to give other functions to the hotspots and even make them inactive. An example of this would be to make a game where the user can click once on a hotspot to send a message to your application, but after that the user cannot use that hotspot again. In more advanced QTVR authoring it's possible to combine flat or perspective overlays (such as image movies or 3D models), specify transition effects, control QTVR's memory usage and intercept calls to some QuickTime VR Manager functions and modify their behavior. This system uses QuickTime file format specifications called **Atoms** that are managed from Atom containers, basically information stored within the QTVR movie that can be used for interaction. You know the writer is going into a lot of detail when he starts talking about Atoms, for the moment, it's suffice to say that QTVR isn't just a pretty picture but also a great interactive multimedia experience!

Shapes and sizes

There are two types of QTVR panorama: **cylindrical** and **cubic**. Cylindrical was the first panorama type to be brought onto the market. The basic difference between cubic and cylindrical is the method used to create the environment in which the images are projected.

Primarily, cylindrical panoramas are a series of photos that are taken in a circle from a central point. Each photo should overlap each other and complete the circle. Although it's possible to make panoramas that are less than 360°, the viewer is then not allowed to complete the circle but can view part of the panorama. This can be favorable if you wish to only show part of a scene, for example a panorama of a spot with a beautiful view of a lake in front and of a rubbish dump behind.

Cubic is essentially made up of 6 photographs, 4 side images, and 1 up and 1 down image. These are brought together to form a cube around the field of view of the user, as if the user was in a box. He can then not only look around but also up and down. With cylindrical panoramas the panorama is made of up to 18 photographs forming a long strip. Because the panorama is more of a strip than an enclosed box, the viewer is only shown the field of view at eye level, with a relatively limited tilt of looking up and down, depending on how the pictures were made and the QTVR movie was constructed.

CubicVR made its first appearance with the introduction of QuickTime 5.0. The advantages of cylindrical panoramas are that they're easier to make and can be viewed properly with older versions of QuickTime. CubicVR can be viewed using older versions of QuickTime but there is a danger of a certain amount of distortion in the image. However, CubicVR panoramas give a much greater feeling of being totally surrounded, of being totally immersed in the image.

There are also examples of excellent CubicVR on the CD made by Ken Turkowski, (see CD Chapter3/QTVR/Stanford_balcony.mov and Chapter3/QTVR/Stanford_organ.mov). These CubicVR's were made in the Memorial Church of Stanford University in the San Francisco Bay Area (see also www.worldserver.com/turk). The QTVR engine distorts the edges and corners of the cube so that you don't see them, unless you are using pre-Version 5 QuickTime, in which case the distortion becomes obvious. It's a much more immersive and richer experience than cylindrical, and is an answer to the iPix panorama product that was introduced a few years ago. Great examples of CubicVR nodes can be found at the Apple site, www.apple.com/quicktime/products/gallery.

Image creation

When making a complex multi-node QTVR movie it is very important to plan ahead. If, for example, you are going to make a virtual reality tour of a house, it is important that you are aware of all the problems that can arise before the shoot begins. A good idea is to make a sketch or map of where you wish to make the panoramas. This map can later be used in your scene creation software to give a graphic representation to help plan and link the nodes. Walking through your area before hand can help give an idea and help solve any problems, for example are there any mirrors that might reflect the camera equipment. Even small details – is the house tidy, will there be people in the house at the time that might get in the way and do you have permission – will all have an influence on outcome on the shoot. The more time you have to concentrate on the photography, the better.

Looking all around

There are several issues, which have to be addressed and that you have to be aware off when creating the images for producing panoramas. If you are using a 3D drawing program you will have a lot more control over the viewpoint and the quality of image produced, probably a panorama export option as well. However, out in the field, there are many things that can influence the shoot. I was involved with taking photographs for a panorama in Venice, but it was incredibly difficult to get a shot without any tourists walking through the picture. If a tourist was in one picture but not in the next overlapping picture (because he had gone off back to his hotel) then the stitching software wouldn't be able to make a fluent stitch and the result would be a ghost or half a man. Once I had the misfortune to take a panorama while a tourist was walking in the same direction as the camera, and he ended up being seen several times in the same panorama... as you can see!

At the Colosseum in Rome, a tourist stood in one picture, then moved slightly so he was in a different

The same problem can occur with cars that pass into shot just as you take the photograph, resulting in a stretched limousine or a car cut completely in two. Another problem I had was taking a panorama in the underground in London. In the dark, the train windows acted as mirrors so you could see the

This particular panorama was difficult to make because the whole carriage was swinging backwards and forwards making it difficult to make a consistent seamless series of pictures. The man in the photograph didn't like being photographed and got very grumpy about it, another problem with panoramas, but I had no choice but to point the camera in his direction. Another problem associated with this panorama

position – the result was twins:

camera equipment and me very easily. These images were then later manipulated in Photoshop. See the following image, or see the CD chapter3/QVTR/underground.mov:

was that... well, quite frankly, I didn't ask for permission, and was thrown out on my ear by the British Transport Police! In places where you could be causing a nuisance, it's better to ask first.

Exposure

When taking a series of pictures, it usually takes a few minutes to complete the shoot, and you would be surprised how quick the lighting changes, even subtly, especially on a semi-cloudy day. You may find that the first photograph you take has a different exposure time, or the setting of the camera for the first photo is too dark or too light for the last. A good example of this is the previous Venice panorama (with the white haired tourist), where there is clearly a dark band in the middle of the picture, as the sun past partially behind a cloud when that single photograph was made. This kind of difference isn't easily perceptible with the human eye, as the eye readjusts automatically to the light change. The exposure settings of the camera however are different, as they must correspond exactly with the lighting settings of the previous photograph. Another problem with lighting in panoramas, especially indoors, is that the lamps you use will be seen in the panorama, unless of course you limit the pan of the panorama. A solution is to use the natural lighting inside the room (such as normal lamps and light from outside), but you also have to make sure that the camera doesn't look directly into the light source, creating glare and light flares.

Parallax

To get a perfect panorama it is important to understand the effects of parallax. Parallax results when the nodal point (also called the focal point) of the camera lens is not the same as the camera's point of rotation. This offset causes foreground objects to appear to move relative to other objects in the background when the camera is moved from side to side, as is shown here. The two lines are the focal point diverging in the lens.

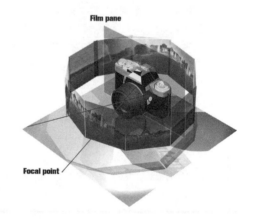

If all foreground features are relatively distant in the view, then parallax effects are not a problem. The focal point is not the area were the light hits the film, called the film plane, but a point inside the lens. Most of the cameras have an attachment socket that is located underneath this film plane making the camera rotate around this point and not the focal node.

If the series of photos is free of parallax it makes it much easier to stitch the photographs later on. Making sure that the camera rotates under the focal node solves this problem and there are several tripods and adapters available on the market, and this is discussed in Chapter 8. This is the ideal situation, but it's not written in law. I once made a panorama from the top of the Campanile in Venice. The point of rotation for this panorama is about three meters from the focal point, as I had to hang over the edge of the four corners of the tower to get a good view. If I had taken the panorama from the middle of the tower you would only see the eight pillars and blue sky. Not only that, I had to take the photographs without the use of a tripod; a common problem when taking pictures in public places. The result was heavily reworked in Photoshop, but was adequate for what it was intended for (see CD `Chapter3/QVTR/Campanile.mov`). Check out the bottom of this panorama, at some places you'll see that the stitcher has made an attempt to fill in the areas where it didn't have enough image material to complete the panorama.

Leveling the land

To make a convincing panorama, the camera has to be level, but it doesn't have to be level with the natural horizon. A QTVR panorama is based on a cylindrical view of 3D space so to ensure the best possible panorama the camera must rotate on an axis that is perpendicular to the axis of the view through the camera's lens.

What this really means, is that when making a panorama you can decide for yourself what the horizon is, but once that decision is made you have to stay with it. For example, I made a panorama in Florence of a building (an example of sgraffito), and in front of the building was a street artist who had chalked a great picture (of Raphael's 'Madonna della Seggiola'). The resulting panorama is a dizzying example of tilt, but it works even though it has no connection with the real horizon. The panorama can be seen on the CD-ROM (see CD `Chapter3/QVTR/Seggiola.mov`)

QTVR objects

QTVR **objects** are in fact the inverse of QTVR panoramas. An object node provides a view of a single object (a speedboat) or a point where a group of objects are, for example, a table with knives and forks and glasses on it. The object node provides a view of an object from the outside looking in, unlike a panorama which looks out. The movie on the CD `Chapter3/QVTR/object.mov` is an example. The user can use the mouse or keyboard to change the horizontal and vertical viewing angles to move around the object. The user can also zoom in to enlarge or zoom out to reduce the size of the object. Object nodes are often designed to give the illusion that the user is picking up and turning an object and is able to view it from all angles. This can be used for technical manuals (for example, showing how a component should look in 3D). It also has commercial purposes as a user can look at something from all directions. I made the example that follows using a 3D drawing package. The object can also be photographed although a lot more preparation and care has to be taken than with panoramas. A good example is the object movie to be found at the Ferrari site www.ferrari.com, which has an excellent object movie of their F355 Spider (which, by the way, is a car).

Creating QTVR object movies

You create a QTVR object movie by taking and digitizing a series of photographs (or rendering a series of computer-generated images) that show an object from multiple perspectives. This is achieved by rotating the object on a turntable or a pedestal (sometimes called a 'Lazy Susan'). After you have created a series of images, and have digitized them, you may need to retouch them with a graphic editor (such as Photoshop) to remove things like the pedestal and/or elements in the background. You can then bring together the images into an object movie using authoring software such as QuickTime VR Authoring Studio, Widgetizer, or PanoWorx. When I created the object movie, I used Strata Studio Pro, a 3D imaging program. It was possible to build my model, and using a virtual camera supplied with the program it was extremely easy to create the images for the object movie.

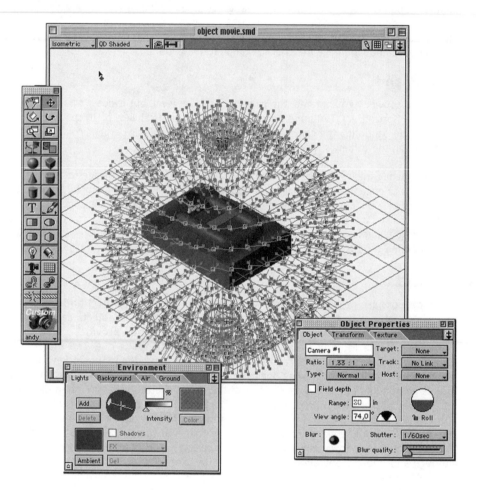

The rendering was first saved as a QuickTime movie, and then using the object movie tool QTVR Edit Object it was converted into a QuickTime object movie. This software is free and is available from the Internet. It's Mac only, though there are PC equivalents available. (http://developer.apple.com/quicktime/quicktimeintro/tools/index.html)

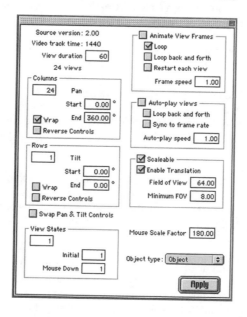

Equipment

If you're not creating your images using 3D software, you need a camera, lights, a backdrop, a turntable or pedestal to rotate the object, and ideally an object VR rig that allows you to position the camera through a vertical arc. The rig is only necessary when you wish to view the object from above as well as from the sides.

A 35-mm SLR camera with a telephoto or macro zoom lens is the standard for high-quality work. These days the quality of the digital cameras is more than enough to achieve a high resolution. Remember that the end product is meant for viewing on the computer and is therefore limited to the resolution of the screen, which is lower than for printed work such as magazines. The only advantage for high resolution is that it gives the user the opportunity to zoom in further before distortion and pixelation takes place. A good digital camera is also much more convenient, as you will not have to digitize the images and can directly load them into your computer for further processing. A digital video camera that can take still frames is also fine for this work, especially if you don't need higher resolution. Another advantage of a digital camera is you take a lot of shots for object movies – 36 exposures for a rotation, and up to 18 rotations to cover an object from top to bottom. That's 648 images in total. A digital camera can download images to your computer in mid-shoot, while a conventional SLR camera has to have its film physically replaced. If your camera is hanging on a rig above an object, lets say a car, that's the last thing you want to do, not to mention the cost of developing 648 photos. A digital camera can also be hooked up to a screen so you don't have to climb up the rig to take a look through the viewfinder. In an ideal situation, when making an object movie, it is best to have a neutral background. When moving the object around, the background will flash past, distracting from the subject of attention. A black background, or alternatively a white background when the object is itself dark, works very well. Also, by choosing a contrasting color, it is easier to remove the background altogether (if so desired) in an imaging program such as Photoshop.

Companies like Peace River (www.peaceriverstudios.com) and Kaidan (www.kaidan.com) sell rigs and motorized turntables that make the process a lot easier. However, if you wish to make a movie of something like a car then you'll need a really big turntable like that made by Emery Manufacturing & Equipment (www.emerymfg.com). There are also studios that hire out this equipment, for example eVox (www.evox.com) that has offices in America and Europe. It is also possible to purchase or hire a rig for vertically aligning your camera and remote-control software that works directly with QuickTime VR Authoring Studio or Widgetizer.

Single-row
The object movie of the Ferrari we've talked about is an example of a single-row object movie; that is, it traverses around the object, but not above or below it. You can use a tripod for these kinds of shots, but it's essential that the tripod remain at the same level, for if there is a slight difference in height, the object movie will jiggle about.

Multi-row
Multi-row object movies need a rig that can swing the camera through a precise arc. A commercial object VR rig is definitely the easiest way to achieve this; again, any differences in the positions of the images in the object movie will result in an irritating jiggle within the movie. There is of course a range from manual models to really expensive motorized apparatus with turntables and remote control software. The main manufacturers are Kaidan and Peace River, and the better models can shoot an entire object movie, top to bottom and round-and-round, under automated control from QuickTime VR Authoring Studio or Widgetizer.

QTVR scenes

As mentioned earlier, it's possible to link up panoramas or nodes, with other nodes, turning one virtual reality view into a virtual reality tour. The creator of the movie can also determine the position and shape of the hotspot. This allows the creator to make hotspots, for example across a door, and when the user clicks on the door it leads to another node, for instance the room next door. This is relatively easy to do, and there are procedures that can help you with authoring, planning, and managing your QTVR scene.

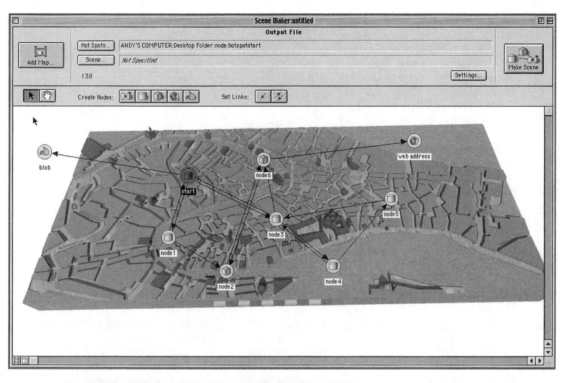

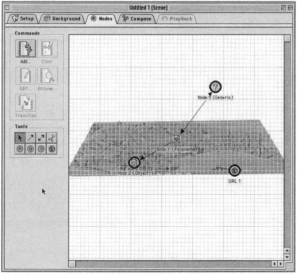

I used Apple's QuickTime VR Authoring Studio to create and manage a scene. QuickTime VR Authoring Studio isn't the only software package that can create scenes and it's Mac only; VR Toolbox also has a scene generator that works in the same way, and is PC friendly.

Firstly, I've created a map to help me visualize the virtual area I wish to manage. With the map as a visual aid (although it is not obligatory to use a map) it is possible to place node icons in relation to one another. The map I created is a 3D map of Venice, but it doesn't have to be so complicated, it could also be a quick pencil sketch that has been digitized using a scanner. QuickTime VR Authoring Studio has

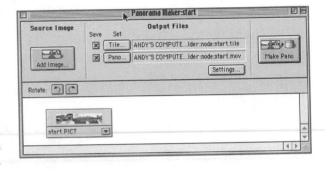

five ways of creating nodes, you can see their icons lined up just above the main window. The **panorama stitcher** links to the images you have created that need to be first stitched to make a panorama. The **panorama maker** takes the stitched image and turns it into a panorama movie:

The third icon is an **object movie node link**. The fourth icon is a **web address link,** when the user clicks on this hotspot, a browser is launched and the specified web page (if the user is connected to the Internet) will be loaded. The fifth and last icon is a **create blob** icon. A blob has a great value in that every hotspot has its own unique number, this number corresponds with the RGB color of the hotspot it self. This unique number can be referenced from outside the QTVR movie by the QuickTime VR manager or in other multimedia authoring tools such as Macromedia Director (this is covered in more depth in Chapter 10). For example, if the user clicks on a blob hotspot, the number referenced can tell the computer to play a sound or perform an action.

There will be a start node, this icon represents the first panorama that appears when the QTVR movie is opened. In the Venice example, from this node there are three links, two linking up to two other panoramas in a two way link (that is, when you have gone from the start node to another node, there is a hotspot in that node to return back to the original node). Also leading from the start node is the third link that links up to a blob. This blob I've used to reference an image file which appears when the user clicks on it. Nodes can be linked with a one-way link; that is, there is no link back to the previous node once one has arrived at our new node.

In our PC map Node 3 is an object movie, so if Node 2 is a panorama taken inside a museum, Node 3 could be an object in that museum that the user can look at from different angles. The hotspots can be created in any shape and positioned anywhere within the panorama. This is done with a hotspot editor.

Here there are three hotspots. The first hotspot is square and has the unique ID of 71; this number is RGB color of the hotspot itself. No two hotspots can have the same color, so there is a limit of 255 hotspots in a single node. There is also the possibility of choosing your own hotspot color from the 255, although the color itself isn't visible to the user.

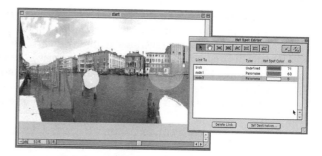

It's also possible to make a hotspot with an irregular shape that covers a specific area in the panorama or object movie.

The final scene once completed can be saved as one large movie containing all the other nodes. It's also possible to save the movie as a small file that simply references the other nodes. These other files are not encapsulated and have to be delivered with the reference file. When building a large scene with many nodes it may be advantageous to reference the other nodes, as a scene can easily grow to be many megabytes and become unwieldy, creating memory management problems. The scene editor file can also be saved for later reference or if any changes have to be made.

An example of such a movie this is on the CD (Chapter3/QTVR/russia.mov). You can see where the hotspots are positioned by clicking on the hotspot button.

Also on the CD is an example of a virtual reality tour of Venice using Macromedia Director, in Chapter3/QVTR_demos/ there are both Mac and PC versions, which will have to be decompressed to your hard drive. This tour doesn't use hotspots, because when it was created, it wasn't possible to create a scene using panoramas made with different lenses. The navigation therefore was created outside of QuickTime using routines called from the Director file itself. It's an example of the control that an author has not only through but also outside QuickTime when creating in this media.

Hotspot button

QTVR embellishments

One of the properties that can be added to a QTVR movie that has a great outcome on the immersive effect is sound. It's possible using either embedded sound in the QTVR movie itself, or outside of the movie (for example using Macromedia Director) to add sound effects. What really enhances the effect of sound is directional ambient audio. Imagine you're looking at a panorama of a scene in a city. To the front of you there is a crowd of children waiting at a bus stop, to the left there is a busy street with cars, to the right is a group of cyclists, and behind you a park with a fountain. It adds immensely to the overall scene if the sound changes when you move the panorama to a specific direction. Imagine seeing the children at the bus stop and also hearing the chatter of children in the background. Move the panorama to the left and the chatter of children dies away while the sound of cars fades in to take its place. Move to the right and the sound of bicycles can be heard. Turn 180° and the sound of a fountain fades in.

There are several ways to do this. One way is to use a product like Macromedia Director, which uses **Lingo** (its own authoring language) to control QTVR. Lingo lets you control how QuickTime VR responds when the user clicks on a QuickTime VR sprite. You can use Lingo to specify how Director handles things like image quality, clicks and rollovers on a QuickTime VR sprite, clicks on hotspots, and interactions with QuickTime VR nodes. Director can also detect the current pan (the angle being viewed) of the QuickTime VR movie. The value is given in degrees and can be set so that the panorama swings to that view. It can therefore also play a specific sound when a specific angle or pan is being viewed. This is also possible with authoring products like LiveStage Pro.

An even easier option is using a tool such as SMGVR's SoundSaVR (www.smgvr.com). With this, it's possible to add several different sound files directly to the QTVR movie, limited only by the amount of available memory. Again we'll delve further in Chapter 10.

Transitional movies

While a panorama is being displayed, it can be either at rest or in motion, and that motion can be automatic or produced by the user. A panorama is in motion when it is being panned, tilted, or zoomed. A panorama is also in motion when a "transition" (defined as a movement between two items in a movie, such as from one view to another view in the same node, or from one node to another) is happening. It's possible change the imaging properties of a panorama to control the quality and speed of display during rest or motion states. By default, QuickTime VR sacrifices quality for speed during motion but displays at highest quality when at rest (at about a 3:1 performance penalty). This is logical, as things tend to have a natural "blur" when moving fast.

When a transition happens, it's possible to specify that a special visual effect, called a transition effect, be displayed. At present, the only transitional effect currently supported is a **swing transition** between two views in the same QTVR movie. When the swing transition is enabled and a new pan angle, tilt angle, or field of view is set, the movie controller performs a smooth "swing" to the new view (rather than a simple jump to the new view). In the future, it's speculated, other transitional effects may be supported. There are some excellent games on the market that give an idea of what the future of QTVR might hold.

Zoom, pan, and tilt

As already mentioned it's possible to zoom in and out, pan (that is look around), and tilt (look up or down). The data in a panorama and object movie imposes a set of viewing restrictions on the associated node. For example, a particular panorama might be a partial panorama (a panorama that is less than 360 degrees). Another example is that the object movie might include views for tilt angles only in a restricted range, for example +30 degrees to -30 degrees (instead of the standard +90 degrees to -90 degrees). The allowable ranges of pan angles, tilt angles, and fields of view are the viewing limits, which can be set for each movie. Viewing limits are determined at the time a movie is created and are exacted by the data stored in the movie file.

The view limits for cubic panoramas perform like those for cylindrical panoramas: the limit is enforced at the edge of the view. The two exceptions are for: tilt = + or -90 degrees; in these cases, the center of the view is constrained to straight up or down. It is also possible to go beyond + or -90 degrees, so that you look upside-down! However, the pan controller acts in mirror image when upside-down.

It's possible to impose other viewing restrictions at runtime. For instance, a game developer might want to limit the amount of a QTVR panorama that is visible to the user until the user accomplishes some objective (such as clicking all the hotspots, or visiting all the nodes in a movie). If the movie file doesn't contain any viewing constraint atoms, and no constraints have been imposed during the playing of the movie, a node's viewing constraints coincide with its viewing limits.

Break out of the real world

The obvious use of QTVR is to view and navigate through a virtual terrestrial sphere, for example rooms in a house, or streets in a city. However, the immersive imagery doesn't have to be based on these worlds; it can also be imagery that is purely based on aesthetics, or has some other educational or informative function.

Surrealism in VR

An example of this is can be seen at http://caroling.holyoak.com/Access/path/immerse/axQubic.htm which is a kind of surrealist's CubicVR. Another example is a CubicVR that I made (see the CD Chapter3/QTVR_demos/cube/cube.mov) shown here:

This uses six checked colored image files (also on the CD in the Chapter3/QTVR_demos/cube/ folder) to create its cubist's CubicVR experience.

Data in VR

There are many great examples of QTVR being used as an interactive graphic representation. One example is the map used by Greenpeace on their web site at: www.greenpeace.org/greatbear.

Another excellent example is the web site tour of New Orleans by Ray Broussard for PhotographicVR.com (http://PhotographicVR.com/neworleans).

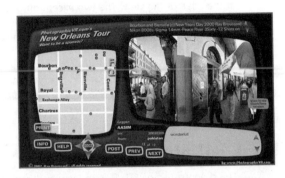

Here QTVR is combined with Flash to give an interactive experience.

Find these!

www.abouthovenweep.com is another example of QTVR being used in combination with Flash. This is a tour made by Dave Krick of the odd structures in the Bisti Badlands of New Mexico:

Orientation maps and compasses

As it's possible to call back the pan angle of a QTVR panorama at any given time, there is the potential to use this information to influence an object or animation outside the movie. An example is a compass, which points in the direction of the panorama. Whenever I make a panorama I always make sure I can place the pan angle in a known direction. That is, I always start taking the first photograph pointing towards the north. A pan angle of 0° in my QTVR movies means that the panorama is pointing north, and 180° is south. This I can use to influence a compass outside of the panorama. An example of this is seen in the QTVR demo on the CD (Chapter3/QTVR_demos/PC (or Mac) /Europe_demo/demo.exe (or demo.sea). When looking around Venice, the eye on the 3D map next to the movie looks in the direction in which the pan angle is pointing.

QTVR as a web site

Another excellent example of a combination of the immersive imagery in QTVR and its many interactive possibilities is www.icimediainc.com/presentations/ici_demos_pres_kel.html, made by ICI media. Here, the navigation structure of a web site has been incorporated into a QTVR movie, so one can "look around" the navigation and has been hotspot-linked to HTML pages within the site. Although this is a very original concept and illustrates the power of the interactivity available from within QTVR, it has a great download disadvantage in relation to traditional HTML pages. In addition, to view QTVR content via a browser, QuickTime has to be installed on the computer and the QuickTime plug-in has to be available to the browser. People accessing the site from their workstations may also have problems with proxy servers and firewalls.

Synchronized VR movies

Another potential within the QTVR movie is the possibility to link QTVR movies up to each other so that they can interact. A cute example is the work created by Eric Blanpied, which shows the various stages of the renovation of his house (www.blanpied.net/workshop/vr/housepanos/panopicker.html).

On the left side you see the house, as it was, on the right the house after the renovation. When you pan the first node, the second node moves in synchronization:

Eric has also used a 3D rendering of his house as a part of the QTVR nodes.

Summary

So, we've investigated the whole sphere (literally!) of QuickTime Virtual Reality and looked at a wide variety of uses for its immersive imaging, from the most basic panoramas to complex CubicVR. We've discussed some of the issues involved in creating QTVR movies – although at this stage we're barely scratched the surface.

Before we can use our new design skills in the real world we need to think a lot more about interaction and delivery of our material, and that's what we'll talk about in the next few chapters before returning to QVTR with a vengeance in Chapter 8.

4 Interactive Media

What exactly do we mean by interactive media? Simply media that responds to some audience activity. Simple examples could include HTML hyperlinks and PowerPoint navigation buttons. In these examples the audience clicks on a hyperlinked word or a conventional navigation icon and a predetermined response takes place; we're shown another page of a web site or another slide in a slideshow.

Is that all there is? Thankfully there's more. When people interact with one another, the responses aren't necessarily predetermined and neither are the stimuli that initiate those responses. People are delightfully complex in this regard and the media we use to express ourselves should strive to be equally boundless.

QuickTime authored media can more closely approximate the complexity that we see in the real world both with human interaction and interactions between and among elements in the physical universe. We can create a movie with a very wide range of possible audience inputs that invoke an equally wide range of responses without always having to script every one of those possible interactions.

Therefore, our definition of interactive media is media that responds conditionally to a range of audience activities. An example of this would be a simple, one player version of the game, ping-pong. Atari did this quite successfully in the early years of video gaming with a video game called Pong.

In the one-player version of Pong, the audience gets to control a paddle moving it up and down along the left of the screen to simulate the wooden paddle in a real game of ping-pong. The object, of course, is to avoid missing the ball with the paddle and losing points. The ball would bounce in directions governed by rules having to do with where on the paddle it struck, whether it collided with a side, etc. The ball might even accelerate in velocity if it were hit squarely.

Even in this rather simple game world, the audience gets an almost infinite variety of possibilities, which is very attractive to them. We might not know exactly how many quarters were spent in Pong machines at the arcade, but you can be sure that the total was impressive. The opportunity to interact where the outcome isn't certain is very attractive to most audiences.

Other examples include problem solving exercises, illustrative physical and conceptual models, fantasy environments, simulations, puzzles, quizzes, and so on. The list of possibilities is really quite open-ended.

A QuickTime movie can be interactive in this sense because it has scriptable tracks (Sprite, Flash, Text, and VR) as well as other tracks (Tween, Modifier, and Source) that scriptable tracks can draw upon for even greater power and flexibility. These scriptable tracks, especially the sprite track, are able to influence and control their own appearance and behavior as well as the appearance and behavior of non-scriptable tracks (See www.apple.com/quicktime/products/tutorials/tracks.html for brief descriptions of all 14 track types). As this is all contained within the same robust architecture, all of the many media types that can be contained in a QuickTime movie can be integrated into a seamless and interactive media experience.

To fully appreciate the potential of QuickTime interactivity, we need to examine these scriptable tracks in some detail. We'll be looking at how these track types make a high level of interactivity possible so that you can see how your authoring goals might be met with in an interactive QuickTime movie. Once you've decided that interactive QuickTime movie making is for you, other texts will guide your journey further.

Sprite tracks

What is a sprite? The contemporary use of the word **sprite** usually tries to evoke references to the quick and nimble movements of an elf or pixie, like Tinkerbell in Peter Pan. Consequently, cars, dog breeds, and other things have adopted the name sprite to convey quickness or nimbleness. Being sprightly is a good thing.

This use of sprite is the same in computer graphics. The nimbleness of a graphic sprite is derived, in large measure, from its ability to move around the computer screen independently of other images. In traditional video or animation, the entire screen or frame has to be redrawn many times per second in order to sustain the illusion of motion even if that motion is confined to a small portion of that graphic image. A sprite, on the other hand, is a visual object that can be moved over top of other graphic layers simply by specifying new locations for its registration point. Avoiding all of that redrawing obviously enables the display device to deliver a better illusion of motion by virtue of the fact that changes in a sprite's location on the screen can be presented in a faster and smoother manner.

QuickTime graphic sprites have many other interesting and useful attributes. We'll briefly refer to the most prominent of those attributes in the next few paragraphs.

Visual attributes

A QuickTime sprite can use any of the hundreds of graphics formats supported by QuickTime (see www.apple.com/quicktime/specifications.html). It can be a raster (bitmap) image or it can be a vector image. In either case, such sprites can be made to do much more than move around the screen. They can be rotated, scaled up or down and distorted in many ways as well as moved around the screen. Moreover, sprites can simultaneously combine more than one of these actions.

Imagine a square rotating clockwise around its registration point, scaling to 200% and exiting stage left, all at apparently the same time! Of course, using vector images would work and look better here primarily because vectors usually have smaller file sizes and don't exhibit exaggerated aliasing when scaled and rotated. Sprites usually contain at least one image even if they aren't visible but may also contain a whole bank of images for the purpose of animations ranging from simple button rollovers to full-screen productions. Layers and transparency are also supported. Finally, more than one sprite can appear and be active at the same time. This is quite a palette to work from but the best is yet to come!

Behavioral attributes

QuickTime sprites, whether visible or not, are able to interact with their environment or "world" as well as interact with one another, with other tracks in the same movie, with other movies, and with the audience. It's here that QuickTime sprites differentiate themselves most clearly from sprite implementations elsewhere. They can be scripted or "wired" to interact with all of these other elements. While there are several ways one can wire QuickTime Sprites with low level coding approaches such as C and Java, our focus will be on the high level solution that is accessible to the greatest number of media producers, LiveStage Professional from Totally Hip Software (www.totallyhip.com). A trial version of this product can be found on the CD accompanying this book.

It's within the sprite track that we find the center of QuickTime media interactivity. Yes, there are other scriptable tracks (Text Tracks, Flash Tracks, and VR Tracks) but the sprite track is where the greatest potential for action resides. So, let's take a closer look at the architecture of the QuickTime sprite track.

Sprites are contained in a sprite track. There can be any number of sprite tracks and each of them can contain many sprite samples arranged along the movie timeline. Each of these sprite samples can contain many sprites and graphic images. Sprites themselves can change their properties and scripts over time. They can even change their graphic face using image overrides, become invisible altogether, and draw data and images from other tracks and remote databases. Sprites can even create other sprites!

When you look at all of these elements as opportunities for making things happen conditionally, it becomes apparent that you've an extremely rich palette to work with. Moreover, these opportunities for change can be time-based or event-based as you decide. That is, something can be scripted to happen at a certain point or points in the timeline or something can be scripted to happen when and if a certain event such as a mouse-click occurs at a certain place. These actions can even be both time and event-based.

Looking a little deeper, we see that there are multiple layers of scripting. Some scripting can be done almost entirely by point and click as is the case with making roll-over buttons. Looking further, we see that some scripting can be done with pre-scripted objects called **behaviors**, which require only that we supply a few parameter values. Peering still further into sprite scripting, we see that common events such as idle, frame, loaded, and various mouse movements can be scripted by selecting them in an event window, dragging script elements from the QScript Reference palette into the script edit window and editing them. Alternatively, one can simply write QScript code from scratch. These scripts can also be saved for later use. If that isn't enough, we can even concoct a custom event and script that! It doesn't take long to assemble a powerful array of behaviors and scripts that facilitate your particular workflow needs.

The QScript scripting language in LiveStage Pro has approximately 176 statements enabling the control of nearly every aspect of a QuickTime movie. Complex scripts that are used frequently can be turned into behaviors and thus become a reusable script object. Perhaps the ultimate reusable object is the LiveStage Pro project folder itself. These can be made general enough so that one need only change the graphic elements in order to create many variations on a single theme. A highly generalized LiveStage Pro project folder can be an extremely valuable asset to busy media producers.

Behaviors, scripts, and entire LiveStage Pro projects are developed and shared freely within the LiveStage community. A good place to find this kind of code and many more valuable resources is the BlueAbuse web site at www.blueabuse.com and the LiveStage Developer Network site at www.totallyhip.com/lsdn. Here, you'll find tutorials, behaviors, project files, scripts, links to exemplary sites, and further resources, and many ways to participate in a community of interactive media authors.

How exactly does all of this work? While we're not going to try to duplicate the many fine "how-to" resources on making wired sprites, an illustration or two will be useful in tying all of these concepts together.

Scripting a button with point and click

First, we use a graphics application such as Photoshop to create three versions of our button. They are named "Down", "Over", and "Up" to represent the three states that our button will be in during the following events:

- Mouse Over and Button Pressed: show "Down"

- Mouse Over and Button Not Pressed: show "Over"

- Mouse Not Over and Button Pressed: show "Up"

- Mouse Not Over and Button Not Pressed: show "Up"

We then launch LiveStage Pro, create a new project, create a sprite track, open the sprite sample, and drag our three button images into the Images tab of the sprite sample.

At that point, we should see something like this:

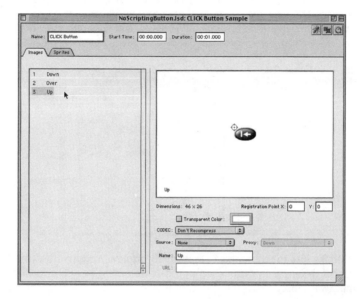

Clicking on the Sprites tab and then the Button tab, we're now able to wire our button images to the states listed above. This is done with a simple point and click. First, we point at the pop-up menus for each button state and select the appropriate graphic. This pop-up is populated with the names of the graphics imported above. Note that we can also determine what kind of cursor appears for each of these events.

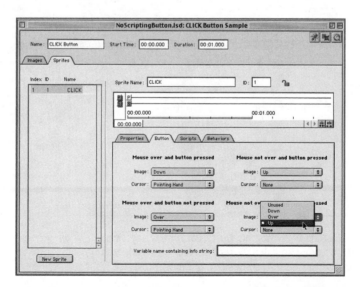

We've now done enough to warrant a quick test to see if what we intended is being carried out. Clicking on the blue Q in the upper, right-hand corner compiles a test movie that we can check out right away. The next three screen shots show what happens when the mouse isn't over the button, when it's over the button but not pressed, and when it's over the button and the button is pressed.

However, that's just the visual part we want to display. We also want the button to actually do something. In this case, the icon used in the button design conventionally suggests a rewind. To affect this, we simply click on the Scripts tab and then locate the appropriate command (GoToBeginning) in the QScript reference palette and drag that into the script window.

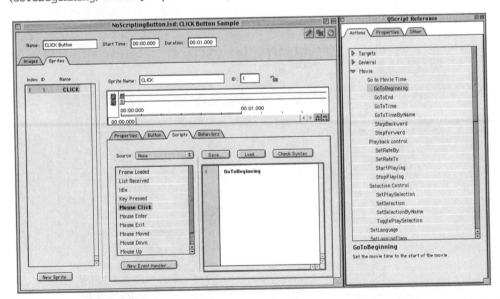

As part of a linear movie this button would be accompanied by others like it, to create a full-featured custom controller. What started out looking very similar to what can be done with JavaScript has turned into something uniquely powerful. As a bonus, we get a single file that works cross-platform/cross-browser instead of many lines of code mixed with HTML, which may or may not work cross-platform/cross-browser.

Using a behavior to automate finding things in a VR Panorama movie

Moving on a bit, we can get very complex activities with minimum effort by using those script objects called "behaviors". In this next case, we have a QuickTime VR Panoramic movie. Let's say that we want to present a panoramic image of several important buildings on a college campus. Even where the audience knows that this is a QuickTime VR Panorama and how to navigate one, they don't know which building is which. Now, while we could come up with a double handful of text to describe which building is which, it's better to avoid that if possible. Here's what we'll do. We'll create a QuickTime movie that contains a QTVR Track and add to it a sprite track with some buttons that cause the focus to pan and zoom in or out to show the building named on each button.

All that this will require on our part is using a LiveStage behavior by feeding it with the data it needs to cause this complex action to take place.

The finished movie looks like:

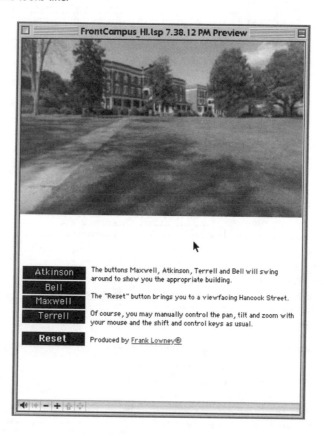

Clicking on the name of the building (a button) swings the view around and zooms in or out as necessary to focus on that building. Whatever sequence the buttons are clicked on, this "smart" movie will calculate what it has to do to bring that item smoothly into view.

How'd they do that? Here's how. In LiveStage Pro, we make a movie whose dimensions are large enough to accommodate both the QuickTime VR Panorama and the text and control buttons you see above. Next, add the VR Track and create a sprite track with graphics for the buttons pictured above. Then create sprites for each graphic and click on the Behaviors tab where we'll add the QTVRSwing behavior by Erik Fohlin (freely downloadable from the LiveStage Developer Network web site www.totallyhip.com/lsdn/resources/Behaviors/index.html). Just drag-and-drop that behavior into place as pictured below:

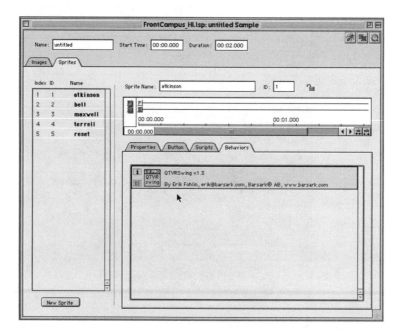

Clicking on the 'i' info icon brings up directions on how to use it and clicking on the parameter button (under the info button) brings up a request for parameter info that looks like:

Your VR stitching software should enable you to easily determine the destination pan angle, field of view, and tilt angle. You can experiment with swing speed by changing this parameter and quickly creating a preview movie until you get the effect that

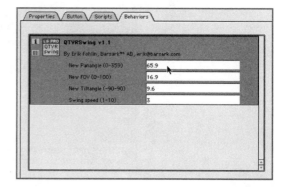

you want. If you'd like to get some insight into how much scripting you've just avoided, open up the behavior in a text editor. This is also a good way to get deeper into scripting, look at how other people have achieved a given effect.

Scripting a MIAM (movie-in-a-movie)

This last example uses the QuickTime Player but could just as well use the QuickTime plug-in to present the movie embedded in a web page. The amazing thing about the movie below is that it weighs in at only 5,738 bytes (6K). Yet, with it, one can watch three 640x480 pixel videos with sound whose duration totals 3 minutes and 10 seconds!

The trick is to use a technique called MIAM. MIAM is an acronym for movie-in-a-movie. The containing movie is called the parent movie and the contained movie is called the child movie. The three videos I spoke of (6.9, 15.3 and 10.4MB respectively) actually exist outside this MIAM and are loaded on demand.

The parent movie contains a movie track containing a child movie and a sprite track. The sprite track has scripted buttons to control starting and stopping the currently loaded child movie and buttons to load the three child movies on demand. This is an excellent way to avoid delay in time-sensitive presentations. If it isn't demanded, it isn't loaded.

The movie track simply contains references to the actual movies using absolute or relative URLs.

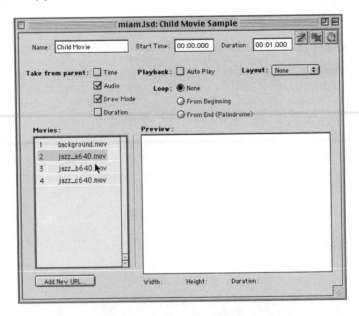

The sprite track contains the button images and the scripting to stop, play, and load movies. That scripting looks like this (see box on the bottom right):

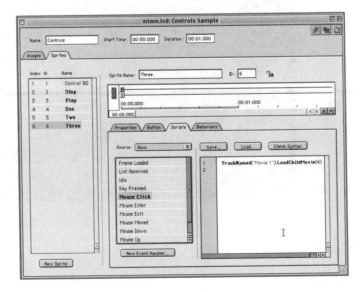

Of course, scripting movies can get much more complicated than this depending upon what your goals are. Other texts can take you down that road as far as you want to go. The point to be recognized here is that wired sprites are within the grasp of most people working in a communications field today. Whether you are doing simple wired buttons via point and click or using behaviors or scripting from the script reference or from scratch, you have a great deal of control over the experiences that your audiences will receive.

Flash tracks

It's not uncommon to perceive some confusion about the relationship between Flash and QuickTime. Many people have mistakenly seen that relationship as an either/or proposition. Now that Flash SWF files can be imported into QuickTime movies as Flash tracks, there is no need to fret over which to use.

There are times when Flash is appropriately used outside of QuickTime and there are times when Flash is enhanced by importing it as a track in a QuickTime movie. The same is true with QuickTime. There are times when including a Flash track adds great value to your QuickTime movie. This is the decision that QuickTime media developers need to concentrate on.

While there's a considerable amount of overlap in what Flash and QuickTime can do separately, it's also true that each has strengths not equaled by the other. Flash excels in the animation of vector graphics and text. QuickTime excels in the breadth and scope of its media reach, including many things that Flash cannot do at all. Seamlessly and appropriately bringing them together in the same movie strengthens both.

Currently, Flash 4 is supported in QuickTime 5, and Flash 5 will be supported in QuickTime 6. Even now, Flash 4 support in QuickTime provides a huge advance in vector animation and text, especially where one scripts the Flash track using LiveStage Pro. Here is a list of the main advantages Flash brings to a QuickTime movie:

- Very efficient vector graphics which: (a) helps keep file size down and (b) scales quickly, smoothly, and without aliasing.

- Flash can send and receive variables from QuickTime.

- Flash buttons can be scripted to execute Action Scripts (much like core JavaScript routines) as well as control any other QuickTime tracks.

- Scalable text with embedded fonts enables consistent and attractive cross-platform font display.

- Flash capabilities in vector graphics and embedding fonts bring smooth and rapid animation well within reach.

Importing QuickTime into a Flash track

Rather than adding a Flash track to a QuickTime movie, I find it's usually easier to do it the other way around and import a QuickTime movie into Flash. This way you can see the QuickTime movie laid out on the time line making it easier to visually set up events on your flash track. However, you can do it the other way and add the completed Flash track to your QuickTime movie using QuickTime-pro, it's just a matter of personal preference. In the following example though, we're going to import the QuickTime movie into Flash. I'm also going to presume that you know the basics of Flash such as how to make buttons and put simple event handlers on them. As mentioned above, QuickTime 5 only supports Flash 4 ActionScript, therefore, until QuickTime 6 is released, scripting must be limited to ActionScript that is compatible with the Flash 4 player.

Importing a QuickTime movie

Use the Import command to bring your QuickTime movie into Flash as you would any other file.

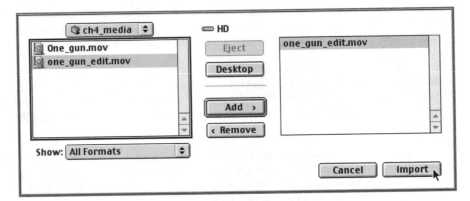

You'll notice though that Flash treats the QuickTime movie as a still image and just places it on the first frame of the timeline, so if we were to publish the result as a QuickTime movie now, we would just get a one frame movie, which isn't much good to anyone!

The first thing we need to do is extend the timeline to the length of the movie that we've imported. To do this we modify the frame rate of the flash movie so that it's equal to the frame rate of the imported QuickTime Movie, which ensures that it plays in synch and that there are no repeated or dropped frames. We need to insert some frames so that we can see the entire QuickTime movie in Flash, and we work out how many frames we'll need, by multiplying the length of the movie (in seconds) by the frame rate

So in the case of this example where the film length = 259 seconds, and the frame rate is 12fps, we just use the equation:

- 259 x 12 = 3108 frames

The next step is to insert frames right up to frame 3108, where the QuickTime movie ends. If we scroll up and down the timeline can see QuickTime Movie in its entirety.

Positioning the QuickTime movie in the Flash frame

One thing you'll notice is that the imported video is sitting in the middle of a large white screen. Therefore, you'll need to position the clip in the desired location, and resize the movie to the size that you want it to be when you re-export it. In this case I need space across the top of movie in which to put some controllers, so I modified the movie to fit in with the QuickTime clips dimensions, leaving an extra strip of 15 pixels at the top.

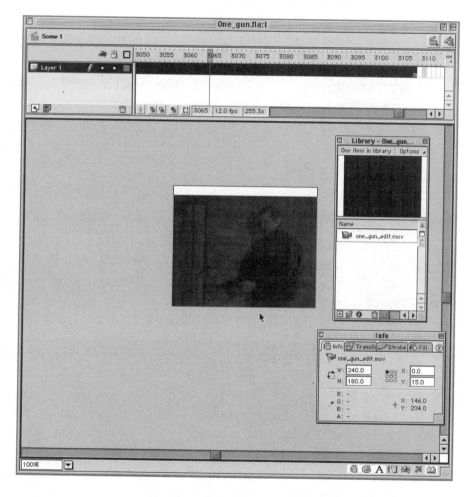

Now the good thing about using Flash (with QuickTime) is that Flash has lovely vector graphics. I'm going to utilise these to create some nice looking controllers for my QuickTime video.

Making a Flash 'rewind-to-start' button

Making controllers for QuickTime movies is pretty basic in Flash. Unlike with Director where there are specific controls for starting and stopping QuickTime movies, in Flash there are no such commands. The commands we have at our disposal refer to the main Flash timeline that our QuickTime movie is now placed on. So basically we can start and stop the movie or go to different locations on the timeline. For this project I'm going to make a simple start and stop button, plus a drop down menu to go to different scenes in the film.

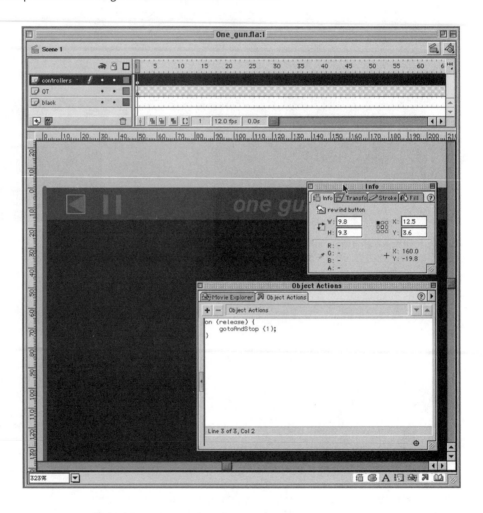

Adding frame labels that correspond to scenes in the film

At this point you can see why it's easier to have imported the QuickTime movie into Flash, as by scrolling the playback head up and down the timeline we can easily see the events taking place within the QuickTime movie. It's now just a case of adding labels to the movie for where we want my different scene buttons to jump to, it saves having to make lots notes on bits of paper, and you're sure of getting your cuts frame accurate.

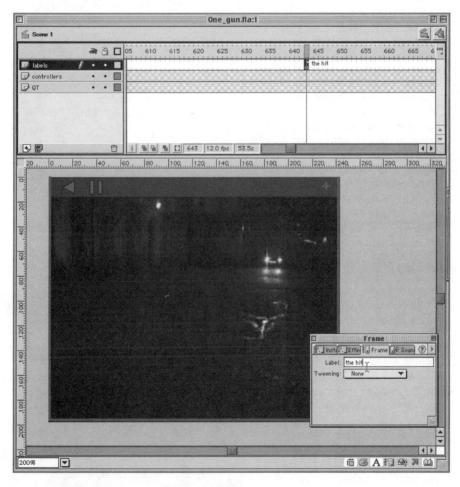

Once we've put the 'go to' actions on all the buttons referring to the labels, we're ready to publish.

Go to File and select Publish Settings. Click on the Flash tab at the top and make sure you select Flash 4 from the version menu at the bottom; otherwise none of the interactivity will work (with anything less that QuickTime 6). Select the Formats tab at the top, and (to publish as a QuickTime movie) check the QuickTime (.mov) box; you'll now see a tab appear at the top for setting the QuickTime preferences.

Click on this tab and take a look at your options:

The main settings you'll be concerned about are the Alpha: and the Layer:. Layer: simply selects which layer you want the flash track to appear on in the QuickTime movie, in this case, because there is a drop down that goes in front of the movie, I have to have the layer set to Top so the flash track appears on top of the video, other wise the drop downs would be hidden from view. Alpha: sets whether the flash track is against a transparent background or not. In this case it needs to be transparent otherwise the Flash track would obstruct the view of the video. I checked the File: box to (there is a similar option in QuickTime Pro) make a self-contained movie that does not need to refer to a separate flash file. Dimensions: is self-explanatory.

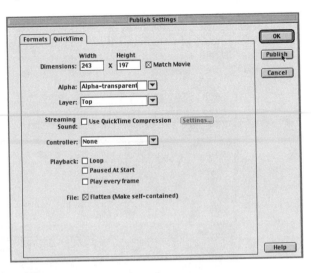

The finished clip with Flash tracks

That's it, you've made a Flash track for your QuickTime movie! Using this method you can add extra interactivity, not just scene selection as in our example, but also extras such as games and hyperlinks to web sites, really anything that you can do in Flash 4, you can have in your QuickTime window.

There are good texts covering the details of what Flash can do and how to access that functionality if you aren't already conversant with Flash, so we won't try to cover that here. Instead, we'll focus on pointing out how Flash functionality is exposed in a QuickTime movie and how those functions can be leveraged to the benefit of the overall audience experience.

Another good feature is that you can add titles and credits to your movies, if you've got the job of compressing someone's film down to 240x180 for the Web, you won't be able to read any original credits that were placed on the film, but using Flash you can embed some fonts that can fade in and out or scroll smoothly across the screen.

Editing a Flash track with LiveStage

Bringing a Flash track into the LiveStage Pro editing environment is a simple drag and drop operation. This brings the entire flash file into your QuickTime movie. We can explore an imported Flash file by opening the Flash track sample and noting a few symbols that may appear on the timeline, which is represented in terms of frames. Selected frames appear highlighted in red. Frames that have buttons will show a small gray dot in the timeline whereas frames that have QScripts will have a small black dot. Selecting a frame that has scripts and/or buttons will reveal detailed information about them in the Object/Event Handler List.

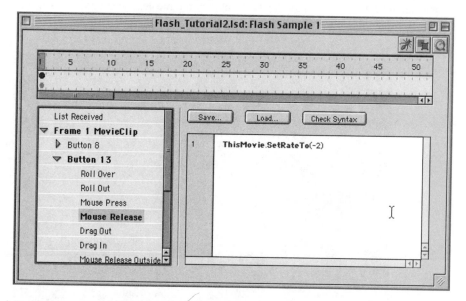

It's here that you can add QScripts as illustrated in the previous screenshot. Your vector graphics animated interface can now control any other QuickTime tracks such as a video track or be controlled by other elements in the QuickTime movie. From the audience perspective, it's all a seamless experience.

Text tracks

The lowly text track is often overlooked because, well, it's just about text and how can plain, old text be at all exciting? Here's how. Lurking under the hood are some pretty powerful capabilities such as animation, hotspots and chapter lists which can be had for just a pittance in file size. The other great thing about text tracks is that you can do all of the things described here with a text editor and QuickTime Pro ($29.95). The QuickTime site has tutorials that explain how to make text tracks that animate (scroll) text, text tracks that make popup chapter lists, and text tracks that load web pages and movies (see: www.apple.com/quicktime/products/tutorials).

If you already have LiveStage Pro, you'll want to use that because it makes this work so much easier as well as enabling you to integrate interactive text tracks with all of the other track types supported in QuickTime, but if you haven't got LiveStage don't despair, you can also create a text track using nothing more than SimpleText on a Mac or Notepad on a PC. So, behold the powers of the lowly text track!

Chapter track

The most visible and dramatic of the interactive text tracks is the chapter track. Whether experiencing a movie in the QuickTime Player or a movie embedded into a web page, the Chapter Track presents a popup menu whose elements are associated with a specific point in the movie timeline, the place where that subject is treated in the movie. The chapter track is shown in a little bar to the right of the timeline.

However, when the bar is clicked on, a list pops up to reveal the titles of all of the points in the movie that you can navigate to instantly. Just select the chapter and release the mouse button and the movie is advanced to that point.

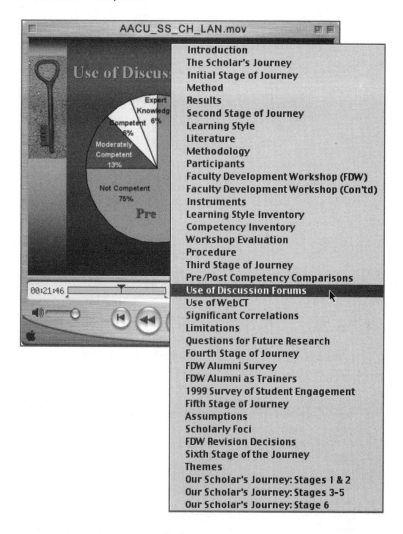

Creating a chapter list is a simple process of associating chapter titles with points on the timeline. In LiveStage Pro, this is a simple matter of creating text samples along the timeline, typing in the chapter titles, disabling the visibility of the track and, finally, associating the chapter track with the track it describes, usually a picture or video track. If you're not flush enough to own a copy of Livestage Pro the following tutorial shows how create a chapter list using just a basic text editor.

1. Open up SimpleText if you are on a Mac or Notepad if you are on a PC, and type out the chapter headings that you want to appear in your movie on separate lines and save the file as a .txt file.

2. Now use QuickTime Pro to import the track. In OS X QuickTime Pro will ask open the track directly whereas OS 9 and Windows will ask you to convert the track, and click on the Options tab before you save. This brings up a dialog giving us full control over the font size, positioning, and the overall dimensions of the text track.

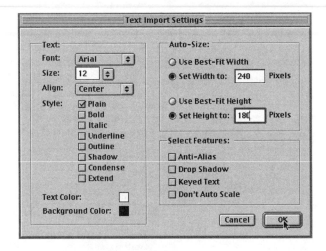

As we're creating a chapter list we don't need to be that concerned with changing any of the settings apart from perhaps changing the font to a standard cross platform font (such as Arial).

3. The next step is to export the text again. Click on File > Export, from the Export: drop down list select Text to Text and then click the Options: button, you'll see these options:

4. We want to have time descriptors visible so click the Show Text, Descriptors, and Time radio button. We also want to set the time scale to 1/30th of a second rather than the default 1/600th of a second if we're going to get our timing information from the QuickTime Pro movie info window. Set these options and then export the text.

5. When we open the text file that we've just exported we'll see a text file that looks something like this:

6. The only bits we need to be concerned with, at the moment, are the time stamps (the bits before each scene title that look something like: [00:00:04.00]). Now if we open up our movie in QuickTime Player we can use the Movie Info (Window > Show Movie Info) window to obtain the timings of the start of each scene and enter the values in the appropriate timestamp. So for instance: if the second scene started at 53 and 15 hundredths of a second we would change the value in the second time descriptor to: [00:00:53:15]. The final timestamp has to contain the total length of the clip, which again you can get from the Movie Info window.

7. So once we've done all that our text might look something like this:

8. Once you've resaved the text file, import the file back into QuickTime Player as we did in stage one. Now when it opens you'll notice that the text appears at the time intervals you just set. Now open the clip that you wish to put the chapter headings on and copy and add the text track to the clip. You need to open the movie properties window (Movie > Get Movie Properties) and select Text Track from the menu on the left. Once that's selected use the menu on the right to select Make Chapter. Click the large button saying Set Chapter Owner Track and select either of the tracks you have on display (it doesn't matter which as long as the track remains in the movie)

9. The final step is to disable the text track, assuming that you don't want the text visible on the screen. Select Edit >Enable Tracks and select the text track and set it to OFF. To finish off re-save the final item as a self contained movie. You should now have a QuickTime movie with a rather neat DVD style chapter selector list!

> *The beauty of this system is that it adds virtually nothing to the file size, so its ideal for using on QuickTime movies on the Web.*

More information about text tracks can be found on the Apple site at the following URL: www.apple.com/quicktime/products/tutorials/.

Hot spots

Hot spots in a text track are called HREF Tracks because they generally follow the pattern of specifying a URL in HTML, the part that says, "HREF=<URL>". Like a chapter track, an HREF track is visually disabled and associates certain text strings with points along the movie timeline.

An HREF track can do one of two things with the URLs it contains. It can either execute them automatically or conditionally upon a mouse click. Since those URLs can have targets such as a frame in an HTML frameset or the QuickTime Player, many interesting possibilities emerge. One simple example uses a frameset to show a linear movie in one frame and HTML text in an adjoining frame. As the linear movie progresses through time, its auto HREF statements load different web pages into the adjoining frame. The following is an example of what it looks like:

Walled Compound (1)

This is a walled family compound in the new territory of Hong Kong. Families have been living in compounds like this for many centuries. You can see that this compound still has its wall with extensive towers.

HREF syntax

The syntax for an interactive HREF track text sample is:

        <URL> T<frame>

(You must click on the movie frame to link to the URL.)

The syntax for an automatic HREF track text sample is:

        A<URL> T<frame>

(The A term indicates that the URL is automatic.)

In the HREF track, an example would be:

```
[00:01:30.15]
A<http://www.apple.com> T<myframe>
```

This automatically loads an HTML frame called `myframe` with the URL `http://www.apple.com` at 1 minute, 30.15 seconds into the movie.

The URL can be relative or absolute for the QuickTime plug-in (absolute only for QuickTime Player), but note that a relative URL is relative to the movie, not to the web page that contains it. The URL can also be the name of a JavaScript function in the current HTML page; loading the URL executes the function. You can also pass parameters or actual JavaScript code this way.

Animated text

Animated text comes in handy for scrolling credits, karaoke, and captioning (including closed captioning). It can even be combined with HREFs to produce dynamic links just like in a web page except that it's moving. The fact that the fonts used are drawn from the host system means that file size is going to be quite small. It also means that there will be variations in font display cross-platform and font substitution if one chooses to use fonts that aren't on the audience systems.

Here is an example that shows many of the options available. Note that in the sample below, we've chosen a nonstandard font, changed its default font size and color, and made the word jumped a hot spot that'll load a web page in the QuickTime Player when clicked on.

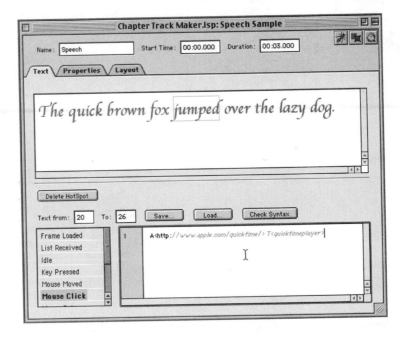

We can do much more than this. The next screen shot shows some of the animation options available to us. We can have it scroll in, out, horizontally, etc. and we can delay the onset of that scroll as well as specify things such as the justification of the text. If we choose Keyed Text, the background will become transparent such as what you'd want with scrolling credits over top of a video or still graphic.

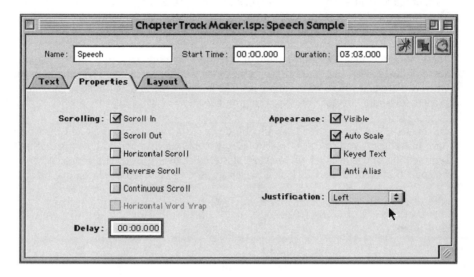

Even with all of these bells and whistles, we wouldn't likely add more than 4 kilobytes to the movie with this track!

QTVR tracks

Of course, QuickTime VR movies are inherently interactive. These nonlinear movies take the form of panoramas, objects, and scenes. The QTVR panorama simulates being in a place and looking around in a cylindrical or spherical plane that is 360° or less in scope. The QTVR object simulates an object that one can turn around as if it were in hand or on a turntable. The QTVR scene combines two or more QTVR panoramas and potentially several QTVR objects as well.

The basic interactivity of QTVR movies can be seen and experienced using only the mouse and the QTVR movie controller if made available by the author. Here, one can click and drag a panorama, or pano, to see up to 360° around a single point. The zoom controls on the controller can be used to zoom in or out to see more detail or more of the location or discover where the hotspots are in order to find more opportunities to interact with the movie. Keyboard equivalents are also available. Similarly, one can use the same tools to manipulate and explore a QTVR object.

Advanced interactivity is also possible. We've already seen how QTVR Tracks can be controlled by other tracks such as a sprite track but the VR Track has powers of its own. Hot spots in QTVR Movies are created by the VR authoring system one uses. Two good QuickTime VR editing packages on the market are Apple's QuickTime Authoring Studio and VR PanoWorx from VR toolbox (www.vrtoolbox.com).

Normally, hotspot creation is a matter of choosing the shape and location of an area that, when clicked, will go to another node in the same QTVR movie. Thus, one can link several QuickTime VR panoramic movies together to form a scene. A scene is where one is "in" a room, for example, looking around with a click and drag motion. At some logical and intuitive point in the pano, a doorway for example, the cursor changes shape indicating that a hotspot is there. Clicking on that hotspot loads another "node" of this QTVR movie representing the adjoining room. This is a scene. The same kind of thing can be done with exterior spaces where you travel from building to building. Here, we are approaching what is called an "immersive" media experience.

These hot spots need not go immediately to the next node in a tour, perhaps another building some distance away, but could trigger a linear movie that simulates traversing the space between where we are and where we're going, just like in the real world. A hot spot could also load a still graphic such as a hotspot over a painting on a wall.

Of course, QTVR movies don't have to be taken from real places at all and their hotspots don't have to transport you to other "real" places. It could be that one could construct a QTVR object representing a huge cylinder with posters plastered all over it. Those posters could be covered with hotspots that opened the QuickTime player and showed a video or played a song or both.

Summary

We've seen how the scriptable tracks can generate a good bit of interactivity just by offering access to their own particular set of capabilities, but the real power of QuickTime interactive movies is in bringing all 14 track types together as a functional unit that offers the audience a seamless media experience. It's this convergence that sets QuickTime apart from the one-trick ponies.

With modern authoring tools such as LiveStage Pro, Flash, and VR Authoring software, it's now possible for people who are not programmers to create works that not long ago could only be produced by teams that included programmers conversant with low-level languages such as C. The significance of this is that ideas no longer have to go through the filtering of as many minds as was the case in the past. The path from creative insight to media expression has been significantly shortened and thereby greatly cleansed of disruptive contaminants. It is even quite conceivable now, where it wasn't before, that one person can go from insight to product without faltering for lack of skill or knowledge. It's also just now conceivable that there can be many more people who are able to vertically integrate all or most of the media production process, end-to-end.

I bet you've got some great ideas for QuickTime, whether interactive or not, by this stage, but before we rush off and create there's thinking to be done. Just who is going to use this stuff, and how are they going to get it? This is what we're about to discuss in the next two chapters.

5 Deployment Options

When you create your QuickTime movies you do it so they can be played, or deployed, somewhere. That somewhere can be one or any of numerous media types that range from linear analogue (like film or videotape) to complex interactive non-linear digital projects (such as you would find on a DVD or on web sites).

Throughout the chapter and the book itself, we refer to QuickTime movies but keep in mind that these can be linear, like video, and non-linear like interactive games. In this chapter we'll focus on the typical deployment options you have for your content regardless of whether it's linear or not. Of course certain media will be linear only, like videotape, but others can be both linear and non-linear, like an interactive CD-ROM.

Once you've read over this chapter you'll have a good idea on where you can deploy your content using QuickTime and what you may need to do to get your content there. We'll start off discussing the deployment media you can use – film, DV, and computer deployment including kiosks, CDs, DVDs and web deployment. Later in the chapter we'll shift the approach from media to the means of deployment as in using dedicated players, embedding your QuickTime movies in HTML, talk about some applications that can contain QuickTime and how QuickTime can help you deploy the best content depending on the user's playback environment. We'll finish up discussing the importance and power of movie-in-a-movie (MIAM) to give you some ideas on how you can use it.

Film to digital video

When we refer to film we do mean "film" as in 8 mm, 16 mm, 35 mm or any other type of film source. I make the distinction because often people refer to "film" when they really mean to say "video". Video refers to the content you shoot on tape. I make this point because dealing with film is very different than dealing with video. With video you shoot and it's ready to be played back. With film you have to develop it after shooting. There are other differences like the quality of the content. Due to the analog and mechanical nature of film (less prone to digital quantization errors), quality tends to by much higher than video. This is because video cameras are limited to the resolution of TV, which isn't that great, while film has no inherent, fixed, resolution as the images are imprinted in the celluloid not captured by an electronic sensor. Having said all this, most of the content you work with won't be shot on film unless you have a very specific reason to do so, for instance if you were shooting a high end TV commercial or feature.

There are a number of reasons why you may want to get film material to digital video. First, having a digital video version of your film allows you to work with the content in a more efficient way, for example when doing your edits. The process is that you shoot with film, digitize it to get a first cut on the computer, and then generate an edit decision list (EDL), which you can then use to cut your actual film material. Of course, once you have your film source digitized you can re-purpose it in a huge number of ways. Once digital you can then print it to video tape or keep it in the computer realm and deploy it on the Web, DVD, CD-ROM, etc.

In some cases film is shot with a different aspect ratio to that of TV. Most film features are shot in widescreen where the aspect ratio is different from that of typical TV. This means that most feature films have wider content than what you can fit on at TV screen. To be able to get widescreen film content to video there are three things you can do: crop the sides of the content to fit in the TV aspect ratio; resize the content to fit horizontally, adding black bars at the top and bottom to keep the original aspect ratio; or make the widescreen content fit the aspect ratio of TV stretching the content vertically making everything look thin and tall.

Another of the reasons why working with film is so complicated is the frame rate. The frame rate of film is 24 frames per second (fps) and each frame is a full progressive frame differing to video that in NTSC has a frame rate of 29.97 fps (PAL is 25 fps) and is interlaced. Interlaced means that each frame is broken down into odd and even lines where one set of lines is displayed first, then the second set.

Getting film into a digital video file often is done by first converting the 24 fps progressive film to NTSC or PAL video and then digitizing that video. As you can imagine, the process of getting the film to video isn't cheap as the content needs to be interlaced and the frame rate increased, but while maintaining synch with the audio. In the case of NTSC converting 24 fps to 29.97 fps is more difficult than with PAL, as in general terms, for every 3 frames of film, a film frame needs to be duplicated to be able to maintain synch. Something interesting is that when converting film to PAL video the frame rate of the film is increased without duplicating frames, so a PAL video counter part of a film clip would be slightly shorter in time. In this case the audio is also accelerated slightly to keep in synch. For an interesting discussion on how film is transferred to video you can refer to the Web: www.cs.tut.fi/~leopold/Ld/FilmToVideo/.

Once you have a video version of your film, then you deploy it on tape for duplication or broadcast. You can also digitize the video to the computer and work with the digital file. Please refer to Chapter 7 for an explanation of the digitization process and required equipment.

The chances are that when you digitize your video QuickTime will be involved. Depending on your process, QuickTime can be involved right from the digitizing process to editing, compression, authoring, and delivery. To give you an example, if you work in Final Cut Pro, when you digitize your content it is captured as a QuickTime movie. All the editing in FCP is done on QuickTime files, then you can export from FCP to a compression program to get your movies in a friendly file size for web delivery, let's say. Then those QuickTime movies can then be enhanced with interactivity also using QuickTime, before finally deploying them on the Web to be seen by your audience with the QuickTime plug-in within a web browser.

Digital video to film

Getting digital video to film uses the opposite of the process used to get film to digital video. If your digital files are video files, you can print them to videotape. The idea is to use the highest quality video like DigiBeta, Beta SP, D-1, D-5, etc. to keep as much detail as possible. The facility that will transfer the video to film will need to de-interlace the content and also drop frames to get the 29.97fps NTSC video to the 24fps that film requires.

Another alternative is to provide high quality digital files to the transfer facility, as in most cases they can transfer the digital images directly to film. Computer generated images are a bit more flexible as you can create them at a high resolution and then provide those big files to the transferring facility. A quick web search will provide a number of transfer facilities near to you.

For example, to display a digital image on 16x9 film the image would need to be about 1828x1028 pixels! For a discussion on how video to film transfers work, you can refer to the web: www.digieffects.com/frames/howtotransfervideotofilm.html

For the most part we wouldn't expect too many people to transfer their QuickTime movies to film unless they need them for a specific reason, like converting a video movie to a feature film. If you're in that situation, try to keep your video at the highest resolution and quality possible. Please refer to Chapter 7 where we talk about what kind of gear you may need to keep the highest quality video.

Digital files

If you're working with QuickTime video files then you're working with digital video. Please note that DV is digital video, but digital video doesn't necessarily need to be DV. Did I confuse you? If so, let me clarify.

DV is a standard codec, an algorithm for compression and decompression and the acronym does stand for "Digital Video". DV is used in a number of digital camcorders so when you shoot with such cameras, the content is recorded in DV. DV being a standard codec means that it has to fit to a specific set of criteria like compression ratio, frame rate, window size, audio sample rate, etc. On the other hand, any video file that you have in your computer is digital video as it's made out of zeros and ones, digital bits, that's why the computer can play it. So, for example, you can have a digital video file that is compressed with the Sorenson codec at a window size of 160x120 and indeed it's digital video, but because the codec is Sorenson and the window size is 160x120, it's not DV.

I make the distinction because DV does mean something very specific while digital video is as generic as any video movie that can be played in a computer. It's important to know the differences to prevent people getting confused.

As mentioned above, DV is a standard codec and does have compression, so if anyone tells you that DV is uncompressed, well, they don't know the whole story.

Now that we know what DV is, lets talk about the more generic concept of digital video. In its most generic definition, video is the ultimate slide show. In NTSC you have 29.97 slides in one second where each slide is a picture. Now, transferring that to computer terms, full video frames often have a width and height of 640x480, 720x480 or 720x486 and a color depth of 24 bits or millions-of-colors. To put it in perspective lets consider an uncompressed TIFF image file exported from a DV movie frame (720x480).

As you can see here, the 24 bit, 720x480 uncompressed TIFF file is about a megabyte in size. Now lets think about NTSC video where the frame rate is almost 30 fps. That would mean that if we were to have uncompressed video, one second of the video alone would take about 30 MB and this is without the uncompressed sound!

Most computers even today cannot cope with so much data. For this reason to work with digital video we need to compress the content so that computers can deal with it. Another alternative to compression is using high-end equipment that can enhance the capabilities of the computer to handle video at this kind of data rate. Often the gear found on high end editing workstations would include a high quality, maybe uncompressed, digitizing board and SCSI drive arrays. For a deeper discussion on this topic refer to the section on capturing video and audio in Chapter 7.

Can you imagine delivering a QuickTime movie online at a data rate of 30MBps (megabytes per second)? You definitely don't want to do that unless you need to transfer uncompressed video for editing, in which case it would be far cheaper to courier a videotape to the destination. The point that I'm trying to make is that for deployment, especially on the Web where the audience may have a slow network connection, you need to compress your content and you want to compress it as much as you can until the quality hit is too high.

The problem is defining how much to compress your content and the answer is: "it depends". I know this isn't the answer you were looking for, but it really depends on a number of factors and you'll need to evaluate each of them. The compression ratio of your output will be determined by your audience playback capabilities, their interest in the content and your objectives. Let's analyze the most used playback mediums and how they impact your compression decisions.

Deploying on hard disk

Dealing with digital video for playback on kiosks is much easier than with any other digital delivery method. The reason why I say this is because often you will have control over the specification of the playback machine, and will at least know exactly the speed of the hard drive. One of the difficulties with other media is that there can be so many variations in hardware and software that the chances are that your work may not play properly on certain machines. But when you work with kiosks, if you don't have control over the hardware at least you are certain what kind of a machine your project will be played back on.

The restrictions that will determine your compression for kiosk playback are the access speed of the hard drive, the power of the CPU and to a less extent the size of the screen.

Delivering video from a hard drive is much faster than delivering it from other devices like CD-ROMs or a network so your limit for bit rate is quite high. With average machines you should be able to deliver video off a hard drive at about 1 to 2MBps If you increase the bit rate chances are that the hard drive would be able to keep up, but the thing that may chug at such bit rates may be the CPU. The processor needs to decode and display the video at least in real time, so if the video requires too much power you may see some frames being dropped on slower CPUs.

Deploying on CD-ROMs and DVDs

Deploying video on CD-ROMs is as old as CD-ROM themselves. The problem was that on one side codecs weren't very efficient and CD drives weren't as fast as they are today. Deploying digital video on modern CD-ROM drives is almost no problem. Deployment gets complicated when you want to target a really wide CD-ROM audience base. If everyone in your audience has a machine less than a year old then you don't need to worry. Depending on your audience, some people may be using an older computer.

So with CD-ROMs, since there are so many types and brands of CD drives out there, then you In the case of deploying your QuickTime movies on either a CD-ROM or a DVD-ROM/Hybrid it's always a good idea to include the full QuickTime installer so if for any case your audience doesn't have QuickTime installed or the latest version, they can always get it from your disk.

You can download the full installer from Apple by visiting:
www.apple.com/quicktime/download/standalone/.
The license for the installer can be found at:
http://developer.apple.com/mkt/swl/agreements.html#QuickTime.

Deploying over a network

Deploying QuickTime movies over a network has become one of the best ways to deliver your content to a wide audience. Most people would want to deploy content over the Internet via a web server but in fact there are a number of other ways like FTP, over a file server, via e-mail and of course, streaming in real time.

In any case, when deploying QuickTime movies over a network the most important consideration is data rate (or bit rate, whichever way you want to refer to it). Most people are concerned about file size when deploying over a network. Yes, file size is important but the truth is that file size is the result of the bit rate multiplied by the length of your movie.

The reason why bit rate is the important consideration and not file size is the bandwidth available by your audience to see your content. For example, if your audience is on a modem connection and they only have, say 30Kbps available, if you want your content to start playing as it starts downloading, then you must keep the bit rate of the movie at a maximum of 30Kbps regardless of the length of the movie.

For the most part there are three ways to deliver your content over a network: download then play, play as you download, and stream in real time.

Download

In a "download then play" situation the audience will need to download the whole document before they can start playing it. For the most part this method isn't used as often, you don't want your audience to wait. There may be a few times that you would want to download the whole clip before playing. One would be if you want to make sure that the content plays without interruption once it starts playing. Another would be if for any reason you need to have the whole clip loaded in RAM for playback, maybe to ensure smooth playback. To download a movie before it starts playing you can use a web (HTTP) or an FTP server.

Progressive download

The correct name for "play as you download" is "progressive download" and in the QuickTime world is often called Fast Start. A Fast Start movie is a movie that you can play as it downloads, so this means that the audience can start watching the content before the whole file has downloaded. What QuickTime does on the client's end is as the movie starts to download, QuickTime calculates how long it'll take to get the whole file at that current download speed. Then it makes a relationship between that download time and the duration of the movie and starts playing the movie when it thinks it can play the movie and it doesn't have to finish playing at the same time as the file finishes downloading.

If you deploy progressive download movies the average bit rate can be higher than the available bandwidth of your audience but the higher the bit rate, the longer the wait before the audience can start playing the whole clip without stopping. The decision on how high the bit rate should be depends on the willingness of the audience to wait. If the topic is appealing to the audience, they'll be more willing to wait. On the other hand, if the audience has little interest in watching the content, they won't tolerate a long wait before they can see your content.

Real time streaming

Streaming in real time refers to when the content is served with a real time streaming server. QuickTime can be streamed off a QuickTime Streaming Server (for MacOS X), a Darwin Streaming Server (an open source project that allows for serving from different platforms like Windows, Solaris, Linux, etc), and other servers based on the Darwin Streaming Server, like a Real 8 server or a Kassena MediaBase server all of which use the RTSP/RTP (Real Time Streaming Protocol/Realtime Transport Protocol) standard instead of HTTP. For RTSP/RTP streaming I like to make the analogy of playing a movie from the server. So you tell the server from where you want to start playing. In the case of a progressive download, the server sends the data, which is cached on the client's machine. When the client plays the movie, it actually plays off their machine.

To better understand real time streaming, let me explain how progressive download works. In a progressive download the server sends the data to the client regardless of how long it takes to arrive. For example, if data is lost in the transfer, maybe because of network traffic or latency, then the server resends the missing data. In a real time streaming scenario the data is sent to the client and if some of it is lost in the process, if there isn't enough time to resend it before that part is played, then the server doesn't send it again. This is because in real time streaming the content plays as it arrives to the client and often there is little time to accommodate for network latency.

This means that for real time streaming the bit rate of your movies cannot exceed the bandwidth available to the user. In a progressive download movie you have the luxury of providing a higher bit rate movie if the audience is willing to wait a few seconds.

Real time streaming can be used for live events, of course, and on-demand streaming. With real time streaming the content is never stored on the user's hard drive (while with Fast Start it is cached on the hard drive for playback) so real time streaming may be a good alternative if you want to avoid the audience duplicating the content.

For very long clips you may want to use on-demand real time streaming instead of progressive download. As an example think of a lecture or keynote that runs for 2 hours. Now imagine that the audience is only interested in the last 20 minutes of the clip. In a progressive download the audience must first download the first hour and 40 minutes to be able to start watching the last 20 minutes. As you can imagine, that download could be a very lengthy one. With real time streaming the client rather requests the server to start sending the data from the 1 hour and 40 minute mark, without having to view or stream the content before that point in time.

Mobile devices and set top boxes

There may be certain applications where you want to provide your content to mobile devices, like training material. Think of a mechanic that has to fix an engine that he has never seen before. With a PDA he could retrieve a video that explains how to access the problematic part on the engine.

In the case of set top boxes the idea mostly is to deploy content that streams on demand, pretty much the same idea as an on-demand real time streaming or a progressive download but being able to pay it back on a regular TV instead of a computer screen.

To be able to deliver content on these devices you would need to transcode your QuickTime movies into something that can be played on those devices. This used to be a little more complicated pre QuickTime 6 as you needed a third party encoder. The solution with QuickTime 6 is deploying your content in MPEG-4 format.

It's important to mention that MPEG-4 isn't QuickTime and that QuickTime isn't MPEG-4. MPEG-4 is a very complex standard that defines video and audio compression as well as a transport mechanism and interactivity, very much what QuickTime offers. The main difference is that it's a standard while QuickTime is still a proprietary technology from Apple. This means that for your audience to play QuickTime movies they need QuickTime installed. With MPEG-4 you can create the .mp4 file in any compliant encoder, like QuickTime 6 and play it any and compliant player like QuickTime 6 but not limited just to QuickTime 6.

Having said all this you can still use your typical workflow with QuickTime but when it comes to deployment you create MPEG-4 files, not QuickTime files, which can then be deployed on mobile devices and set top boxes that have support for MPEG-4. If you need to stream your MPEG-4 content in real time, QuickTime Streaming Server 4 and Darwin Streaming Server 4 have support for streaming MPEG-4 to any device that has a compliant MPEG-4 decoder.

For a deeper discussion on the different deployment transport methods please refer to Chapter 6 where you'll find more detailed information.

Digital file vehicles

So far in this chapter we've talked about the different ways of getting your content to the end user. For the rest of the chapter we'll talk about different ways of presenting your content once it's on the client's machine.

Web page embedding

With QuickTime, just like with the other major media players, you can embed your QuickTime movies in HTML to be viewed in a web browser. The main difference is that QuickTime offers the same playback support on both Macs and Windows machines while the other players often have inferior performance on the Mac.

For your audience to play embedded QuickTime movies on their web browsers they'll need to have QuickTime installed as well as the QuickTime plug-in or the QuickTime ActiveX control.

It's a good idea to always point your users to where they can get the QuickTime installer before they get to the content. It's much better if they're informed that they'll need QuickTime ahead of time, than they hit a web page that shows a broken icon as the QuickTime plug-in isn't installed. You can and should point your viewers to Apple's web site to get the installer: www.apple.com/quicktime/download/.

Tag team

Embedding QuickTime movies is as simple (or complicated, depending on your point of view) as embedding any other piece of content like SWF Flash files or DCR Director files. For browsers version 4 and older you could do with just the <embed> tag, but Microsoft dropped support for Netscape style plug-ins in Internet Explorer from version 5.5SP2 and newer. This means that the <embed> tag alone doesn't work on those browsers.

This is a bit of a problem for people that had a lot of QuickTime movies embedded in HTML just using the <embed> tag. The good news is that Apple wrote an ActiveX control for QuickTime that works in IE 5.5SP2 and newer. For the ActiveX control to work you will need to use the <object> tag when embedding your QuickTime movies.

For any new movie that you post on the Web by embedding it in HTML you should always use both the <object> and the <embed> tag. This way it will work on older browsers and the Mac with the <embed> tag and the plug-in and newer versions of IE on the PC with the <object> tag and the ActiveX control.

The official documentation on how to use the <embed> tag with the QuickTime plug-in can be found at: www.apple.com/quicktime/authoring/embed.html. There you'll also find a link to the documentation and notes on using the <object> tag with the ActiveX control that point to: www.apple.com/quicktime/products/tutorials/activex.html.

For consistency with Apple's web site I'll start explaining the use of the <embed> tag and then move on to the <object> tag.

When embedding your QuickTime movies with the <embed> tag you need at least three attributes to go with it; src, width, and height. For the following examples we'll use a QuickTime movie that is 192x144 pixels.

The minimum `<embed>` tag for our sample movie would be:

```
<embed src="Coquitlam_video.mov" width="192" height="160"></embed>
```

Please note that I'm adding 16 pixels to the height. This is because we need to fit the 16 pixel height controller.

If you leave the height with the original value of 144, the controller and the top of the movie are cropped by 8 pixels each. In the above screen shot you'll notice how the controller is cropped and if you pay attention to the top of the clip you'll see how a few pixels are also missing there.

So if you want to have the QuickTime controller you must add the 16 pixels to fit. On the other hand, if you don't want to show the controller for some reason you could use the attribute `controller` and a value of `false`. There are times when you want your movie to merge perfectly with the background or to create your custom controller with sprites or Flash and you don't want to display the standard QuickTime controller. Here's a sample snippet of code:

```
<embed src="Coquitlam_video.mov" width="192" height="144"
➡controller="false"></embed>
```

You can add more attributes to the embed tag and have total control on the way the movie is embedded. For example, with the `volume` tag you can specify at which volume level the sound of a movie starts. There are over 30 attributes that can be used in conjunction with the `<embed>` tag. For a description of each of them, please refer to Apple's site. There you'll see the list and descriptions of these attributes. Keep in mind that embedding QuickTime doesn't only mean embedding linear movies. You can also embed QTVR movies as well as any other type of QuickTime movie. On Apple's site you'll find how to use some attributes for these kinds of movies too.

It's always a good idea to include the `pluginspage` attribute that directs the user to Apple's site when the plug in isn't installed. For our example and for any movie for that matter it would look like this:

```
<embed src="Coquitlam_video.mov" width="192" height="144"
➥controller="false"
➥pluginspage="http://www.apple.com/quicktime/download/"></embed>
```

Explorer objects

Now that we know how to use the `<embed>` tag let's talk about the `<object>` tag. In general for the `<object>` tag you need to duplicate any attribute and it's value that you use in the `<embed>` tag with some minor differences.

First, the `<object>` tag needs to enclose the `<embed>` tag and must start with the `object classid`, `width`, `height`, and `codebase`. Then, for every attribute, except the `pluginspage`, in the `<embed>` tag you must have its counterpart in the `<object>` tag with the format of `<param name="attribute" value="attribute_value">`. For our sample movie above the full correct HTML code would be:

```
<object classid="clsid:02BF25D5-8C17-4B23-BC80-D3488ABDDC6B"
        width="192"
        height="144"
        codebase="http://www.apple.com/qtactivex/qtplugin.cab">
    <param name="src" value="Coquitlam_video.mov">
    <param name="controller" value="false">
    <embed src="Coquitlam_video.mov"
           width="192"
           height="144"
           controller="false"
           pluginspage="http://www.apple.com/quicktime/download/">
    </embed>
</object>
```

- Please note that the `classid` must be: `"clsid:02BF25D5-8C17-4B23-BC80-D3488ABDDC6B"`

- The `width` and `height` must be the same as in the `<embed>` tag.

- The `codebase` must be: `"http://www.apple.com/qtactivex/qtplugin.cab"`

- The `pluginspage` in the `<embed>` tag must be: `"http://www.apple.com/quicktime/download/"`

Any attribute in your `<embed>` tag needs to be duplicated as a `param` with it's value being the same in the `<object>` and `<embed>` tag.

On the CD `Chapter5\embed.html` demonstrates this.

For a thorough discussion on the use of the `<object>` tag and why we need to use it refer to Apple's web site, Chapter 12 also includes some discussion on this.

Dedicated players

With dedicated players we refer to applications that are meant to play QuickTime movies. The most important player is the QuickTime Player but there are other third party players as well as custom made players that you can do with applications like Director or iShell. Keep in mind that any player or application that displays QuickTime will need to have QuickTime installed for it to work. That is why we suggested including the QuickTime installer when your project is deployed on a CD or DVD-ROM.

A dedicated player breaks the web browser barrier. This means that you don't need to use the web browser to display your content. In most cases you would want to use dedicated players to leave the user the ability to use the web browser for what it was designed: web browsing.

> *By launching the QT content in a separate player the user can navigate away from the specific page they were on, without losing the movie.*

Having a dedicated player means that you have much better control on how your movies are displayed. On the web browsers you have to deal with multiple versions and platforms and setups that may not always be what you expect. With dedicated players you have the same concerns, but they tend to be more predictable than web browsers. Also with dedicated players you can take advantage of features not possible with a web browser, like being able to save (maybe using Director) or to use a custom window shape for your movie via a media skin.

The QuickTime Player

Chances are that if QuickTime is installed, then the QuickTime Player application is installed. The QuickTime Player application is a full-featured player and also an authoring tool when you use QuickTime Pro.

With the QuickTime Player by default you get the brushed metal interface that surrounds your movies. This interface is sufficient for most linear projects where you don't need a custom controller.

You can also remove the default controller all together, and create your very own.

Custom skins and controllers

As we learnt in Chapter 2, it's very simple to remove the standard QT controller and to add skins to your movies. Adding a custom controller is a little more difficult but not too much! First we have to lose the brushed metal, there are a number of ways of doing this, but the fastest maybe would be to do it in the QuickTime Player Pro as we have before.

To program your own controller you have a few options that all require a 3rd party application. In order of importance you can use LiveStage Professional, mixing Flash with LiveStage Professional (creating the Flash interface in Flash and programming the logic in LiveStage Pro), Flash alone (designing the interface and doing the programming in Flash) or Cleaner 5 using EventStream to create hot spots that set your movie to play or to stop. In general LiveStage Professional would give you all the control you need, but if you rather design your interface in Flash and then program the behaviours of the interface in LiveStage Pro, then you'll be mixing two very powerful applications.

Blue Abuse's site has a smashing tutorial on how to create a controller in Flash, refer to http://blueabuse.com/flash/04/.

Here you'll find a tutorial on how to label your Flash button so you can program them in LiveStage Pro: http://blueabuse.com/flash/18/.

Another great alternative introduced in QuickTime 5 is what Apple calls QuickTime Media Skins which in simple words means they just change the shape of your QuickTime movie, as we did in Chapter 2.

To do a skin you need to have a QuickTime movie and two mask images; one that defines the shape of the window and what areas will be visible and invisible and another mask that is a subset of the window mask that defines which areas the user can click and drag the movie around the computer screen.

When creating a skinned QuickTime movie we recommend you also program an interface for your movie as we have here, as when you use a skin there is no QuickTime controller so the user has no playback control and also very importantly, doesn't have a close button where they can click to close your movie. We've provided two pre-made close buttons on the CD-ROM (close_button_1.mov and close_button_2.mov in the folder Chapter5 if you want to use them in your projects.

The controller here was made purely in LiveStage Pro via programming a series of sprite buttons, similar to the way it was explained in Chapter 4.

As you can see in this example, media skins allow you to customize the way your content is displayed. In fact there is a strong emphasis on the word "media" as your movies carry the skin with them. Different to other players, a media skin is always used to display your movie on the QuickTime Player 5 and newer.

Feel the width
Yet another feature of the QuickTime Player is that you can have your movies going full screen. Some people, like myself, don't like movies that go full screen as often there is no warning before they take over the screen, but nevertheless it's a great way of showing your work without the typical computer desktop.

There are a number of ways you can make your movie go full screen. One is in LiveStage Professional selecting Full Screen (Auto) from the Window: pull-down menu in the Info tab for your project.

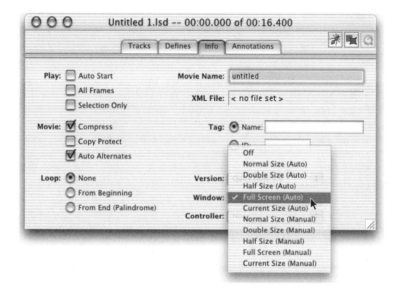

Another way is using Cleaner 5. From the Output tab check Autoplay when open in QuickTime Player and select Present Movie-Full Screen from the pull down menu.

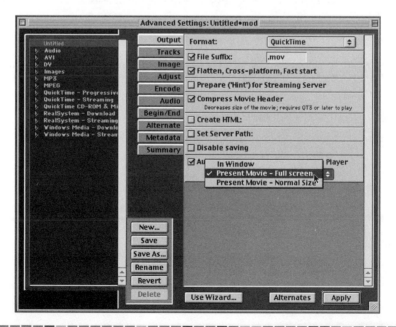

Yet another way that only works on the Mac is using AppleScript. You can download a huge collection of AppleScripts from Apple's site at: www.apple.com/applescript/qtas.html for OSX or www.apple.com/applescript/scripts/scripts.00.html for older systems.

In the collection there is an applet called *Save As Presentation File*, which allows you to set your movie to play full screen. Just drag and drop your movie on top of the applet.

Custom players

Apart from applying media skins to your content to customize the player, you can make custom players with other applications such as iShell and Macromedia's Director and even in Java using QuickTime for Java. Usually you would consider authoring these custom players if the QuickTime Player or the QuickTime plug-in cannot offer a specific requirement, like allowing your audience to save to their hard drive, or other capability not possible without a custom player.

Macromedia's Director may be one of the oldest applications out there that offers support for QuickTime. As such it has a legacy amongst multimedia authors of being one of the most used ways of playing QuickTime content embedded in multimedia CD-ROMs.

A great recent example of use of a custom player for QuickTime content in particular is the BMW Films site (www.bmwfilms.com), which uses a custom made Director player used to present a series of QuickTime movies showcasing some BMW car models. This project is particularly interesting because the producers took advantage of both what QuickTime and Director can do best. The videos are QuickTime movies, which by themselves are full blown film (shot on film) feature productions. Director is used as the player as it offers the ability to save the QuickTime movies to the user's hard drive for later playback without the need to connect to the Internet again. This is quite useful as the hi-resolution QuickTime movies tend to be above 20MB in file size on average.

QuickTime and Director

If you decide to work with Macromedia Director here are a few guidelines that should keep you free from headaches.

Check Direct to Stage in the Property Inspector for the QuickTime cast members. What this does is to give QuickTime the responsibility of rendering the video instead of Director. Think of it as if QuickTime was overlaying the video on top of the Director stage. This option doesn't allow for any other sprite channel to be on top of the QuickTime movie, but offers much better playback performance, as Director doesn't have to work hard compositing the video with other sprite channels. Rather, the application doing the rendering of the QuickTime video is QuickTime directly.

Set Playback: to Sync to Sound in the QuickTime Property Inspector for the QuickTime cast member. Sync to Sound will allow QuickTime to drop frames when playing the video on slow CPU machines so the video can keep synch with the audio track of your QuickTime movie. Setting Playback: to Play every frame (no sound) as the pull down menu suggests, won't play the sound track but will play every frame of the QuickTime video track regardless of how long it takes the CPU to decode each frame. This play every frame option may be good if you want to have a slideshow type of QuickTime playing within your Director project.

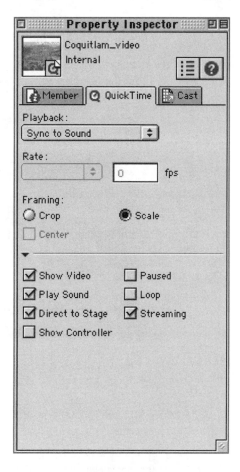

Size is important
If you need to resize the QuickTime video don't do it within Director, rather do it in the QuickTime Player and then import the resized movie into Director. If you resize your movie in Director, then Director will be the one rendering the QuickTime movie instead of QuickTime itself, making it more CPU intensive and increasing the chance of a performance hit, especially on slow CPU machines.

If the movie itself has the resize information within, when played in Director and with the Direct to Stage options selected, QuickTime will be doing the rendering and not Director, making it more efficient.

For example, lets say you have a QuickTime movie that is 192x144 and want to display it at 320x240 on your Director project, you may be tempted to put your QuickTime cast member on the stage and resize it there. What you should do is:

1.   Open your 192x144 QuickTime movie with QuickTime Player Pro.

2. Select Get Movie Properties from the Movie menu. From the left pull down menu select your video track, and from the right pull down menu select Size.

3. Click on the Adjust button and from the red handlers on the player resize your movie to the size you want (320x240 in this case).

4. Once you're done click on the Done button on the movie properties window and save your movie.

Now you can import the movie that will display at 320x240 instead of 192x144.

One other option to explore with Director is the behavior library which contains drag and drop scripts for media elements including QuickTime. A behavior named QuickTime control button, can be dragged onto any sprite and using a drop down menu the developer can choose to make the button, rewind, play, fast forward, stop and pause. It also has a slider behavior.

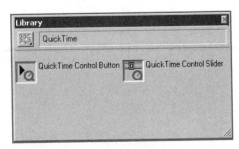

QuickTime inside other types of files

Similar to playing QuickTime movies with custom players you also have the ability to embed QuickTime movies inside other types of files like MS Word documents or even PDF documents. To add your QuickTime movies to PDF documents you'll need Acrobat from Adobe (the authoring environment, not Acrobat Reader; Acrobat Reader is used to open PDF files which can contain QuickTime Movies). Please refer to the documentation included with Acrobat.

QuickTime in MS Office
To insert a QuickTime movie in a MS Word or Excel document on the Mac just select Movie... from the Insert menu. On PowerPoint select Movies and Sounds > Movie from File... from the Insert menu.

> On Windows certain QuickTime movies won't work as the Windows version of Office only has support for an old version of QuickTime.

If you want to display audio/video QuickTime movies inside a MS Office documents on the PC you may be better off saving your movie as an AVI file. To do this, open your QuickTime movie with QuickTime Player Pro and from the File menu select Export... In the dialog box select Movie to AVI from the Export: pull down menu and click on the Save button.

Then you'll be able to embed the AVI on MS Office applications on the PC. A workaround to the problem of MS PowerPoint not supporting newer QuickTime codecs is to make an action button in your PowerPoint presentation that launches your movie on the QuickTime Player. Another less elegant way would be to open your QuickTime movies on the player before the PowerPoint presentation starts, and while you do your presentation you press ALT-TAB to switch between the PowerPoint presentation and the QuickTime Player. For deeper integration you can use the QTVRControlX ActiveX control, instructions on how to do this are in Appendix B.

QuickTime in e-mail
For distributing QuickTime movies another alternative is via e-mail. Some e-mail applications will be able to render and display QuickTime movies, like Eudora. You just need to attach your QuickTime movies to your e-mail messages and send them off.

The problem with QuickTime in e-mail messages is that some e-mail clients either won't be able to display QuickTime files or they may have that option switched off. For example, anyone on a Unix text based e-mail program like PINE won't be able to play your content. Further more, some people find it intrusive when they receive a large file (as QuickTime movies tend to be larger than your average attachment). You could make a reference movie and send that instead of the actual media. A reference movie could be a QuickTime movie that contains no media but that has a reference to the URL where the media can be found. With these kinds of reference movies, when you open them they start fetching the media from the URL if there is a network connection. The nice thing is that the file size of a reference movie that only has a URL is very tiny.

To make a reference move that points to a URL you can use MakeRefMovie, a free application from Apple. You can download the latest version from: http://developer.apple.com/quicktime/quicktimeintro/tools/.

1. Open MakeRefMovie and in the dialogue box enter the name of the reference movie you are creating. Don't forget to add the .mov extension.

2. From the Movie menu select Add URL…

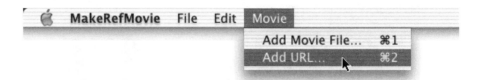

3. Then enter an absolute URL for the movie you want to point to. Don't forget to enter the protocol prefix (which by default is) `http://`. This will tell `MakeRefMovie` to make a link to that URL you entered. Once the URL appears in the `MakeRefMovie` you don't need to change any of the values in the interface if you're making a reference to only one movie. For a deeper discussion on reference movies please refer to the next section in this chapter.

4. At this moment we're almost done. Just select Close… or Quit from the File menu in MakeRefMovie. This will save the URL in the tiny reference movie you just created.

To test it out, just double-click on the reference movie off the desktop. The movie that is at the URL you specified should start loading on the QuickTime Player. If you get the properties or Get Info for the reference movie on the desktop you'll notice that the file size is very small. You can now attach this tiny movie and send it to your e-mail audience. In fact you can work with this reference movie as if it was any other QuickTime movie, so you can take it to your Director projects, your Word documents, your HTML web pages, etc.

Having said all this about QuickTime movies in e-mail messages, my personal recommendation for sending QuickTime movies in e-mail is not to do it. As I said above there is a high chance that your audience may not have an e-mail client that can display QuickTime movies or that they've disabled the feature. Rather, it's much better to send the actual URL of the movie or site in the body of your e-mail. That gives your audience the option of checking out your movies without having to download a large attachment.

The bottom line when adding QuickTime movies to other file types is that certain applications support QuickTime and often you can embed your QuickTime movies to documents created with such applications, while other applications cannot. The good news is that if the applications do have access to ActiveX controls, then movies can be added via ActiveX controls like the QTVRControlX we mentioned earlier. Other applications would not have support for QuickTime nor ActiveX controls, though.

Alternate & reference movies

QuickTime is one of the most flexible technologies for multimedia authoring and deployment, as you have seen in the past few chapters. One simple example is the reference movie we created in the section before, which doesn't contain any media but rather the reference of where that media is stored on a web server.

QuickTime by design can give the user the correct content depending on a number of playback environment variables. Some of these variables include (but aren't limited to) connection speed, CPU power, installed version of QuickTime, language preferences of the audience, etc.

Alternate tracks

One of QuickTime's most powerful features, and often underused, is what is called "Alternate Tracks". Alternate tracks are meant for multilingual deployment.

For example, let's think of a movie that you want to deploy for two types of audiences, English and Spanish speaking. Now, to better illustrate my point, imagine that the video should be the same for both audiences, but the audio track needs to be localized. Therefore you would need an English and a Spanish version. The typical way to solve this dilemma would be to make two movies with the same video track and different audio tracks and give your audience the choice of an English or a Spanish version.

Well, with alternate tracks you can make the whole playback process much more transparent to the user. The idea is that you create a movie that contains 3 tracks, one video track, one English audio track and one Spanish audio track where the Spanish track would be an alternate to the English track. The way this works is that QuickTime knows what language it is running under, so if the user has an English OS or set the preferred language to be English he'll get the English track playing. If the user has a Spanish OS or Spanish in the Language settings for QuickTime, he'll get the Spanish version. Last, if the user has a non-English and non-Spanish OS or preferences, they'll get the English version.

Alternate tracks with QuickTime Pro

This is how you create audio alternate tracks with QuickTime Player Pro. In this section we use the QuickTime Player Pro to do the authoring and the alternate tracks are contained within the movie. In Chapter 7 we make a reference movie with MakeRefMovie which points to totally different movies. The examples are similar as they both check for language, but the approach is totally different. You don't need to have differing language versions of course, two different music tracks will work just as well for this exercise.

1. Create a movie with one audio track (English for this example) and one video track.

2. Create a second audio track (Spanish) the exact same length as the one on the other movie and make it so it synchs with the video.

> *In fact, the second audio track does not need to be the same length nor be in synch of the video track, but for any project where you would want to have multiple languages synched to the video you would want to make them the same length.*

3. Open the second audio track on QuickTime Player Pro and from the Edit menu choose Select All. Then choose Copy from the Edit menu.

4. Open the movie that has the video and the first audio track.

5. On the video/audio movie make sure the playback head is at the beginning of the movie and select Add from the Edit menu in QuickTime Player Pro. At this moment if you play the movie both audio tracks will play simultaneously along with the video track.

6. Open the movie properties widow for the movie with the three tracks by selecting Get Movie Properties… from the Movie menu.

7. On the left pull down menu select the first audio track English and on the right pull down menu select Alternate. By default it has English as the language and None for the alternate.

8. Since this will be the English track, leave the Language: alone but click on the Set… button for the Alternate: and select the second sound track.

   This tells QuickTime to: "use the first sound track for machines that are set to English; if they're set to another language, try the second sound track".

9. From the left pull down menu in the movie properties window select the Spanish sound track. On the right pull down menu you should still have selected the Alternate option.

10. For the Language: click the Set… button and then choose Spanish from the list of languages (take a look at the long list of languages that QuickTime supports). You'll see that by default the Alternate is the first of the two sound tracks (the English one).

    This is like telling QuickTime to "If it is not set to English, check to see if the machine is set to Spanish. If so, then use the second sound track, otherwise use the alternate track of this Spanish track that is the English track".

11. From the File menu select Save As…, choose Make movie self-contained and give your final movie a different name.

In the example above we only had two sound tracks being each alternate of the other. In the case that there were three alternatives, for example English, Spanish and French, one track needs to be an alternate of another always.

So English would have Spanish as the alternate. Then French would be the alternate of Spanish and last English would be the alternate of French. As you can see they cycle. In other words, if the user has English as the preferred language, the track(s) that is(are) associated to English will play instead of any other alternate. If the preferences are in Spanish, then the Spanish takes over, if the preferences are in French the French track plays, and if the preferences are in another language from English, Spanish or French, then the alternate would be the English track in the diagram.

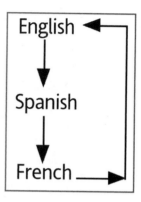

Reference movies

Opposite to alternate tracks, reference movies are used very often by a number of producers. In general terms a reference movie is a QuickTime movie that refers to media somewhere else. This definition is very broad but also very powerful. It's very powerful because the way a reference movie refers to media somewhere else could be called "intelligent". By "intelligent" I mean that QuickTime can select the media somewhere else by matching predefined criteria like the version of QuickTime installed on the user's machine, language preference, a specific component being installed, the CPU power of the host machine, network status (like connected, or not connected to the network), etc.

We've already made a reference movie in this chapter and we'll make a language selection reference movie in Chapter 7.

There are a number of ways you can create reference movies that can select media depending on a specific criteria.

Cleaner 5 can be used to create this kind of reference movies, for example. You do this with the Alternate tab of the Advanced Settings window and choosing multiple settings for one movie. For more information on how to create reference movies with Cleaner 5 please refer to the manual about *Alternate movie display requirements* in Appendix A of the Cleaner 5 manual.

You can also use a free application written by Peter Hoddie called XMLtoRefMovie. This application is freeware and can be downloaded from Peter's web site where he also has an excellent documentation page (www.hoddie.net/xmltorefmovie/). The logic behind XMLtoRefMovie is that you write an XML document with a text editor where you define the criteria and the movies or

URLs that the reference movie should point to. Then you just drop the XML document on top of XMLtoRefMovie, which with no user interface will create a reference movie based on the criteria in the XML document.

Yet another alternative is to use a free unsupported application from Apple called MakeRefMovie (which we used early in this chapter). This application does have a user interface and it's very simple to use and is available for Mac OS 9, Mac OS X, and Windows. As mentioned earlier, you can download it for free from Apple's site at: http://developer.apple.com/quicktime/quicktimeintro/tools/.

MakeRefMovie can choose a movie from a reference movie based on the users Internet connection speed preferences, language preferences, the power of their CPU, and the version of QuickTime installed on the user's machine. You could have complex selections made from one reference movie, for example by mixing a number of options per referred movie like connections speed and CPU speed at the same time. Another thing you can do is branching with reference movies, so a reference movie refers to another reference movie that in turn refers to the actual media.

Speed
Speed alone refers to the Internet connection speed of the user's computer. This value is determined by the user's preferences and not by their actual connection speed. The user sets their preferences in the QuickTime control panel (Mac OS 9 and Windows) or in the QuickTime preferences pane (in Mac OS X). This selection is usually made when the user installs QuickTime, but in some cases people just leave the default which is set to 28.8k/33.6k modems.

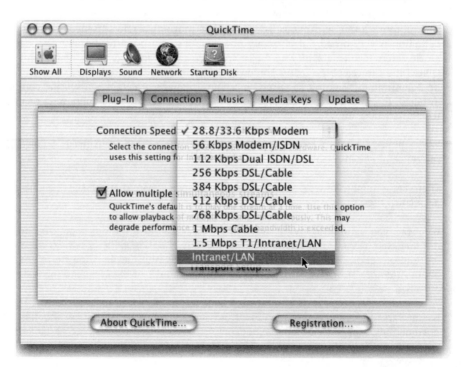

The idea is that with the different speed settings you can give your audience a movie where they won't have to wait too long on their connection. Use the speed setting with care because some people may have the default set to 28.8/33.6 k modem or in other cases if the audience is really keen on the content even on a slow connection they may be willing to download a larger movie just to get the better quality.

Language

As you can imagine using the language option to create reference movies is similar to creating alternate tracks. The difference is that in an alternate track all the alternate tracks need to be added to the movie making it larger and viewers must download the whole thing even when only one track is played. So the more alternate tracks, the larger the movie. With reference movies rather different movies are selected depending on language settings and preferences so you would make a movie per language you want to offer but such movie will only contain the tracks that it needs to play, not all the other alternate tracks.

The language preference is taken from the language version of QuickTime installed or from the selection made in the QuickTime control panel in MacOS 9 and Windows. For example, you could have an English OS but a preference for Spanish content. The language setting in the QuickTime control panel takes precedence over the installed language version of QuickTime. For an example of creating a movie reference depending on language settings please see Chapter 7.

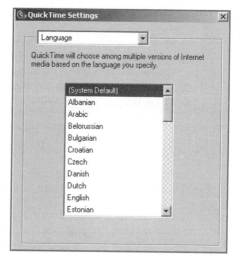

CPU speed

CPU speed refers to how powerful the CPU of the host machine is. The problem with this setting is that there is no documentation of what 1 (slowest) means in relationship to 5 (fastest). In general you could say that 1 refers to machines about 100Mhz and 5 to machines running at about 600Mhz or faster.

You may want to use the CPU speed setting instead of the Speed setting in some cases. What happens is that a lot of broadband users got their broadband connection a few years after their computer. So for example, if a reference movie selects the media solely on connection speed and the user is on an old machine but on broadband, chances are that such user will get a larger version movie. The problem is often that larger movies also require a faster CPU to play smoothly. So someone on a fast connection, but on a slow CPU may get a movie that would choke the processor and drop frames. A good solution would be to use the CPU speed in conjunction with the speed settings to better deploy the correct media to the different audiences.

Version

The version of QuickTime installed can also be quite useful especially with QuickTime 5 and QuickTime 6 component download program. The component download program is where third party developers create components that enhance QuickTime in some way or another. Think of these components as plug-ins for a browser. The way the component download works is that if the user's QuickTime doesn't have such a component installed needed to play the movie, the user gets prompted to download such component from Apple's server to play the content.

> *The problem with this component download program is that it started with QuickTime 5 so if your audience is on QuickTime 4 or older for some reason, the whole component download will not work for them.*

Some important components would be Sorenson Video 3 for one, and any other specific component like On2's VP3 codec that also offers great quality-file size ratio. Sorenson Video 3 was introduced in QuickTime 5.0.2 and is not available in earlier versions of QuickTime. On2's VP3 can be used in QuickTime 5 and previous versions too, but if the user has QuickTime 4 or older he won't get prompted to download the missing component as it happens on QuickTime 5.

Version dependant reference movies using MakeRefMovie

So, for example, you could have a movie that uses Sorenson Video 3 as it offers great quality-file size ratio but there is a slight chance that some of your audience may still have QuickTime 4 installed. In this case you can make a second movie that is compressed with Sorenson Video 2 (which plays fine in QuickTime 3 and newer) that doesn't have a nice compression-file size ratio but would work on older versions of QuickTime. Then with a reference movie you deploy both Sorenson Video 2 and 3 to the correct audience depending on the version of QuickTime they have.

1. Create the two movies to be used, in this example a Sorenson Video 2 (sorenson2.mov) and a Sorenson Video 3 (sorenson3.mov) movies will be used, then open MakeRefMovie. A movie showing anything you like will do.

2. As you open the application it will prompt you to save. This will be your reference movie. In this case we'll call it version_reference.mov.

3. Drag and drop the Sorenson Video 2 version of the content from the desktop to the blank window in MakeRefMovie.

4. From the Version pull down menu select QuickTime 3 and from the Speed menu select 28.8/33.6 kbps Modem so that the connection speed doesn't limit our audience.

5. Drag and drop the Sorenson Video 3 version of the content to the MakeRefMovie window.

6. For this second movie also set the Speed to 28.8/33.6 Kbps Modem but change the Version to QuickTime 5.0.2.

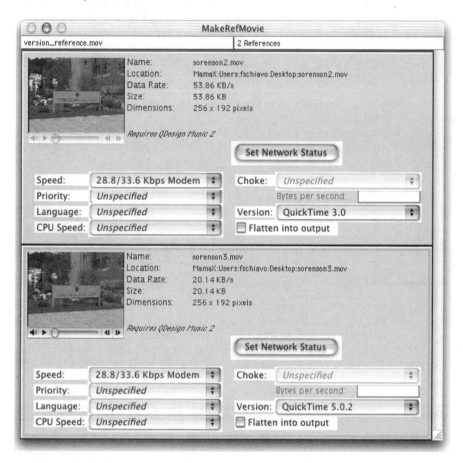

7. Quit MakeRefMovie and save your version_reference.mov file in the process.

Now you can deploy the 3 movies (the version_reference.mov, sorenson2.mov, and sorenson3.mov). The movie you use, say in your embed tag in HTML, would be version_reference.mov.

To try this reference movie out you'll need to open it in QuickTime 5.0.2 or later and in any older version to test if you get the Sorenson Video 2 or 3 accordingly.

Movie-in-a-movie (MIAM)

Since QuickTime is track based it has been able to handle a number of tracks at the same time even at different sample rates. For example, you could have a QuickTime movie that has two video tracks playing simultaneously, one playing at 10 fps and another at 15 fps and a single graphic behind both tracks for the whole duration of the movie. This is a great feature as you can have the best settings for each track, for example, the single image in the background for the duration of the whole movie is just one sample, making it really light in terms of bandwidth requirements.

In QuickTime 4.1 a new type of track was introduced: a movie track.

A movie track is one of the most powerful features of QuickTime as it allows you to have content playing simultaneously or not. This means that for example you can have two video tracks on the same movie and each playing (or not) independently from each other. So you could have one stopped while the other plays, or both playing or both stopped or whatever combination possible.

The way I like to think of a MIAM is like having a movie with a hole and playing different content inside that hole. Let me see if I can explain. In a MIAM situation you basically have one movie playing inside another movie and each can have its own clock, meaning its own timeline and playback state. The movie that contains the second movie is called the parent movie, in my analogy, the one with the hole. Then the movie that plays within the parent movie is referred to as a child movie, or the one that plays in the hole.

This great QuickTime feature allows you to create QuickTime movies that can be used as players or full-featured applications, but they are still a QuickTime movie. Why is this so great? Well, for one you don't have to be a C++ programmer to create a very complex and powerful media browser, for example, and the other is that since QuickTime is cross platform your application (movie) should play the same on Windows, Mac OS 9, and Mac OS X. Even better, if you apply a media skin to your movie, then you customize not only the capabilities of the player but also the way the player looks or if you feel so inclined the parent movie can be deployed on HTML too! Yet another major benefit of MIAM is that you give your audience the choice to download or not content. For example, in a normal movie (a movie with no MIAM) you need to download the whole thing to see the last few seconds of the movie regardless if you watch that part or not. The same thing happens when you use alternate tracks, all the tracks are downloaded, but only one is played. With MIAM you can author your movie so that if the user doesn't select a specific child movie, well its not downloaded keeping your project lean.

There are a few ways of making MIAM. One of them is using SMIL (**S**ynchronized **M**ult**I**media **L**anguage) and authoring your movies with a text editor. For more information on writing SMIL for QuickTime please refer to Apple's site: www.apple.com/quicktime/authoring/qtsmil.html.

MIAM with LiveStage Pro

A much more powerful way to author and program QuickTime movies that use movies-in-a-movie (MIAM) is to use LiveStage Proferssional.

1.   In the Track tab for your project select Create > Movie from the Tracks menu.

2.   In the track header for your movie track make sure that the height and width are big enough to fit your MIAM.

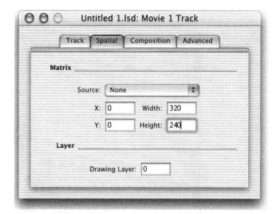

3.   Double-click on the movie sample to open the sample settings.

4.   At the bottom left of the sample settings window click on the Add New URL... button.

5.   Enter the URL of the child movie you want to load in the MIAM. The URL can be an absolute URL or a relative URL but note that it has to be relative to the parent movie.

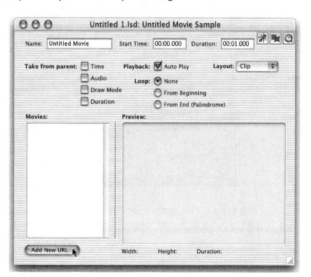

If you want you could add more URLs to the list of Movies: but you'll need to use QScript to load them dynamically and then play them. If you do so you'll need to use the LoadChildMovie(ID) command in QScript.

If you want to see some clever use of MIAM go to the following URL and click on either the enhanced or standard versions: http://kellybrock.com/qt_splash.html.

This is a QuickTime movie that has a QuickTime VR MIAM child that acts as the navigation to the content. You can see Kelly's video and listen to her music. These movies (the video and the music files) are also child movies that are only downloaded to the client if they request them. Even more interesting, the child movies also use reference movies, so if you're on a modem connection you'll get a different version from those on broadband.

There is a QTVR embedded inside a parent movie which represents the main UI for the movie. You pan around and click on the different hotspots to take you to content within the parent movie.

One hot spot takes you to a child movie playing in the parent movie. In this case it's like a flip card of Kelly's pictures. I got here by clicking on the pictures hot spot on the main QTVR UI.

Summary

As we've seen in this chapter you definitely have a large selection of deployment to choose from. Your choice will depend on your project of course, but being aware of what QuickTime can do should help you make the correct choice. As we have seen in this chapter QuickTime can be deployed to film, to video tape (analogue or digital) and a powerful array of digital media, hard drive playback, CD and DVD (DVD-Video/ROM/Hybrid) to web sites and other network deployment like from a file server.

We covered concepts like dedicated players for QuickTime content. In this particular section we talked about media skins and how they can help you brand your content using the QuickTime Player and of course we talked about other deployment media like the web browsers (via the QuickTime Plug In), applications like the MS Office suite, and authoring environments like Macromedia's Director.

Building on the deployment media we also talked about reference and alternate movies and how QuickTime can react to the viewer's (audience/client) environment ranging from language, CPU, bandwidth and other deployment variables. This is a great feature of QuickTime as it allows you to better tailor your projects to cater a wider audience base. Finally we talked about the recent concept of movie-in-a-movie (MIAM) which can basically turn a QuickTime movie into an application capable of loading other movies within it and controlling them independently from the parent timeline. But after all that we *still* haven't got our content to our audience, there are a few more decisions to make first.

6 Transport: Delivering to the Audience

QuickTime has been at the heart of media delivery since its inception. In the early days of CD-ROM development it competed with the AVI format for delivering synchronized audio and video to the desktop. Since version 3.0 its been completely cross-platform compatible and offers equivalent features on all Windows operating systems along with its native Mac environment. Today, your application determines how you deliver your QuickTime since all its functionality is inherent in all forms of transport, whether you're creating educational CD-ROMs, corporate presentations or documentaries on DVD, setting up trade show kiosks, or delivering your media over the Internet.

This chapter will explore the details of transport for your QuickTime media. We'll offer a detailed description of what it takes to deliver your content on all forms of fixed media and all types of networks. We'll offer you a true alphabet soup of acronyms that will get you ready to deal with the IT department in your office, Internet service providers, and content distribution vendors, as you'll need to deliver your QuickTime reliably to large audiences.

Setting up a kiosk for a QuickTime presentation

Fixed media and basic hard disk playback is where QuickTime began back in the early 1990s. Apple's MoviePlayer, now QuickTime Player, has always been the medium for playback and content creation, as you learned in the previous chapters, and has evolved tremendously over the last decade. Kiosks can be based around hard-disk playback, which offers great functionality and full screen presentations due to the processing speeds of today's computers. They aren't encumbered by limited data transfer rates or storage space restrictions as are fixed media options.

Most kiosk presentations will benefit from advanced authoring applications as discussed in the next sections but all QuickTime content, all types of media, and all of QuickTime's functionality can be offered in a kiosk presentation running from a hard drive. Using CDs or DVDs in such an environment will be discussed later in this chapter.

Your considerations for setting up a kiosk include where the media will be stored, how fast the processor, bus transport, and graphics cards are, and making sure there are no incompatibilities between drivers and other physical components installed in the computer. Since you have control over the playback environment, it's a relatively easy task to set up and deliver a kiosk-style QuickTime presentation.

The presentation can run from a laptop or standard desktop computer, depending on the application. The former is more mobile, but you can generally get more processor speed and hard drive space on a desktop as well a better processor and graphics cards. If you're setting up a trade show exhibit, a large monitor and a hidden computer will offer a higher resolution and more viewable experience to your audience than the smaller LCD displays on a laptop.

Specialized kiosk manufacturers can also provide systems for stand-alone applications, such as retail stores, hotels, and hospitals. While media can be stored, played back, and interactively controlled from the system, they are also often capable of accessing online information over a network. This leads to a great advantage in remote maintenance of these systems via a browser-controlled interface.

In addition to large screen playback of video in a kiosk environment, you can also utilize high quality audio tracks. Stereo sound systems, and even surround sound systems can be connected to your computer to add impact to the presentation as well. The next chapter discusses production considerations and codec options for creating audio content at this level.

You can store the content on the hard drive of the computer or in an external drive that connects to the computer via SCSI, FireWire, or USB connections. The following table shows the maximum data transfer rates of each of these connections:

SCSI-2 (Legacy)	Ultra160 SCSI	FireWire/IEEE 1394	Universal Serial Bus (USB 2.0)
20 MB/s (160 Mb/s)	160 MB/s (1.2 Gb/s)	50 MB/s (400 Mb/s)	60 MB/s (480 Mb/s)

"MB=Megabytes, Mb=Megabits"

Most processors over 500 MHz can easily play back full screen video at these data rates, although a kiosk may benefit from other features of QuickTime such as QTVR, sprites, and hotspots for use on a touch screen. All of these components are less taxing on CPU and bus transfer rates than full screen video, and can add exciting features to your kiosk presentation.

Having an external drive or using fixed media options, which will be looked at next, allows you to transport the media and utilize computer resources that are available on location. Of course, it's always recommended that you specify the exact computer configuration you require to anyone supplying your system. The advantage of a kiosk is that it's a controlled environment, and therefore you can set-up and test the system that will playback your QuickTime media in advance.

As you'll see later in this chapter, when we discuss network transport, that old adage of "Test early, test often" doesn't have to be taken to an extreme for kiosk delivery. It is more like, "Just test" before any presentation is offered that's critical to your business application in front of a real audience.

CDs as a transport media for QuickTime

QuickTime was developed for delivering digital media files on CDs, in the early days of 1x CD-ROM drives. Today we have drives capable of reading data at 24x and 32x, as well as CD-R writing data at 8x and 12x. The "x" refers to the speed of the reading mechanism on those very first drives, equivalent to 150 Kilobytes/sec. So today's drives are capable of reading at 3.6 Megabytes/sec and writing at over 1.2 MB/s. A sustained 3.6 MB/s isn't usually achieved, however, so full resolution video such as DV wouldn't necessarily play back from these disks and drives. In addition, the higher the data rate of your video, the less you can store on a single CD.

In general you first define your audience and then the lowest common denominator CD drive this audience would have, in the case of a kiosk, you know exactly. With users' CD drives running at different speeds, the best way to determine this is by experience as it's very difficult to find statistics on installed CD drives, especially broken down by the different type of audiences you may want to target. I personally like to analyze the target audience by the year they bought their computer:

Year	Average CD drive	Theoretical data rate	Target data rate
Before 1995	2 X	300 KBps	180 KBps
1995-1996	8 X	1,200 KBps	720 KBps
1997-1998	12 X	1.75 MBps	1.0 MBps
1999-2000	24 X	3.5 MBps	2.0 MBps
2001 and after	40 X	5.8 MBps	3.0 MBps

Please note that the data rate target is the theoretical data rate minus 40% to accommodate for hardware/software discrepancies. You should make sure the data rate of your movies is below the target data rate. Also note that the data rates in this chart are in kilobytes and megabytes per second and not kilobits or megabits per second.

You can think of any fixed media storage as a bit bucket that fills up from a faucet. Turn the flow of bits up by raising the data rate, and the bucket fills up faster. Lower the flow rate by lowering the data rate and the bucket takes more time to fill up. Hence, you get a longer movie clip on one disk with lower data rates. The following table shows some typical types of content and data rates associated with them, and how each might fill up a CD:

Data Type	Data Rate	CD Capacity
MP3 Audio	16 KB/s (128 Kb/s)	10 hours
CD Audio	176 KB/s	1 hour
Broadband Video	60 KB/s (480 Kb/s)	3 hours
MPEG-1 Video	200 KB/s (1.6 Mb/s)	54 minutes
MPEG-2 Video	500 KB/s (4 Mb/s)	21 minutes

One thing you can do if you want to offer the best to people on slow machines as well as to those on faster machines is to use QuickTime's capabilities. With QuickTime you can determine the speed of the CPU so you can make a reference movie that refers to different video files on the CD depending on the power of the CPU. For a full tutorial on how to make reference movies with MakeRefMovie please refer to the end of Chapter 7.

CD-R drives have become as common place as floppy drives, and CD-RW technology is now affordable to the masses for creating CDs with music, videos, or multimedia content. I find it to be the perfect media for archiving client projects and documents and sending clients samples of compressed media. QuickTime content in any form can be written to, read from, and played back from any CD drive on any Windows or Macintosh platform.

One of the many advantages of CDs for transport is that they can be programmed to auto-start so your end user simply puts them in their CD drive and the program begins execution. For Macintosh playback, the disk must have specifically designated information at the beginning of the HFS volume, and the file that will execute at start-up, such as an installer or application, needs to be in the top level directory of the disk. Adaptec's Toast software (now available from Roxio, www.roxio.com) offers these options when burning CDs.

For Windows playback, an `autorun.inf` file is used instead. More information on how to create this file and use the auto-start feature on Windows is available at http://msdn.microsoft.com/, should you run a search for "`autorun.inf`".

You can also create one hybrid disk that will contain content for either platform in two distinct volumes, one HFS (for Macs) and one ISO 9660 (for PCs). Shared files, such as long video or multimedia projects, are placed on the Windows partition, but can be accessed by the Macintosh operating system and be used in conjunction with its platform-specific files. The CD in the book is a perfect example of this.

Another advantage of CDs is that the full QuickTime installer can be placed on them so end users are not prompted to go to Apple's web site in order to download the QuickTime components they need to play back your content. New codec technologies can also be installed from the CD, but be forewarned that QuickTime versions and codecs can be superceded, though QuickTime is always backwards compatible. Licensing agreements are fairly straightforward for distribution of QuickTime in this manner, and you can find out how to do this at the Apple web site.

The most common application of CDs is multimedia projects using Director or other authoring platforms, especially in the gaming and educational markets. I use them to archive data files, but for storing large quantities of media, they've been outpaced by Jaz drives, DVDs, and DLTs as removable storage devices. That's where we'll go next in our discussion of fixed media options.

DVD options for transport and archiving

Apple was the first manufacturer to offer a built in drive for writing DVDs, which they marketed as the SuperDrive in conjunction with the introduction of DVD Studio Pro. DVD recordable and re-writeable technology is still evolving, and here we'll explore the various formats and media options and their applications for your QuickTime projects.

DVD-R

The SuperDrive in its first incarnation was a limited capacity DVD burner for creating write-once disks or DVD-Rs. Analogous to CD-R, and now capable of holding the standard 4.7 GB on a single disk, they're fast becoming the low-cost, high density replacement for CDs in the computer world.

You can burn standard DVD Video projects to a DVD-R using authoring packages that have also become very affordable. Today's DVD set-top boxes, and all computer DVD-ROM drives should be able to read a standard disk, but older drives may have some compatibility problems. As with CDs, testing prior to an important presentation is imperative if you have any concerns about compatibilities, or you can check with the drive's manufacturer about known issues.

DVD-Rs are best used for short-run projects. If you need large quantities of disks for distribution, you are best off selecting a replicator. They may require you to deliver your project on DLT (Digital Linear Tape) in order to create a perfect master prior to replication. DVD-Rs are sometimes accepted, but have been known to create errors during the copy process at the replication facility.

Other applications of DVD-R include archiving content and transporting your media to other locations for playback. Just as in the case of CD-Rs, a DVD burner will come with software to format and burn disks for the most common applications. Authoring applications, as discussed in Chapter 11, may also be included. Keep in mind that standard DVD – Video disks are not QuickTime based. You'll most likely use QuickTime as a container for your source files going into a DVD authoring application or software MPEG encoder. However, as a transport mechanism, DVD-R will hold any type of data and computer DVD drives will be able to read and playback your QuickTime, even from the disk, at sustained rates up to 10 Mbits/sec.

DVD-RAM

DVD-RAM technology was one of the first to reach the computer market, but as such isn't necessarily compatible with newer standards. A DVD-RAM is more likely to be used as a computer storage or archival format rather than a transport and playback format. Early drives required disks in cartridges, just like the early CD-ROMs, and some disks weren't even removable from their cartridges. Disk capacities have reached the standard 4.7 GB, and most drive manufacturers are fully compliant with the DVD forums standard format. DVD-RAMs won't play back in set-top boxes, making them limited for project creation and distribution.

DVD-RW and DVD+RW

There are two competing formats for re-writeable DVDs today, DVD-RW and DVD+RW. They're supported by two different groups of manufacturers, and discussions about them look so much like the old Beta vs. VHS wars. The former has been proposed as Book F of the DVD standard by the DVD Forum, while the latter is backed by a group of manufacturers that included Sony and Philips.

Similar to CD-RWs, rewriteable DVD media will be more expensive then their DVD-R counterparts. They have the advantage of being re-usable, although both are capable of writing multi-session data, meaning you can write data to them at different times without overwriting the existing contents. For this reason, they're better used as storage for ongoing projects, but their higher cost makes them less desirable as an archive format or as a transport medium.

This discussion really only touches the surface of DVD media options. Ongoing developments of this technology and perhaps new, competing technologies, means that you can never be guaranteed of complete forward compatibility with any of these choices. Choosing a media option that works for your application today, and staying within the guidelines of the standards created will assure you of a reasonable level and length of time when that application will be useful.

To follow-up and stay on top of developments, I'd recommend the general DVD forum site, www.dvdforum.org and for more information on the DVD+RW technology, also take a look at www.dvda.org.

Apple has an extensive list of DVD drives that have been tested with DVD-Rs burned on their SuperDrive at www.apple.com/dvd/compatibility/.

Network transport of QuickTime content

QuickTime is certainly the longest running format for delivering media over networks. Originally, media files were simply treated like any other data file and were downloaded to the end user's computer before playback could occur.

Beginning with QuickTime 3.0, Apple released their progressive download implementation, Fast Start. This offers the user a media file that was still downloaded to their computer, but could begin playing before the download was complete. A streaming server technology was introduced in conjunction with QuickTime 4.0, QTSS (QuickTime Streaming Server), allowing media to be delivered to the user without the need to save it to disk, and playing it back in real time. Live events can also be streamed using this technology, and Apple offers the server software core as an open source project under the name Darwin Server (see www.apple.com/quicktime/products/qtss/).

Today, media is delivered over networks in various forms and using various methodologies, including progressive download and streaming of live and on-demand content, or many hybrid ideas. Your application will, in part, determine how you should deliver QuickTime over the network available to you. Understanding the protocols of each of these transport methods and defining the terms of delivery is the purpose of this section.

Protocols and formats

Server technology and network protocols are the mechanisms that can deliver QuickTime assets reliably over networks to users connected anywhere from 56k modems to T1 leased lines and beyond. The server software rearranges the media file into packets that are more easily transported over the network. This **packetizing** makes efficient use of the available bandwidth on the network, while adding some overhead for handshaking protocols that assure that the data being sent can be properly received and utilized.

The protocols are the language of networks, allowing communication between network components as well as servers and client computers. They're organized in layers and operate differently depending on whether you are delivering web pages, progressive downloaded movies, or true streaming media. This discussion gets pretty technical, but I think it helps to understand some of the underlying technology, so you can choose the method of delivery that best suits your application.

Let's first take a look at how these protocols relate and operate on a basic level:

Protocols for Viewing a Web Page and Streaming a Movie

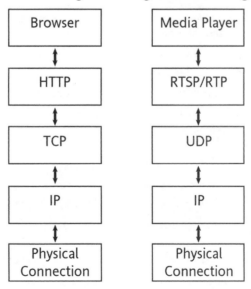

Browser software such as Internet Explorer or Netscape uses the application protocol HTTP to communicate to a server using the transport protocol, TCP, over the network protocol layer, or IP. A media player, or plug-in software used by the browser, uses the application protocols, RTSP (Real

Time Streaming Protocol) and RTP (Realtime Transfer Protocol), to get real time data streams using the transport protocol, UDP over IP.

QuickTime supports the delivery of media to the client computer using HTTP and RTP. A standard web server can deliver any QuickTime content using HTTP. QuickTime can stream video, audio, text, and MIDI using RTSP/RTP from a QuickTime Streaming Server or Darwin Server. A QuickTime movie can also reside on the HTTP server, but contain **streaming tracks** that reference content on the streaming server, so that a movie with media types that cannot stream, such as Flash and Sprites, can take advantage of the streaming capabilities for video and audio as well.

The advantages of using HTTP delivery for your QuickTime movies are:

- All packets are received and lost packets are retransmitted automatically.
- The movie is stored locally and play back begins when enough of it has arrived.
- All QuickTime track types can be delivered over HTTP.
- Firewalls will generally pass HTTP data through to the requester, rather than block the transmission from the server.

The advantages and some consideration for using RTP and RTSP for delivering QuickTime movies are:

- RTP doesn't attempt to retransmit lost packets, for a live stream this can prevent a bottleneck and the viewer won't miss as much content.
- The movie isn't stored locally, so it won't take up disk space on the viewers computer, or be easily copied and reused.
- RTSP allows the viewer to skip ahead without downloading the entire movie.
- RTP can deliver single tracks, or streaming tracks, contained within a movie on an HTTP server or even on a CD or DVD.

> *Firewalls will often block UDP traffic, so streaming QuickTime over RTP might not reach viewers behind firewalls.*

HTTP and RTP each have their advantages in specific applications, which I'll explore in the next few sections.

Progressive download vs. true streaming

Progressive download, or HTTP streaming, is beneficial if you have shorter content that requires a high quality assurance factor during playback. If you know the end user will tolerate longer wait times, then your media can be encoded at bit rates that are higher than their real network connection. This is particularly useful for delivering higher quality video to 56k modem users, 56k is so limiting that usually you need to make your movies larger to look good.

True streaming over RTP offers the end user a real-time experience, with little wait time and hardly any need for buffering if you have a reliable network in place. When the user clicks on a movie link, the player or plug-in begins negotiating the stream delivery with the server, either a QT Streaming Server or a Darwin Server (although RealNetworks can also serve QuickTime from their proprietary server systems). The player animates the progress slider and tells the user it's "Negotiating", "Connecting", and "Buffering" before it begins streaming the movie. Usually this happens in a matter of seconds.

True streaming is beneficial for long, continuous transmissions, without requiring the client's computer to store the media file. It does require that the encoded bit rate is lower than the actual network connection. Encoding to meet this requirement and other considerations are discussed in the next chapter.

Since the content needs to be played back in real-time, there is no opportunity for error correction and retransmission of lost packets while delivering true streaming media. Network congestion, and overloaded servers, switches, or routers, may cause transmission errors. Thankfully, network providers are raising the bar on Quality of Service guarantees in order to stay competitive. Errors in the transmission may appear as glitches in individual frames of the movie, or dropped frames while the movie is playing. The audio track may also pause if re-buffering is required under heavy traffic conditions. There are methods of encoding and transporting that prioritize the data so that audio flows more smoothly during playback, as this can be quite disruptive to the user. These generally involve codecs and media servers designed for network transport of the QuickTime files.

You can also combine HTTP delivery with RTP delivery, which is useful for some types of QuickTime content that aren't supported in true streaming, tracks that can be streamed are video, audio, text, MIDI, and MPEG-4 (as of QT6).

In QuickTime Pro you can set your video and audio tracks as a streaming track, place their content on the streaming server, and reference them from a file on a web server that contains the non-streaming tracks that need to be delivered over HTTP. Pictorially, it works like this:

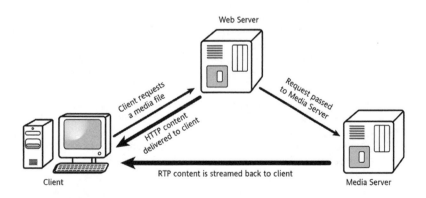

The client computer requests the media file from the web server, where it is stored as a QuickTime movie. The movie contains a streaming track in a QuickTime movie file, so the web server sends a request to the media server to retrieve that part of the media file. On the client's computer, QuickTime receives the HTTP content and the RTP streaming content and packages it together for the viewer. In essence you can stream the Flash or Sprite tracks from the HTTP server because their bandwidth requirements are very low.

Live streaming vs. on demand streaming

Using a streaming server you can offer live events as well as audio or video on demand, sometimes called VOD. A live event requires a broadcaster as well, such as the new QT Broadcaster or Sorenson Broadcaster discussed briefly in Chapter 10. For VOD content you can use any encoding tool to save the media to a file that is then uploaded to the streaming server.

Some live events are necessary for impact, but they will also tax the streaming server since all users connect simultaneously. Today's QuickTime Streaming Server is capable of delivering up to 4000 simultaneous streams in one 1GHz box, but some events may require even greater capacity and edge serving networks should be considered for such large capacity projects.

On demand projects offer the user a choice of when and where they view your content, one of the many benefits of Internet delivery of media. The server demands are also reduced because the likelihood of simultaneous connections is lowered. Often, live events are archived to a file as well, so that they can be delivered as VOD in the future. More thoughts on encoding considerations for live and on demand delivery are discussed in the next chapter as well.

Unicast vs. multicast

In order to relieve the burden on the server and networks, you can use a multicast-enabled network for delivery of your content. Multicast is a method of delivering content from one-to-many as opposed to the standard unicast, or one-to-one delivery that I've been discussing up until this point. In this method, one stream originates from the server, and many users can pick it up by intelligent routing technology as it traverses the network. This does mean that it serves the needs of simultaneous viewers, such as a corporate presentation or distance learning application. There must be a scheduled multicast for viewers to log into, but it doesn't necessarily have to be live.

Running through walls

Firewalls are designed to protect computers from unwanted traffic, especially in corporate environments. Home networks and even individual computers connected to the Internet using an "always on" device such as a cable modem or DSL line, will also have firewalls set-up on them. Firewalls block UDP (User Datagram Protocol) traffic, so users behind them may not be able to view your QuickTime streams.

Individual users can set their QuickTime preferences for delivery even through firewalls by opening up the QuickTime Settings control panel on their computer and selecting Streaming Transport from the pull-down menu. (In OS X it reads Transport Setup and is found in the Connection tab of the QT Preferences pane.) A dialog box will appear on their screen:

Clicking on the Auto Configure button will allow QuickTime to establish a connection and determine the best method of delivery, either UDP or HTTP. If QuickTime fails to make a connection you'll receive an error message that your network connection may not be properly set-up or operational, or your firewall is blocking the RTP/RTSP traffic. In the latter case, you can follow the link at the bottom of the pop-up shown above, which will guide you through the steps needed to set-up proxy servers and ports IDs so that the QuickTime streams can get through your firewall.

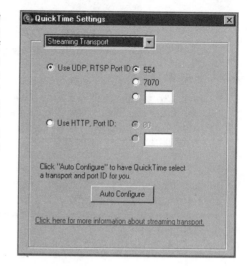

All this information is useful to tell users, it may be appropriate to have a 'how to set up your computer if you are behind a firewall' link on the web page you are hosting the QuickTime movie on.

If you've made it this far and are confused, you probably want to get a system administrator involved who'll have first hand knowledge of the servers and networks that you're dealing with.

Controlling and communicating during playback

The QuickTime framework allows many sophisticated features for the communication and control of different media elements and files within the context of web delivery. While it's beyond the scope of this chapter to go into detail, I'd like to highlight a few of these features and offer some resources to probe further.

Setting up playlists

QuickTime can understand MP3 playlists for simulating a live radio feed over the Internet. You'll need to create all of your audio content as MP3 files, which will best be streamed using HTTP or icy (Icecast protocol) with QTSS 4.

A playlist is simply a text file with special formatting so QuickTime can read it. The file extension that QuickTime will recognize as a playlist is .m3u. A poster movie on your web page can be used with a link to the playlist M3U file. Then QuickTime takes over and plays back the list of media files in the playlist.

Playlists can be m3u files, but also a playlist of video and/or audio QuickTime movies that can be looped. QuickTime Streaming Server 4 also has support for MPEG-4 playlists both video and/or audio.

A simulated live event or delayed broadcast is when you set a playlist to only run once at a specific time. So all the listeners/viewer get the same content as the same time, as in a live event, but from a prerecorded movie file. You can also have a playlist of MP3 files that uses the icecast (icy://) protocol to stream to any compliant player like iTunes, MacAmp, WinAmp, or SoundJam.

For more sophisticated control over the look and functionality of a custom player for a playlist application, you should think about using skins and look into learning Totally Hip's LiveStage Pro authoring application further.

XML importer

A link to a QuickTime movie on a web page can be a text file containing XML (eXtensible Markup Language) commands. XML is a more expandable set of commands beyond HTML for controlling the look and functionality of web pages. In the context of QuickTime, it allows you to combine elements from different files into a skinned custom movie player as described in the previous chapter.

You can also use XML to create a reference movie that passes attributes and playback functionality parameters to the QT Player, such as `AutoPlay` or `View as FullScreen`. Both of these techniques benefit greatly from the advanced authoring capabilities of LiveStage Pro, but here are some beginner's resources to get started and learn more:

- The XML FAQ at www.ucc.ie/xml/

- QuickTime API Documentation: XML Import at (deep breath) http://developer.apple.com/techpubs/quicktime/qtdevdocs/REF/whatsnewqt5/Max.2a.htm

JavaScript

QuickTime can execute JavaScript functions wherever it can reference a URL in order to control the playback of your media elements. JavaScript is a relatively simple programming language used in conjunction with HTML web pages. The functions will be programmed into the web page and QuickTime will look there for the code it needs to execute. An example of this would be:

```
<EMBED SRC="poster.mov" HREF="javascript:openMovie('Movie1.htm')" >
```

Which would call the JavaScript function `openMovie` that you've defined in the current HTML page when the poster movie is clicked on. You could use this method to pass parameters to a QuickTime playback function. Be careful when using JavaScript, Internet Explorer and Netscape can have differing reactions to fairly simple code, the best advice is to test every line in as many different browsers as possible.

Some beginner's references and tutorials for JavaScript are:

- The JavaScript Primers at www.htmlgoodies.com/primers/jsp, they hope to offer "30 Steps that make JavaScripting fun to learn!"

- QuickTime API Documentation JavaScript Support is at: http://developer.apple.com/techpubs/quicktime/qtdevdocs/REF/QT41_HTML/QT41WhatsNew-72.html

Summary

After Chapter 5's discussion of what you can do with QuickTime media once it's out of your hands, here we've looked into more depth of how best to get that media into someone else's. If you're not in the enviable position of being able to control the exact specifications of the eventual host machines, then we've hopefully given enough information for you to be able to decide the best storage, delivery, or transport methods.

In the involved case of Internet delivery there really are an awful amount of compromises to be made, and it'll depend heavily on your target audience as to what you can realistically do with your QuickTime content. The next chapter will be of even more help in making your decisions, as we discuss the process of creating QuickTime linear media, right from it's inception to final delivery. Including all you'll ever need to know about codecs!

7 Linear Media, Capture to Delivery

During this chapter we'll talk about each step in the production process of linear media. For the most part linear media means content that has a beginning, middle, and an end and the content is viewed in that order. A typical example is a video based QuickTime movie where there is a beginning, middle, and an end, and the viewer is expected to watch the whole piece in order. Other examples could be audio files like music tracks, narration, or maybe ambient sounds from the Amazon rain forests. For the most part when we refer to linear media we mean video and/or sound.

Usually linear media is used to tell or enhance a story, be that artistic, communication centric or commercial. Linear media created in QuickTime can be deployed in a variety of ways via QuickTime, and also be deployed with other technologies. Think about some of the ways linear media is deployed in QuickTime. How many times have you seen a movie trailer online or listened to a live streaming radio show? You must have watched CD-ROMs that contain digital video, or have seen information or shopping kiosks that play video and/or music? Well, in every case QuickTime can be used to deploy the linear media.

This chapter will discuss the process of creating linear media content, but it's important to say that linear media often becomes part of a larger project. Projects may have a collection of linear media content or by being interactive make the linear media not too linear anymore. An example is a DVD where you have a mix of interactive media (the menus) with linear media (the actual video clips). Another example of a project involving a collection of linear files would be an interactive piece that has access to multiple video files, for example, a QuickTime movie that has a movie in a movie track where different movies could be loaded in one by one. In this case, each loading movie would be considered linear media, but the 'parent' movie displaying them wouldn't be linear media. As an example of making linear media not linear, consider a two-hour lecture video file, and a student who needs to access the last 20 minutes of the class. The student jumps to 100 minutes from the beginning and watches the last 20 minutes. In this case, even though the two-hour long clip is linear, the student is accessing the content in a non-linear fashion.

One of the beauties of the QuickTime architecture is that it can be present throughout the whole production process for linear media from capturing, editing, compressing, and deployment. One of the major advantages of QuickTime is that the linear media you create can easily be part of other types of interactive media as mentioned in the examples above. In Chapters 9 and 10 we'll cover some ways of mixing the linear media with the interactive logic.

Producing linear media

OK, so now we have an idea of what we can do with this linear media, let's now get into the production side of things.

In a nutshell producing our linear media can be broken down into a few sequential steps:

- **Pre-production:** Everything has a beginning and the best way to start is by having a solid plan to help you minimize surprises and strategies to overcome them when they appear.

- **Capture:** Which means getting the content in a digital form on to the computer for processing.

- **Edit:** Most often your raw content needs to be edited to better tell the story or just to better get the message across.

- **Compress:** Once you have your digital content captured and edited you need to get it to a small file size so it can fit on a CD or through a network connection.

- **Deliver:** Having the compressed media isn't enough, now you need to deliver it, maybe over the Web, or maybe as part of an interactive CD-ROM.

Each part of the process has its intricacies that you have to know and keep in mind if you want to achieve the best results both from your workflow and with the quality of the finished product. We'll look at a number of concepts that should help you make the right decision as you go through your own process, but keep in mind that each step in the process can be individually very complex.

Web video myths

There are a lot of misconceptions about web video and most of them are just fueled by ignorance. We'll demystify some of these myths, so that when you're working in your pre-production process you're aware of what other people may think about web video.

- **Myth: If it's video on the Web, the audience will watch it.**
  Fact: Well, the only reason why some one would rather see a smaller size video on a computer screen, rather than a film on a TV screen is due to the content; if the viewer thinks that the content is valuable to them, then they'll watch. When thinking about your video projects always question what will make it more interesting than the content on TV.

- **Myth: If the user doesn't have QuickTime installed they won't download it.**
  Fact: For the most part this is a myth. If the subject is appealing enough to the users, or they know that the content is valuable, they'll download the installer if they don't already have QuickTime running on their machine. When you design your project make sure that the audience has a good understanding of what they may expect. Also, when selecting the content, make sure it adds value to the audience.

- **Myth: Windows Media and/or Real Networks are better.**
Fact: In certain cases Windows Media and/or Real may produce better looking video but that doesn't mean that they're better. Windows Media and Real are mostly used for streaming video while QuickTime is mostly used for progressive downloads, which offer better quality, although with the delay of a download. Being better means being better overall. QuickTime movies can have not only audio and video, but also a collection of more than 200 media types. Try viewing QuickTime VR on Real or Windows Media, or try integrating a streaming video track with a simple Flash interface and pictures that come from a web server! Furthermore, QuickTime offers much better cross platform support both for encoding and for playback while Windows Media and Real usually offer worse performance on the Mac than on PCs. Certain projects would benefit from using Real, Windows Media, QuickTime, or all 3 depending on the objectives and audience. It's best to be aware of what is best for what, and how they relate to your specific projects. QuickTime may not always be the best option, but it certainly is one to consider.

- **Myth: Anyone can create great looking web video.**
Fact: This is a good one. Yes, the technology allows anyone to make a video and put it on the web for a few dollars, but great looking video? To create great looking video it takes a team of experts, not just a person with a camera. Great looking web video starts with production values like a story, lighting, camera work, editing, audio, compression, delivery, etc. When you decide to start a project make sure you gather the expertise needed for every aspect of the project. Keep in mind that shooting for the Web may be different from shooting for TV, so the videographer must be acquainted with web limitations, some of which are covered in this chapter.

- **Myth: My $300 camera and my old computer can achieve professional quality.**
Fact: Just like the myth above, you need the best to create the best. If you start with bad quality sources, such as what you'd get from a $300 video camera, then you're bound to produce web video that's less than professional quality. For the most part you should get the best gear for your projects as your budget allows. The good news is that with today's technology you can achieve very good results for a fraction of the cost five or seven years ago.

- **Myth: Streaming on the Web is the best way to deliver video.**
Fact: Streaming is great for some projects, but definitely not for every project. Depending on your objective and audience the best way to deliver the content may be streaming, progressive download, CD, or on VHS in some cases. You can even use a combination depending on your project. The downside to streaming is that you'll need to cap the average bit rate of your files to fit in the users' bandwidth.

- **Myth: I managed to compress my 4 GB original movie into 10 MB, so I'm really good at compressing!**
Fact: Although file size is important, file size is the result of multiplying data rate by the length of the content. Therefore, you shouldn't ask how big a QuickTime movie file should be. Rather you need to ask yourself what the data rate of a specific audience

will be. Once you figure out the data rate you can use, you can then calculate the file size by multiplying the duration of your content by the data rate.

Pre-production; thinking about delivery

Pre-production of anything is simply the preliminary arrangements that are made upon the inception of a project and in this case the project is creating your linear media for delivery. The whole idea about the pre-production phase is to ensure that there is a plan to follow during production and that everyone involved knows what to do and when. Having a great plan will help you minimize unexpected problems and if they do arise, you'll also be well prepared for them.

The very best way to go about getting pre-production right for your projects is by gathering experience. As you produce more projects you'll learn what the expectations of your audience are, and how the technology works under certain circumstances. The problem is that if you've no experience then you're in a Catch 22 situation, but that's why we're here! Hopefully our experiences can help you in your projects.

First and foremost, the most important thing to consider in your pre-production process is your intended audience. Yes, your *audience*, and not the technology. The better you define your audience, the better you'll know what you need to deliver and how best to deliver it. In turn you'll be able to plan and execute towards that objective you set. Once you know what you need to deliver, then you can deal with the right technology or choice of technologies to achieve that goal. Whenever you have a question for yourself in regards to your project, just think about what the audience would expect, and the solution to your question should become that bit clearer.

Often, inexperienced producers ask the question: "how do I get the best quality?". Well, there is no simple answer to that question. In most cases the question is incomplete, and therefore will lack an answer. Rather, the question should be "how do I get the best quality for a specific audience, when I want to achieve a specific goal?".

For example, if the objective is to target the widest possible audience you may want to use a codec that is widely available, like Sorenson 2 instead of 3 (Sorenson 3 requires QuickTime 5+). Also, to cater to a wide online audience you'll need to compress your videos to fit on a 56k modem, but this yields a small video window and quality that may be too low. However, if the target audience is on broadband and you know that they have QuickTime 5, then you can deliver much better quality by making your videos larger and using Sorenson 3.

Now, these decisions will vary from project to project. There'll be a number of technical constraints dictated by your audience, and these constraints will have a direct impact on your production decisions.

As an example of how from analyzing your audience you can reach some answers about the technology you'll need to use let's suppose that you decide to make a video to be delivered on the Web. Let's start thinking about the audience. You want this audience to have a wide base, meaning lots of people in different locations, maybe with very different interests, without considering their interest in your content.

Let's look at some of the technical constrains first. We know that the audience needs to have some sort of web connection, as our video will be deployed on the net. Now, we want a wide audience base and the chances are that a large percentage of that audience connects to the web via a 56k (or slower) modem, (possibly from home or from a hotel room). At the same time, a smaller percentage of the audience will have a broadband connection (perhaps because they'll be seeing your video content while they're at work on a corporate network).

We also have to consider the type of computers that a wide audience base would have. These will range from really old stinky machines to new powerful workhorses. For the most part, the chances are that the larger percentage of the audience have relatively slow machines for today's standards, but that aren't too old. We'll assume that the majority of the audience will have a computer bought between two and three years ago.

Thinking about the interest that a wide base audience would have on a specific topic, we can safely say that the average interest level wouldn't be too high! The logic is that the wider the audience base, the interest level on specific topics tends to be lower than for audiences interested in targeted niches.

If we consider bandwidth, hardware, and interest we arrive to the following pre-production conclusions:

- First you'll need to make sure that your audience has QuickTime installed. You should offer a web link to Apple's web site from your site, or if your project is on a CD then include the full installer that you can license from Apple for free.

- Secondly we need the QuickTime video files to load quickly without too much delay. The main reason for this conclusion is that the average interest level of a wide base audience isn't too high. So, if the audience is waiting for something they aren't that interested in, it's likely they'll hit the back button on their web browser. If that happens, then you've lost your audience and the value of your project is reduced.

From understanding what QuickTime (the technology) can do, we can create different versions of our movies. One of these versions could be compressed for users on 56k modems and slower connections, another version could be compressed for viewers on ISDN lines (128kbps is often common in Europe), and a larger version could be compressed for customers on broadband connections. Even better, knowing that QuickTime has the capability to select tracks depending on client machine language settings, multiple QuickTime movies (or movies with multiple tracks) could be used in a number of languages to try to cover not only English speaking people. We'll touch on how to create these reference movies at the end of the chapter.

As you can see in this previous example, by first understanding the needs of the audience and then the capabilities of QuickTime, then we can make the right decisions for our production process.

When you're in the pre-production stages of any video project for the Web, CD-ROM, or kiosks you need to know what the limitations of the authoring technologies are, as well as the technical constraints that the audience may have. When you create the storyboard for your computer-delivered videos, you need to consider what affects the quality of the output. Delivering video over the Web or CD-ROM means that you need to juggle between quality and file size. The higher the quality of a QuickTime movie, the greater its file size will be. The greater the file size, the longer the audience has to wait on the Web to get your content, or the greater the chance that the QuickTime player will skip video frames when playing on a slow CD or hard drive.

Looking for masking and blue screening opportunities

When talking about the limitations of the technology, especially with digital video technology, we have to deal with compression. Video in particular tends to be very demanding on both computer power and file size, which has a direct relationship to bandwidth requirements. If you think of video as the ultimate slide show, it means that in one second a large number of frames need to be displayed. To be able to handle so much content we need to use some sort of codec (**CO**mpression – **DEC**ompression algorithm). The interesting thing is that codecs don't like changes from frame to frame. If you can keep the frames of a video without changing, like a static image, then it's easier for the codecs to compress. As you can imagine, this is the antithesis of video and in most cases you cannot have static video! Why would you have video when you could use an image?

The good thing is that you can help the codecs do their work if you keep the changes to the minimum. In terms of the pre-production process there are two video compositing tricks that could have a positive impact once your video is produced: **masking** and **blue screening**.

The idea behind blue screening is that you shoot your subject against a blue screen, which can then be replaced with some other backdrop during post-production. This technique allows for a less expensive production process, as your backdrop could be a static image of a location that would be difficult to gain access to. If your blue screening results in a background that has little changes over time then you'll be helping the codec do the compression by allowing it to focus on the subject and not on the static background.

Similar to blue screening, the concept of masking can be used to improve the quality of your compressed videos. The difference between masking and blue screening is that with masking you don't replace the background, but rather you grab the first frame and keep the background of your subject consistent through out the timeline. This way, if the background had some minor changes throughout the timeline with masking, those changes are removed keeping the background constant. Another approach to masking is being able to remove the background all together with a static mask. As an example, think of a project where you want a standing narrator to be in front of a white studio that should match the white background of your web page. As you can imagine, shooting someone against a perfect white background is very difficult. The idea is that you shoot your subject on the white studio to the best of your ability, and then in the post-production process you add a white mask that covers any problem that you may have had in lighting the studio. In this case, a white mask around your subject will ensure that the background matches the white of your web site.

The reason why we mention both blue screening and masking in the pre-production process is that you may want to think of some clever ways of how you could use these methods right from the storyboarding phase.

Capturing video

To be able to create your QuickTime movies with audio and video you need to turn your content into a digital file so you can manipulate it with a computer. The process of getting an analogue signal (like the one from a microphone or a VHS tape) onto a digital file is called **digitizing**. As the name implies, the process converts an analogue signal to a digital one. On the other hand, digital cameras store the content in a digital fashion. Getting the digital content from the digital tape to the computer is called **capturing**, as the data is already digitized. In this section we'll discuss some of the considerations you should have, both when thinking of the gear you may need and when going through the process of digitizing or capturing.

The bottom line is that you should try to get the best quality that you can with your budget. The reason for this is that once the content is digital you'll need to compress it for delivery to a computer by CD-ROM, the Web, or a kiosk. If the source you compress for delivery is of bad quality, there is no way that you can improve it. In fact, bad quality source that is compressed will turn into *really* bad quality compressed video and this is true not only for QuickTime but for any other compressed format. It's as simple as the old adage "garbage in – garbage out".

Non-digital sources

Some common examples of non-digital sources include film, Betacam SP, Hi8, VHS, etc. Of these formats, some will yield much better quality than others once the content becomes digital. For example, the highest quality will come from film and the lowest from consumer level VHS.

There are two sides to the coin when dealing with *professional* non-digital sources. The first is that it can get complicated and expensive, while the other is that you'll start with sources of great quality. Similarly, *consumer* level non-digital sources and equipment aren't too expensive, but the quality of your content won't be the best.

In summary, to turn your non-digital source into a digital file to work with on a computer, you'll need a source like a camera to shoot with, a playback deck unless your camera is suitable, a computer with a digitizing board and a lot of hard drive space.

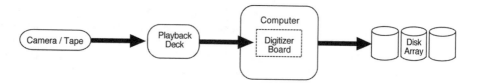

As these formats (film, Betacam SP, Hi8, VHS, etc.) are analogue they require a computer with a digitizing board to get the content stored in a digital file. Digitizing boards range in price and quality from a couple of hundred dollars up to tens of thousands of dollars depending on the specification, quality, and the manufacturer. In some cases some vendors like Avid offer full solutions that include everything you need: the computer, monitors, hard drives, digitizing board(s), etc.

Usually, the higher the quality of your source material, the higher the quality of your decks and your capturing boards. It would be impossible to suggest a specific system, first because different people would have different budgets and needs, and second because the technology advances so fast that certain products may become obsolete relatively soon. Rather we can talk about some general considerations and characteristics that you should look for.

Starting at the highest video quality, if you can afford it or if your projects justify the investment you may want to consider using **uncompressed capable boards**. These digitizing boards take in video and audio without applying compression, capturing the source at a really high quality. On the same note uncompressed means a lot of data, usually in the range of 30 Megabytes per second. This means that a minute of video would take about 1.75 Gigabytes on the hard drive, which by the way needs to be fast enough to deliver so much data. Fast SCSI drives or even dual channel disk arrays, depending on the capture card, are often used for these needs. As you can see, dealing with uncompressed audio and video will require an expensive digitizing card plus other expensive goodies. As mentioned above, due to the data rate, uncompressed video will require a lot of hard drive space that often is solved using disk arrays which are a number of high performance hard drives connected in parallel. Usually with these kinds of expensive digitizing systems people use really high quality source decks, Betacam decks for example. In some cases film is turned into video and then digitized with a board like those described here.

QuickTime can handle uncompressed video and audio. Some systems like CineWave from Pinnacle use their own proprietary uncompressed codec, which is an addition to QuickTime. This means that you can take a CineWave captured file as a QuickTime movie to Discreet's Cleaner 5 or to After Effects without the need to transcode to another codec. This means that depending on the uncompressed system you use QuickTime can be involved from the original stages throughout your whole workflow.

Going down the food chain of digitizing boards you'll find boards that compress the video in real time to an intermediate codec. Most high end digitizing boards that compress as they digitize use some variation of a Motion JPEG codec or M-JPEG (not to be confused with MPEG). One of the neat features of M-JPEG is that it can apply varying degrees of compression. As you can imagine, the idea is to use a board or card that applies the least compression possible. The thing is if you apply too much compression to the source, then the quality will suffer. You want to work with the best source and then compress at the end of your process. A good M-JPEG board today could yield about 10 Megabytes per second, which is about one third of uncompressed. As with uncompressed video, high quality M-JPEG needs large amounts of drive space and high performance hard drives, though not as much as with uncompressed. On the same note, usually professionals using this kind of equipment complement their capturing process with professional grade video decks like Betacam decks.

On the next level of digitizing boards down you'll find boards that apply further compression to the source. At this point we start to get into the consumer or low-level prosumer gear that often uses some sort of M-JPEG or MPEG compression. Usually these cards will yield data rates below 5 Megabytes per second and their price tend to be under USD$1,000 but the quality tends to be too low for professional looking video. Consumers and beginners may end up using this kind of digitizing equipment with low-resolution sources like VHS, Super VHS, or in some cases Hi8 decks.

In a typical high-end professional production environment you would have an NTSC/PAL monitor connected to the computer to be able to preview your work. A professional deck to play back high quality sources would be connected to a high quality digitizing board inside the computer which would often have two computer screens (to enlarge the desktop) and a disk array to store lots of video files. Depending on your own budget you may not be able to have such a complex system, but most high-end studios would. For an alternative, using DV gear, please refer to the "Digital sources" section below.

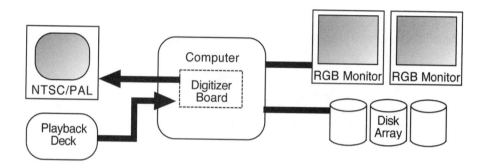

Digital sources

Working with digital sources offers interesting challenges as well as some great workflow advantages. Contrary to non-digital sources, the content is stored in a digital medium right from the time it is shot. All digital sources share the benefit that you don't have to digitize your content once shot with any of the digital formats; you just need to capture it. The main advantage of digital sources is that there is no or little generation loss when you copy digital media. For example, if you have a VHS tape that you copy to another VHS tape or that you digitize to a computer, the resulting version will be of lower quality than the original; this is what we call generation loss. When you capture or copy a digital source to another digital medium then the result is identical to the source.

Just like with everything in the video world, digital sources range in format, price, and capabilities from professional and industrial D-1 Digital Video down to consumer level miniDV or even Digital 8™ but in this section we will focus on DV.

The main reason we focus on DV for the digital sources is the price-quality ratio that you can achieve. Other digital and even non-digital sources offer much higher quality than DV but usually their prices compared to DV equipment tends to be too high for most people, including a lot of professionals.

To DV or not to DV

As mentioned above, one of the best strengths of DV is the price. Most DV cameras offer good quality while the price of the hardware is not too high. This translates to good-looking QuickTime movies without having to spend a lot of cash on a very expensive camera. For example, today you can spend some $3,500 on a camera, $3,000 on a computer, $2,500 in software and for about ten grand you have a system that can challenge some TV stations in a number of places. The only thing you'll need at that point is *creativity*.

With the advent of FireWire, DV has the great advantage that it's very easy to capture. For example, all Macintosh computers from a few years back include at least one FireWire port and more and more PCs are also including FireWire ports as standard equipment.

FireWire is not DV and DV is not FireWire. DV is the format in which the video is store digitally, and FireWire is a connection used to transport the digital content from one device to another, for example from the camera to the computer. So if your computer has a FireWire port or card and your camera or deck has also a FireWire port, then you don't need a digitizer. You can transfer the media without any generation loss from the source to the computer.

The size of most DV cameras tends to be smaller than other types of professional cameras. For some people having a small camera means that they can get to the action with more ease and without being too conspicuous. On the other hand, for some experienced professional camera people, a small camera is not necessarily the best as they feel they don't get enough stability from it.

Now, DV isn't perfect and although it's great for certain things it has its problems. One of the most important limitations of DV is the color space that it records which is 4:1:1 for NTSC. This means that for every 4 pixels, there are 4 samples of luminance (Y) and 1 sample for each type of chrominance (Cr and Cb), the color components of an image. This means that DV is not your best option when you want to use blue screen for chroma keying.

Another limiting factor of DV is its compression. Yes, I hate to break it to you, but DV isn't uncompressed. If someone ever tells you that DV is uncompressed then that person isn't sure what he's talking about. DV has a compression ratio of 5:1 which means that for certain content there is a bit of noise in the video caused by the compression algorithm.

As you can imagine, if DV doesn't take all the color samples and then it adds compression, then the whole idea of chroma keying suddenly seems more difficult. Most video professionals would not bother trying to key out a blue screen if it was shot on DV. Now, having said this, it doesn't mean that you cannot chroma key a DV file, rather it means that it may be a bit more difficult than if it wasn't DV.

The bottom line then is that DV offers a great value for your buck, is very flexible to work with, but it may not be your highest quality source.

Typical DV gear

As mentioned above, with DV as with any other digital source you don't need to digitize your content, just capture it. So what do we mean with this? Well, let's explain it here:

With a digital camera the light comes through the lens and it's captured by a number of photosensitive sensors. These turn the light into an electrical impulse, which is the representation of whatever the lens was seeing. Here is where it gets interesting. This signal is then passed through a compressor, a codec, which compresses the media in real time. Finally this compressed digital media is stored on the DV tape as a series of ones and zeros (hence the digital name). Therefore, in the end the camera not only shoots, but it also digitizes and compresses the data on the fly.

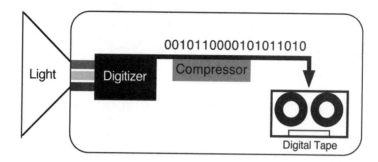

Because of all this pre-processing that is done on board the camera, once you have your content shot on DV then you just need to copy that data to the computer.

Well, to copy the data to your computer you'll need a few more things. Lets start from the source. You'll need a deck or a camera that can play the digital tape. Most often you connect this device to the computer via FireWire, so you'll need a FireWire cable that goes from the camera or deck to the computer. If you have a recent Macintosh, the chances are that you already have a FireWire port. If you have a PC that doesn't have FireWire, then you'll need a card (there are a number of options with varying qualities and prices). The official name of FireWire is IEEE-1394, which is the number of an international standard. If you're shopping for a FireWire card make sure you get an **OHCI** card. OHCI stands for **O**pen **H**ost **C**ontroller **I**nterface, so it's not a brand, but rather a type of card. An OHCI card should work without any extra drivers on Windows 98SE, ME, 2000, and XP. The last thing you'll need is the software to capture your digital media from your DV tape. Most NLE (Non Linear Editing) software like Premiere, EditDV, Final Cut Pro, etc. has the capability of capturing DV using the FireWire ports on your computer.

Since most DV cameras and decks can send both analogue and digital signal at the same time, you can use your DV gear to connect an NTSC monitor to the camera or deck directly instead of the need for a video card that can play to NTSC. This makes DV slightly less expensive and more flexible as you don't need so much gear.

Editing linear video

Editing video and audio for computer delivery is often different than for other kinds of delivery like broadcast or VHS. There are a number of reasons for this. One is that computers represent color very differently to TV screens. Another is that video on a computer screen often is smaller than what you get on TV and that mostly depends on the capabilities of the playback machine. Depending on the project, video for the web in particular, needs to be very compressed. This translates to even smaller window sizes and the possibility of having to loose a lot of quality for playback sake.

The idea is to achieve a good balance between compression and the quality of the content. The good news is that if you understand how compression works then you can take a number of steps to avoid quality loss even from the pre-production and storyboarding stages of a project. When you start paying attention to the details they build up, often translating into better looking video on a computer.

Storyboarding for content

As explained at the beginning of the chapter, the better you plan your project, the better you'll be able to deal with surprises along the way. Where planning is very important is in the storyboarding of your shoots. For multimedia developers using QuickTime in a project this is analogous to doing mockups of what the end project should look like. Most of the recommendations that follow are drawn from experience and understanding how video and audio is compressed for computer delivery. One thing video codecs don't like is changes, so you need to avoid or minimize changes on the screen.

Tight shots

You want to keep your shots tight and to the point. In most computer delivered video the size of the window tends to be small, so if your subject is small in relationship to an already small window, then it'll be very difficult to distinguish. The idea is that if you're shooting a person, an activity, or an object, the subject should cover a large percentage of your viewfinder.

Avoid pans, tilts, and zooms

When you have camera pans, tilts, and zooms the content of the screen changes quite a lot in just a few seconds. In these cases the codecs have a harder time trying to keep up with these changes. For example, if you pan, the pixels on every frame will change, making it difficult for the codecs. With so much changing on the screen, the code may blur or pixelate the content resulting in unclear video.

Use straight cuts

As stated in the recommendation above, using straight cuts usually yields better results. The main reason for this is that newer codecs like Sorenson Video are "intelligent" enough to detect the changes on the screen and react to those changes. Therefore, if you have a scene that is fairly constant, and then you cut to a different angle or scene, the changes from one frame to another are so great that these "intelligent" codecs are able to insert a key frame at the cut. Inserting a key frame ensures that the new scene is taken in consideration by the codec improving the way it looks.

Avoid hand held/use tripods

If you hold a camera by hand, it doesn't matter if you're the best cameraman out there, the camera will shake at least slightly. Again, having these changes on the screen happening so often is bad news for the codec, especially when using a telephoto lens, as every tiny move is amplified by the camera. However, if you use a tripod, the amount of movement is minimized letting the codec focus on the subject and not on lots of changes happening at once.

Light your scenes

Amateur videographers are almost famous for having scenes that are under lit and dark. This typical mistake is magnified, as video often looks lighter on TV than on a computer screen. So if you have a dark scene, chances are that when it's compressed for computer delivery, then it'll get even darker. Make sure that your scenes and subjects are well lit. This will ensure that your video looks more vivid and interesting.

Shooting text

This is kind of a subset of the "Tight Shots" recommendation above. Text in particular tends to blur and pixelate when it appears in compressed video. So if you need to shoot a sign, a diagram, or a billboard, make sure that the shot is tight enough to still be able to read the content after quality has degraded from compression.

Avoid noisy backgrounds

Imagine you're shooting a person doing something, and behind this person there is a beautiful tree that takes up a large percentage of the background and that swings to the rhythm of the wind. Once you've pictured that in your mind, imagine it made smaller, and with a mosaic effect on top of it. You end up having something that looks like random tiles moving behind your subject making it difficult to differentiate the foreground from the background. Well, this is kind of the way the codecs tend to work. As every frame of the video changes a lot when the leaves swing, this is similar to a hand held shot or a zoom. There are too many changes on the screen happening for an amount of time. In the screenshot above you can see that the trees in the background have completely blurred.

Using blue screens

Now, imagine that you shoot your subject on top of a blue screen and then you key out the blue and super impose a picture of the tree we mentioned above. In this case, since the tree isn't moving the video would look better than if you had shot against the real life moving tree.

Avoid audio noise

So far we've talked mostly about video as video takes the highest percentage of bandwidth from a movie. The truth is that audio is often as important or even more important than the video. Whenever you shoot or record the audio for your projects think that any noise added to the recording will take away from the actual content. Psychologically it's very important to have the best audio, and in terms of compression it's as important. Audio codecs work by the same principals as video codecs. If there are too many changes, it just makes it more difficult to compress. So if your recording has the noise of a fan, the street, or a nosy party, the sound wave will be so complex that the codec won't be able to be very efficient. Therefore when you design your scenes, keep in mind the noise from the shooting/recording location.

Use the best microphone and camera

Although this isn't too related to storyboarding it's related to the production and quality of your QuickTime video and audio files. Using the best gear, may that be microphones and/or video cameras, will ensure that you minimize noise from the actual shoot. Remember the concept of "garbage in – garbage out"; you want to start with the best source, so you must use the best gear that your budget allows.

Editing for bandwidth

Just as the storyboarding and production process can have a huge impact on the quality of your compressed QuickTime video and audio files, the editing stage also offers a number of circumstances that can either yield better or (if not considered) worse quality. Just like in the storyboarding step, when you're editing you want to keep the changes to the minimum and keep anything that needs attention large.

Avoid dissolve transitions

Ah, transitions. Most video professionals would choose to have a dissolve transition in very specific cases, like when you want to give the sensation of time passing by. On the other hand, amateurs tend to have a dissolve transition for every cut they make! Apart from not being the best technique for cutting in most cases, having dissolve transitions for the video codecs are as bad as shooting a noisy background or a pan. Everything changes on the screen from frame to frame making it very difficult for the codec to keep up. In general straight cuts work better both aesthetically and technically.

Avoid very dynamic Special Effects

Having lots of dramatic dynamic special effects can also be detrimental to the quality of your compressed QuickTime videos. The same logic applies if a large percentage of the screen is changing from frame to frame; it's not too efficient for compression.

Avoid scrolling or fading text

Text needs to be of high quality to be able to read it. At the same time text tends to have complex shapes, at least from a codec point of view. So if you have text that moves around, because it scrolls or it fades in or out, then we get to the same problem we've been banging our head over. Lots of changes and detail are difficult to encode. Having large static contrasting text on the screen makes it easier to read once compression has been applied.

Avoid a lot of cuts

As mentioned above having a static image for a long period of time is the best you can give a codec. Now we know that this isn't possible if we want to have video, but if you can keep the scene changes to a minimum, then that does help the quality on the compression. If you have a clip that changes scenes too often, like a music video or a movie trailer, then the codec needs to create a large number of key frames making your video file larger. Have you ever wondered why the movie trailers in QuickTime are so large?

Color/Gamma correction

As mentioned in the storyboarding section of the chapter, TV video tends to look darker on a computer screen. In most cases either the colors need to be adjusted or the gamma boosted a little, especially if you're authoring on a Macintosh and the content will playback on a PC. PCs often have a darker gamma than Macintoshes. This means that everything will look slightly darker on the PC. So if you are working on the Mac and you think your video is bright enough, and you haven't tested it on a PC you should. Often you will need to boost the gamma so the video doesn't look too dark on the PC. You can increase the gamma of your videos with the Gamma filter in Cleaner 5 or by applying a Gamma change in the filters when you encode your QuickTime movies. If you don't have a Gamma filter you can increase the brightness of the video to encode slightly.

De-interlace

This is more a compression tip than an editing tip, but it can be applied during editing. Most of the content that you see on TV is interlaced. The problem comes from the fact that as computer screens are so much better than TV screens that they don't need to use interlaced video and instead use progressive scanning. So what does this have to do with your QuickTime videos? If you play interlaced content on a computer screen you'll notice some interlaced artifacts, especially on sharp edges on fast scenes. To avoid this problem you can de-interlace your content from the time line of your NLE system (by applying the de-interlace filter in Final Cut Pro, After Effects, Premiere, etc). Another alternative is to de-interlace your source just before you do the compression. Cleaner 5 from Discreet can help you out with de-interlacing your interlaced content. Another alternative you have is to shoot the source in progressive mode. This is great when you know that your content will be mainly deployed on a computer. This will avoid the de-interlacing step making it easier for you to work with.

Compressing linear video/audio

As mentioned through out this Chapter, audio and video need to be compressed for delivery from a hard drive, CD-ROM, and particularly from the Web. We've also mentioned the word codec in a number of topics. A codec is an algorithm that **CO**mpresses and **DEC**ompresses data. There are audio codecs and video codecs, some of which are specifically used for web or CD delivery. Most codecs are lossy, which means that the compressed version is different from the original. A few codecs are loss-less which means that the compressed version is almost identical to the source. Loss-less codecs tend to yield very large file sizes and aren't good for deployment.

One of the characteristics of QuickTime that makes it such a superb technology is that third parties can write their own codecs for it. A classic example is the Sorenson Video codec which was developed by Sorenson Vision (now Sorenson Media) as a component for QuickTime, so the Sorenson Video codec, although part of the default installation of QuickTime, isn't owned by Apple.

QuickTime includes a plethora of codecs in the default installation and can also use third party codecs written for QuickTime. Now, this translates in having as having a lot of options to choose from, and then each codec has its own set of parameters to tweak when compressing. On one hand this is great, because you can choose a specific codec and tweak its settings to better match your needs. On the other hand too many choices and options often overwhelm the users when they're not acquainted with encoding and/or the lingo used in such field.

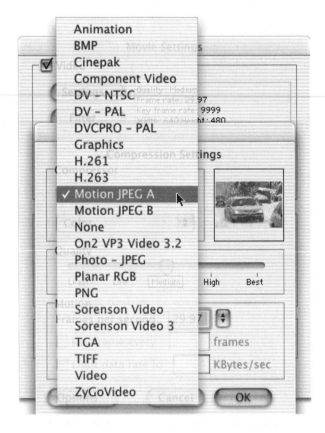

For encoding you can use a number of applications that range from QuickTime Player Pro, to NLEs (like Premiere or Final Cut Pro), to encoding specific applications like Sorenson Squeeze, Totally Hip's HipFlics, and the famous Cleaner 5 from Discreet. Each one of these applications offers varying options and capabilities for your encoding.

Choosing codecs

Although QuickTime includes many codecs, here we'll just explain some of the major and most often used codecs. Depending on where you're in your workflow you may need a codec for editing and another for deployment.

Authoring codecs

Authoring codecs are meant for editing and transporting high quality video/audio by applying some compression. These codecs don't offer a very high compression ratio but also don't degrade the content as much as deployment codecs. You would use an authoring codec when you capture or digitize content, when you're editing in the time line of your NLE, when you are rotoscoping, and when you're playing back for delivery on tape or broadcast. You wouldn't want to deliver authoring codec compressed video, as the file size and data rate would be too large for most audiences.

Motion JPEG

Most digitizing video boards use some variation of Motion JPEG (or M-JPEG). This codec has a number of advantages. One is that you can set your compression ratio. The more you compress your content, the smaller the file size, but also the lower the quality. Another advantage is that it's designed for interlaced or progressive content, so if your source is interlaced, M-JPEG understands it. At high quality this codec will require relatively large amounts of drive space for your video. You can use M-JPEG as an intermediate codec, for archiving purposes, for example, or to take your video from your NLE program like Premiere or Final Cut Pro to another program like Commotion or After Effects without loosing too much quality in the process, and keeping the ability to create manageable files sizes.

Photo JPEG

Just like M-JPEG this codec is great as an intermediate codec. The main difference between Motion JPEG and Photo JPEG is that Photo JPEG is meant for progressive video and not interlaced video. So if you shoot content that will be deployed on computer with progressive video, using Photo JPEG as the intermediate codec will work very well.

DV

DV is very similar to M-JPEG. It can be interlaced or progressive as well as supporting NTSC and PAL. However, a difference is that you cannot control the amount of compression. DV always uses a 5:1 compression ratio with a data rate of 25 mega bits per second (mbps) which means that about 5 minutes of DV would take about 1 Giga Byte (GB) of space on your hard drive. The main advantage of DV is that you can capture it directly via FireWire to the computer. Another workflow advantage is that with DV you can shoot, capture, and edit without too much generation loss. DV has the disadvantage compared to M-JPEG, that the color space is 4:1:1 (NTSC) or 4:2:0 (PAL) which makes it a bad option for blue screen.

Uncompressed audio

Audio takes far less bandwidth than video, so for authoring purposes you should always use uncompressed audio with at least CD quality (16 bit, 44.1 KHz stereo). You should never work with compressed audio files in your authoring stages, so forget about that bootlegged MP3 that you downloaded as the background music for your project!

Delivery codecs

Opposite to authoring codecs, delivery codecs have a very high compression ratio and in most cases they achieve this by sacrificing quality. All delivery codecs are lossy which means that they discard data to compress the content. For delivery that is fine but for editing, delivery codecs are very slow and don't have enough data to create high quality edits. What I'm trying to say here is that if you get a video, from the Web for example, that has been compressed with one of these codecs and try to edit it, you'll end up with really low quality output. Remember "garbage in – garbage out". It's always a good practice to work with the highest quality through out your process until you need to deploy. Another good practice is to keep your sources in a safe place in the case you need to use them later.

Don't get me wrong. Using delivery codecs to deliver your content doesn't mean that you will be producing bad quality outputs. For web, CD-ROM, or kiosk delivery, these codecs offer great file size to quality ratio, but you shouldn't use them for other purposes. Web or CD video is often lower quality than TV video, so keep your expectations realistic.

Sorenson Video

Sorenson Video has been the premiere delivery codec for QuickTime since it was introduced with QuickTime 3. Although Apple didn't develop Sorenson Video, it's included by default in the installation of QuickTime. The Sorenson Video codec is mainly designed for low bit rate movies so you should think of using it when making video for the Web and CD. It's important to note that Sorenson Video 3 requires a relatively fast machine to decode, especially if the bit rate is high (above 500 kbps).

Sorenson Video is currently in its version 3.1 (at the time of printing), which plays on QuickTime 5 and newer, and there are two 'editions' of the codec, a Professional edition and a Basic edition. When you download QuickTime you get the Basic edition, which allows you to play back Sorenson Video compressed content. When you buy QuickTime Pro it allows you to compress to the Basic edition of Sorenson Video and offers a few tweak settings.

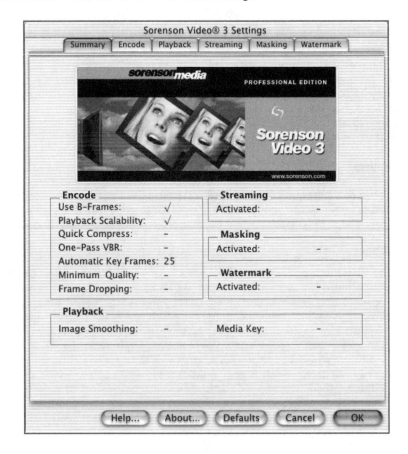

You can also buy the Professional edition of Sorenson Video 3, which offers a lot of control over your compression. Having more control means that you can achieve better quality. The main advantage of the Professional edition of Sorenson Video is the ability to use **VBR** (Variable **B**it **R**ate) encoding. With VBR the codec analyses the content and assigns more or less data depending on the complexity of the content. To keep the quality, the codec assigns more data to scenes that have many changes, and conserves bandwidth in scenes that are fairly static.

Sorenson Video 3 Professional Edition also offers 2-pass VBR encoding which is even more efficient than 1-pass VBR, but at the time of writing only Cleaner 5.0.2 and Sorenson Squeeze have access to the 2-pass VBR encoding in Sorenson Video 3 Professional Edition.

You would want/need 2-pass VBR if you want to encode QuickTime movies with the best quality possible for delivery as progressive download over the web, CD-ROM, or Kiosks. The only time where you would not use 2-pass VBR is for RTSP/RTP streaming. Please refer to "Differences between Progressive Download and RTSP/RTP Streaming" later in this chapter for more information on progressive download and RTSP/RTP streaming.

MPEG-4

MPEG-4 (not to be confused with M-JPEG) has received a lot of attention lately. MPEG-4 isn't just a codec but also a whole ISO standard that combines video, audio, and images with interactivity. The idea for MPEG-4 is that computers, consumer appliances, and mobile devices will support it. In addition you'll be able to author it with any MPEG-4 compliant encoder and it will play on any compliant MPEG-4 player. As simple as that!

QuickTime 6 is the first version of QuickTime to offer both an MPEG-4 encoder and decoder. This means that you can create and play compliant MPEG-4 video and audio files in QuickTime 6. This is a major advantage for production, as your workflow can be kept all in QuickTime from capture to deployment, and it's also a great advantage for deployment, as your MPEG-4 files (created with QuickTime 6) will play on QuickTime 6 players and any other player that supports MPEG-4, such as Ericsson's phones, Real Player, etc. In fact QuickTime is one of the very first technologies to offer the whole deal when it comes to MPEG-4. The QuickTime Streaming Server 4 can serve not only QuickTime files but also standard compliant MPEG-4 files to MPEG-4 players! With QuickTime Broadcaster you'll also be able to stream live with any codec QuickTime supports including MPEG-4. In the MPEG-4 arena there are a number of encoders (Envivio, for example), decoders (Real Player is one), and servers (Sun offers MPEG-4 streaming servers) but few products or companies offer the whole gamut. All this allows you to author once (with QuickTime) and deploy anywhere, through QuickTime or not.

The quality of the video codec part of MPEG-4 is comparable to that of Sorenson Video 2. This means that Sorenson Video 3 offers better quality, but MPEG-4 has the major benefit that your audience doesn't require QuickTime to be installed for them to play your MPEG-4 content. They'll only need an MPEG-4 compliant player, and these will eventually make it to PDAs! That is definitely something that Sorenson cannot give you.

MPEG-1

MPEG-1 is an older standard that QuickTime can play right out of the box. Contrary to Sorenson Video Basic Edition, you can't encode MPEG-1 with QuickTime Pro without buying an encoder.

MPEG-1 was designed for computer delivery, more specifically on CD-ROMs. The best feature of MPEG-1 is that being a standard there are a lot of compliant players including QuickTime. The major draw back with MPEG-1 is that since it's an older standard, the quality of the output isn't as good-looking or efficient as that of other codecs like MPEG-4 or Sorenson Video 3.

H.263

The H.263 codec is another standard and also part of the QuickTime installation. This codec was originally designed for video conferencing so it's very efficient at low bit rates and often used for live streaming. With QuickTime Pro you can encode to H.263 without having to buy a professional or commercial edition.

VP3

The VP3 codec was first developed by the On2 company, as an additional component for QuickTime. In 2001 On2 released the source code as an open source project so that developers could freely use and modify the code to make it more efficient.

In general the quality of VP3 is great, even compared to that of Sorenson Video 3 Professional Edition in some cases. VP3 produces really nice quality video at web data rates, as well as for CD-ROM deployment.

The major drawback with VP3 is that it's not part of the default installation of QuickTime. This means that if you encode your content with VP3 and your QuickTime 5 audience doesn't have the codec installed, they'll be prompted to download it. The problem, and it is a problem, is that most people, as soon as they see a dialogue box they don't understand or have never seen, they'll click on the Cancel button without giving it a chance to install. If that happens, then the audience won't be able to see your VP3 compressed video content.

IMA 4:1

IMA 4:1 is an audio codec that as its name implies, it has a compression ratio of 4 to 1. This compression ratio isn't massive, but produces very clean compressed audio. IMA 4:1 is better used for CD-ROM movies rather than web movies. The reason is the compression ratio isn't efficient enough for web bit rates.

QDesign music codec

QDesign Music codec (QDMC) is the Sorenson counter part for audio codecs. Also introduced in QuickTime 3 by a company called QDesign, the QDMC has a Basic and Professional edition where the Professional edition offers better encoding and more settings options.

Although the codec has the word "music" in it this is a general-purpose codec so you can use it to compress music, narration, etc. For any type of content that has anything apart from voice, you should be thinking about QDesign. If it's voice only, and I mean *only* voice, Qualcomm PureVoice may be better.

QDesign Music codec offers good results at lower bit rates. Almost anything below 96 kbps can be encoded with QDMC, for anything above 96 kbps, you may want to use MP3.

Qualcomm PureVoice

The Qualcomm PureVoice codec is the same kind of codec you find in cell phones. This codec is specifically designed for human voice where there is no need for a large dynamic range. As you can imagine, this codec excels at narration but tends to sound like "cardboard" when there is some other type of sound in the audio track, for example the noise of a street, or the music of a band. Have you ever tried to talk to someone on a cell phone when they're in a noisy place? When you encode with Qualcomm you may want to try the different settings so you get a first hand feel of what the codec produces. Keep in mind that audio is very important for the playback experience.

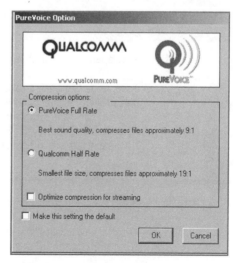

MP3

MP3 stands for MPEG-1 Layer 3, and is a subset of the MPEG-1 standard. Just like the video MPEG-1, MP3 is an older codec that may not be very efficient but that can play on compliant players such as QuickTime Player. Again, like MPEG-1 you won't be able to encode MP3 audio with QuickTime Pro without getting an MP3 codec. The good news is that you can use other encoders like iTunes.

MP3 is great for CD-ROM audio and for high bandwidth web movies. As mentioned above, if you need a bit rate lower than 96 kbps you may be better off using QDesign, but with anything above 96 kbps MP3 will sound better.

Testing to save time and money

When you are encoding your movies, especially when you are new to compression or to a codec in particular, you don't want to compress your whole clip to figure out that the settings were wrong. This happens so often. You grab your source movie, make your settings for compression, let the compression go for the whole clip taking a really long time to finish, to then find out that the output is not the best, then go through the same process over and over.

The idea is to set a testing ground before you commit all that time to encode the whole clip. What you should do is just compress a few seconds of the source file and test your different settings on that selection. This way you can see the results of your settings much faster than encoding the whole clip.

When you choose a selection to encode, grab a few seconds of the "difficult" areas of the movie. One way to learn what's difficult and what's easy for the codec to compress is to encode the whole clip once. Where you see that the quality degrades a lot, you know that you've found a difficult area of your clip. Grab a selection including a few seconds of that difficult area and test your settings. Once you create the settings that make the difficult areas look good, then the easy areas are already taken care of.

To encode a selection with QuickTime Player Pro you can make a tiny reference movie and apply your settings to it.

1. First open your source movie in the QuickTime Player.

2. Then, using the small arrows in the lower part of the time line, make your selection. You can click and drag these arrows to make your selection that is represented by the gray area in the timeline.

    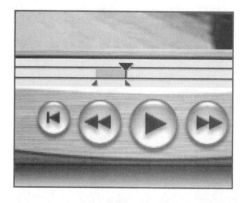

3. Then from the Edit menu select Copy.

4. From the File menu select New Player.

5. On the new empty player select Paste from the Edit menu.

6. Select Save As... from the File menu, give your movie a name and save as Save normally (allowing dependencies).

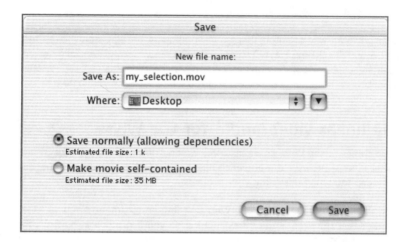

At this point you'll have created a reference movie that only plays the selection you made from the full clip. This reference movie requires the original clip to be on your hard drive as it was saved with dependencies. If you delete the original, then the reference movie won't play anything.

Now you can try your different settings on this reference movie. Once you find the best combination of settings, just apply that to the original movie instead of the reference movie.

You can also set in and out points if you use Cleaner 5. Just open your movie in Cleaner 5, move the playback head to whereever you want to start encoding, select Set In Point from the Edit menu, move the playback head to whereever you want your selection to end and from the Edit menu select Set Out Point. Once you want to remove the in and out points, select Edit > Clear In/Out Points.

Batch processing & workflow

Often you'll need to compress not only one movie but also a number of movies. Having to compress one by one could get quite tedious especially if it takes a long time to compress each of these movies.

One of the ways professionals improve their workflow is by first trying out their settings on short selections of the clips. Then, once the settings have been fined tuned, they apply those settings to a large collection of movies that need to be encoded. The encoding starts and a number of hours later, after all the clips have been encoded, the output files are uploaded to the delivery servers (possibly a web server or a streaming server).

There are a number of tools out there that can help you create a smooth workflow. The most known tool is Discreet's Cleaner 5, which has the ability to encode large batches of files with different settings all at once. Another tool less known, but more accessible is Totally Hip's HipFlics. Instead of creating a batch list with HipFlics you create applets where you can drag and drop a number of source movies to be encoded with that applet. In the case of HipFlics an applet is just a collection of settings that when activated, launches HipFlics and encodes the sources with those settings.

Another powerful way of automating your workflow is by using AppleScript on the Macintosh. Both Cleaner 5 and QuickTime Player Pro are AppleScript aware and can take advantage of this amazing automation-scripting tool. If you don't know AppleScript you can still download more than 100 AppleScripts from the Apple web site and put them to work for you in no time. You can also open the scripts and learn from them by reading how they were done at www.apple.com/applescript/qtas.html.

Delivering linear video/audio for the Web

When it comes to the Web, as we all know we end up dealing with a lot of uncertainty. Questions like what kind of browser the audience has, or how fast an Internet connection they have should all be addressed when designing your projects.

Delivering video and audio over the Web isn't limited to embedding QuickTime movies in HTML. Remember that the Web is the infrastructure, so you can move away from the limitations of the web browser and deliver your QuickTime movies over the Web to the QuickTime Player by other means. Web browsers are great for web surfing, and in some cases to see some video content that's part of a larger page. Often though, video and audio can be better delivered on just the QuickTime Player. Some projects are based on the QuickTime Player turning movies into full-featured applications. For an example take a look at www.toddishere.com where the movie gives the user more capabilities that you would get on a web browser.

If you want to see an example of an organization that understands what QuickTime can do without the use of the web browser for the most part, click on the TV button in your QuickTime Player and click on the WGBH hot pick button. These guys manage to deploy very interesting QuickTime content all over the web often without the need of a web browser.

Differences between progressive download and RTSP/RTP streaming

In a progressive download situation you, as the author of the movie, have the luxury of time. What I mean by this is that if the audience is willing to wait, regardless of the connection speed they have, then you can give them better looking video. To give you an example, when the first Star Wars movie trailer came out it was about 26MB in size. A friend of mine, on a 56k modem started the download and went for a round of golf. When he came back he had the large movie on his hard drive and enjoyed it every single time he played it.

In the case of RTSP/RTP streaming, the data arrives in real time (**RTSP/RTP** stands for **R**eal **T**ime **S**treaming **P**rotocol/**R**eal **T**ime **T**ransport **P**rotocol), so if the user doesn't have enough bandwidth to get the content in real time, then they won't get the content. This means that you as the author need to compress the content enough so it can fit in the audience's available bandwidth. For a 56k modem audiences this is very challenging.

To give you an idea here are some typical data rates from different Internet connections:

- **28.8K modem:**   20 Kbps

- **56K modem:**   40 Kbps

- **Dual ISDN:**   90 Kbps

- **DSL:**   256 Kbps

- **T1:**   340 Kbps

Someone on a T1 connection *should* have about 1.5 Mbps of bandwidth. The complication comes when part of that bandwidth is used for other things as the audience tries to get your QuickTime movie. A safer assumption would be to consider that the audience of a T1 connection may only have a data rate of about 340 Kbps available.

Here's an example that compares RTSP/RTP streaming with progressive download. Imagine that your audience is on a 56K modem. If you were to give them an RTSP/RTP streaming movie, then you would need to compress the QuickTime to a maximum of 40 Kbps, which wouldn't yield the best quality. Now, if you deploy that same movie as a progressive download, depending on the willingness of the audience to wait, you could compress the movie to say 100 Kbps giving the audience a better looking video, but with a longer download wait.

When you compress for RTSP/RTP streaming you shouldn't use the 2-pass VBR feature of Sorenson Video 3 or any other codec that supports 2-pass VBR. The reason is that 2-pass VBR often produces large spikes in the data rate when the content changes dramatically. If that happens and you're delivering your movie via RTSP/RTP, the chances are that those spikes won't fit in the available bandwidth of the user.

RTSP/RTP streaming can be used for live streaming as well as for on-demand streaming. As the names imply, for live streaming you need to compress the content in real time as it happens. In this case you'll need broadcasting software like Sorenson Broadcaster or ChannelStorm's LiveChannel.

On the other hand, on-demand streaming means that the movies are compressed and made available via the streaming server. When you play an on-demand streaming movie it's like asking the streaming server to play the movie for you.

When encoding your clips you may want to use these guidelines:

Often used window sizes:

Width x Height	Connection
320x240	High broadband
256x192	Broadband
240x180	Low broadband
176x132	Low bit rate
160x120	Low bit rate

Typical frame rates for NTSC sources:

Frame Rate	Connection
5 to 10 fps	High motion on slow connections
10 or 15 fps	Low motion on slow connections
10 or 15 fps	High motion on broadband
15 or 29.97 fps	Low motion on broadband
29.97 fps	High or low motion on high broadband

Typical frame rates for PAL sources:

Frame Rate	Connection
5 to 8.3 fps	High motion on slow connections
8.3 or 12.5 fps	Low motion on slow connections
12.5 fps	High motion on broadband
12.5 or 25 fps	Low motion on broadband
25 fps	High or low motion on high broadband

The idea is that you have a bit rate limit that you don't want to exceed. If you have a lot of motion and a fast frame rate, each frame will receive fewer bits making it look bad. If you reduce the frame rate you'll have more bits per picture, making each picture look better. When you have less motion, since there are fewer changes on the screen you can increase the frame rate making it look smoother without increasing the need for many more bits.

Progressive vs. real time delivery

To deliver progressive-download QuickTime movies you need either a web (HTTP) or FTP server, although most people use a web server. Progressive-download doesn't require a streaming server and can often yield better quality than streaming, but depending on the connection speed of the audience you may need to wait to get the content. For RTSP/RTP or Real Time streaming of QuickTime you'll need a QuickTime Streaming Server (QTSS), a Darwin Streaming Server (DSS), or a Real 8 streaming server (which can stream QuickTime content to QuickTime clients). Both servers do exactly the same thing except with the difference that a QTSS runs in MacOS X and a DSS runs in any other platform like Linux, Solaris, Windows 2000 Server, etc. For MPEG-4 streaming you can use any compliant server like QuickTime Streaming Server 4 or Darwin Streaming Server 4. QTSS/DSS 4 can also stream MP3 files using the Icecast standard, which means that you can stream regular MP3 files to any Icecast player (like WinAmp, SoundJam, iTunes, MacAmp, etc.). Just as with MPEG-4, you can wrap these streams around a QuickTime movie to enhance it with other media types like Flash 5, QTVR, Sprites, etc.

Unlike the Real Networks server, QTSS and DSS have no per stream fee. With Real if you want to serve 100 connections at the same time you have to pay a steep license fee. When the numbers add up the cash starts to run down. QuickTime Streaming Server and Darwin Streaming Server are open source, which means that you can download the source code and change it to suit your needs. It also means that you can use it without paying license fees to Apple.

RTSP/RTP streaming movies are better suited for live events and long clips where you don't want the user to get a copy of your content or if you want to set up an unmanned online TV or radio station.

For live events there is no way to get the content as it happens better than RTSP/RTP/RTP streaming. In any other case the content would need to be recorded first and then served, getting rid of any "live" factor.

For long clips streaming is good because the user doesn't need to download the whole large file to see the end. For example, imagine that you've a one-hour lecture and that someone in the audience is only interested in the last 15 minutes of the clip. Instead of having to download the first 45 minutes of content to be able to start watching the interesting content, they can start streaming the movie from the 45-minute mark.

In a progressive download the content is always downloaded to the viewer's machine. This means that a copy could be made and then duplicated without your permission. In the case of RTSP/RTP streaming only a few seconds of content are kept on the client and then they're discarded. This means that making a copy of your content isn't as simple as in a progressive download situation.

With RTSP/RTP streaming you can program a streaming server to sequentially play audio or video files. The sequence could be ordered or random. If you have a couple of thousand clips and you set it to random, you can have a streaming radio or TV station that doesn't require anyone doing the programming of the content. A good example of this is the heavy metal radio station, HardRadio.com at www.hardradio.com.

Having said this, most web projects can happily make do with progressive download movies as often content isn't long enough to justify streaming. If your content is short, say a few minutes long, progressive download may be a best alternative.

With a QuickTime Streaming Server or Darwin Streaming Server you can only stream out audio, video, text and MIDI. With a progressive download you can send any file format that is supported by QuickTime including Flash and QuickTimeVR.

In fact, in lots of cases you can deploy a movie that's a hybrid between RTSP/RTP streaming and progressive download. An example of such a movie could be a Flash interface where you control the volume and the playback of a streaming audio track. As mentioned above, you cannot stream the Flash track but you can certainly mix the streaming audio track with a progressive download Flash track that controls playback on the streaming track.

Choosing the number & kind of movie versions to make

Depending on your audience you may want to provide them with more than one version of your movie. One of the powerful features of QuickTime is that you can create multiple versions of your content and you can create what is called a **reference movie**, which intelligently selects the correct movie for the correct situation. You'll see the term "reference movie" mentioned in a number of places through out the book. A reference movie is a movie that refers to other files to access the media.

A typical case is to create a movie for audiences on a 56K modem, another version of the same movie for audiences on ISDN, and a third version for audiences on DSL or T1 connections depending on the audience.

The more alternatives you create, the more work it is to create them, but at the same time you give your audience a customized experience.

QuickTime can use lots of factors to choose which alternative movie to show, so you could create a movie for an English speaking audience and another version for francophone audiences.

The idea is that you should assess your audience(s) and objective(s) and depending on the combination of both, you can decide on how many movies and what kind of movies you need to create.

Reference movies & heterogeneous audiences

As mentioned above, with QuickTime you have the flexibility to create movies that are "intelligent". In more technical terms, these are reference movies that can contain logic. To create these types of reference movies Apple offers a free application for MacOS 9, MacOS X, and Windows called "MakeRefMovie" that you can download from: http://developer.apple.com/quicktime/quicktimeintro/tools/.

There are a lot of different ways you can use these reference movies but they're mostly used to provide a customized experience to your audience. Earlier in this chapter we described the example where a reference movie could choose from 3 bit rate versions of the actual content depending on the connection speed of the user.

MakeRefMovie can differentiate the user connection speed, the user's language preferences (from more than 40 languages), the performance of the user's CPU, and the version of QuickTime installed on the user's computer. So with MakeRefMovie you can create a reference a movie that "intelligently" selects the appropriate content depending on any combination of the above variables.

However, when would you want to make a reference movie? Well, it'll depend on your project, but for the most part your audience can benefit from reference movies in most projects, but yet most people don't know about them and how they work. Here you'll learn when to use them and how to create them.

Mind your language

Maybe the best way to understand reference movies and learn how to make them is if we go through the process of creating one. Let me set the scene for this example. In a typical video-for-the-web project you would end up having movies with an English audio track. Lets say that in your project you could extend the reach of your audience if you could also offer the movies with a Spanish audio track.

You could think of making an English and a Spanish version of your movies and then give the audience the choice from your web site. Rather, let's not confuse the audience with too many choices. It would be less complex for the users if they hit the page or the link to your movies and depending on their language preferences, the movies would start in English or Spanish accordingly.

Although a large part of the Internet audience understands English, there is also a significant part that doesn't. Making content in multiple languages increases the range of your covered audience.

To create the reference movie we'll need an English and a Spanish movie.

1. Create your English and Spanish movies. If you want we have provided two tiny text based movies (`english.mov` and `spanish.mov`, which can be found on the CD at `Chapter_7\Sources`) that you can use. If you use the provided movies, copy them to the desktop.

2. Open MakeRefMovie.

3. As soon as you open the application it'll ask you to save a file. This file will be the reference movie that we'll create. Save the reference movie in the same directory as the `english.mov` and `spanish.mov` files. In this case we'll call it `reference.mov`.

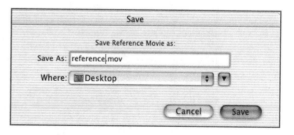

4. From the desktop drag and drop english.mov to the MakeRefMovie window. This will make the reference to english.mov. Now we need to set the criteria to load this movie.

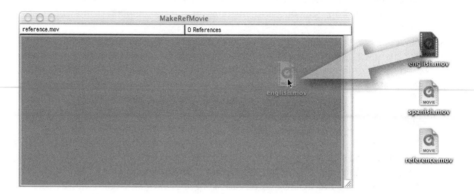

5. At the Language: drop down menu select English. This will make the reference movie select english.mov if the user has an English OS or if QuickTime has English set as the preferred language.

6. At the Priority: drop down menu select First Choice. This is to break any tie that there may be with another movie. For example, if the user has a French OS neither english.mov or spanish.mov take precedence over the other. Selecting english.mov as First Choice ensures it will be selected by default with OS other than English or Spanish.

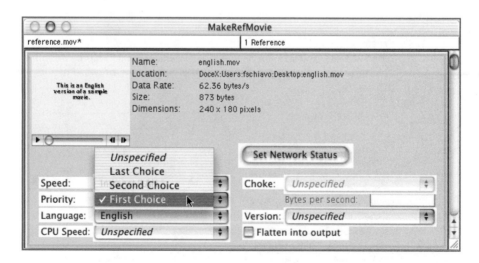

7. From the desktop drag spanish.mov and drop it on top of the MakeRefMovie window. This should bring spanish.mov to the list. If you don't see it, scroll down inside the MakeRefMovie window.

8. For spanish.mov select Spanish from the Language: drop down menu and Second Choice from the Priority: drop down menu.

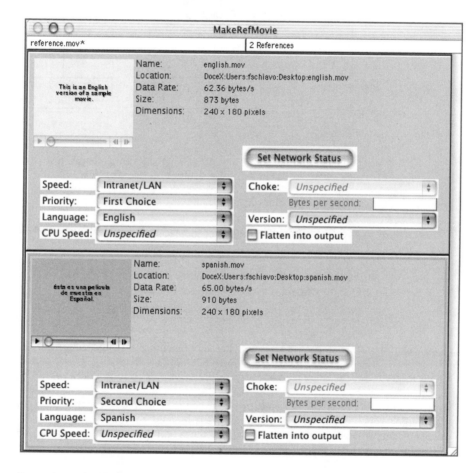

9. Once done select Quit or Close from the Edit menu to save your work. If prompted, click on Save.

That's it. You just created a reference movie that will select english.mov on English or any other OS that's not Spanish, and spanish.mov if the OS or the QuickTime language settings are Spanish (the finished example can be found on the CD at Chapter7/Done).

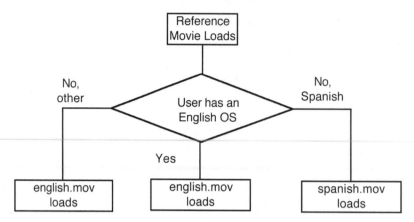

Now let's see how it works.

1. If you're in an English OS or any other language but Spanish, just double click on `reference.mov`. You should see the content of `english.mov`.

2. Close the movie.

3. Go to the QuickTime control panel in MacOS 9 or Windows and from the menu select Language.

4. From the long list of languages (this will give you an idea of how many languages you can use) choose Spanish and close the control panel.

5. Open up `reference.mov` again and this time around you should get the Spanish version.

If you select any other language that is not English or Spanish you should still get the English version.

Don't forget to set the language back to your preference once you're done with the exercise!

As you can see in this simple example, by using the reference movie capabilities in QuickTime you can deploy your content in a more transparent manner to your audience. By doing so your audience gets the best content for them. In a sense you are customizing the experience of the different audiences out there.

The same logic of offering more languages to expand your audience base can also be used by offering your content to a multitude of audiences, not only based on their language but in other environment variables, like those that MakeRefMovie detects.

With more and more complex technologies hitting the markets, chances are that when you create your content it may or may not work for everybody out there.

With all these heterogeneous audiences it's up to you to foresee their requirements so you can tackle them and deliver your content successfully.

To illustrate the point lets go back to the example of someone creating multiple versions of a movie for audiences of three different connection speeds. Usually what people do is have a larger, high frame rate, high quality movie for the audience on broadband. Because their connection is so fast, the producers can deliver larger movies. However, there is a small flaw in this thinking. Some broadband users will have got their Internet connection a few years after they got their computer. What I'm trying to say is that some broadband users, although they can download large movies in no time, have computers so old or underpowered that they can't decode large, high frame rate, high quality movies quick enough. In these cases the user's experience will be far from perfect as their computer will choke with movies that are too demanding.

A producer that understands his audience and the capabilities of the technology, QuickTime in this case, can plan ahead and take the necessary steps to provide the best possible experience to his audience as heterogeneous it may be.

A solution to the problem above would be to use reference movies that not only choose the content to display depending on the connection speed, but also on the power of the CPU of the audience. Do you want to offer a more customized experience? Then you may want to consider language settings, or the version of QuickTime installed.

As an example of why you may want to check for the installed version of QuickTime is if you're using Sorenson Video 3 to compress your movies. The reason is that, although Sorenson Video 3 offers an excellent compression to quality ratio, it requires that the audience has QuickTime 5 or newer; QuickTime 4 and previous can only decode Sorenson Video 2, so won't be able to play back Sorenson Video 3.

Therefore, in the spirit of offering the best quality possible to your audience, you may want to check for the version of QuickTime running in the viewer's machine. You could compress a Sorenson Video 2 movie for your QuickTime 4 audience, and a Sorenson Video 3 for anyone with QuickTime 5 or newer. This way you don't limit yourself to only QuickTime 5 audiences, but if they do have QuickTime 5 then can get a better-looking movie.

Summary

Very many of the uses of QuickTime that you'll see will involve at some time what we're calling linear media, even the most interactive uses that we can think of will have portions of linear content. Looking at your target audience will help you make many of the decisions about how best to create your media, from the use of the appropriate camera equipment right up to choosing exactly which compression codec and delivery method will be best.

We're going to spend much of the rest of this book discussing the tools and methods that we'll need in more detail.

8 Creating Images in QuickTime Virtual Reality

Because there are three different types of QTVR (cylindrical, cubic, and object movies), there are three separate methods used to create these movies. On top of this, the images can be created using a different technology. It can be created traditionally using a camera, or created with modeling software (such as 3DS Max). Let's take each movie type individually and look at how these two techniques are applied.

Film or digital?

Photography is an art form, and much has been done in the last hundred years to increase the quality of the cameras and the caliber of the film. At a professional photography shoot there isn't just an expensive camera, but also a team of people making sure that the conditions are optimal to produce the best images possible. The same conditions can also apply to QTVR panoramas and object movies, although it must be remembered that the final product is a digital image shown on a computer screen. A digital image is always confined to 72dpi (dots per inch) when shown, and this resolution is much lower than the 300dpi to 1200dpi used in the printing industry. There are other issues involved as well when the traditional photographer translates their work to digital images. Color management is an art form in itself. Getting the colors to be perfect depends upon many factors. Printed images are built up of ink, usually the primary inks **CMYK** (**C**yan, **M**agenta, **Y**ellow and Black, black being called the **K**ey color by lithographers). Mixing some or all of these colors together produces the other colors of the spectrum. Ink color is different from light in that it is a subtractive color process. That is, if you add all the CMYK inks together then eventually the end result will be black. Light on the other hand is additive; its primary colors are **RGB**, **R**ed **G**reen and **B**lue. If you shine these colored primary lights at one spot the resulting color is white. By mixing these colors it's also possible to create the other colors of the spectrum.

As many in the multimedia industry will know, the task of producing quality work that will be run on different platforms can be very frustrating. Not only are computer monitors of different qualities and settings, but also different platforms, such as Macintosh and PCs, handle their images differently. For example, images on the Macintosh tend to be a shade lighter.

The nature of QTVR (computer based) gives digital photography a great advantage above traditional photography. It's possible these days to purchase cameras with resolutions of 3 mega-pixels and higher, but this is not necessary for QTVR. Images of 800x600 pixels captured at 72 dpi are perfectly acceptable for QTVR. Higher resolutions are of course better, the extra information will help the stitcher to make more convincing blends and a better compression of the total image. Also, if wished, there'll be more detail in the panorama when zooming in. However, if you wish your QTVR panorama to function at an acceptable speed on all computers, and especially be small enough to be used on the Web, then the end image will be a relatively small low-resolution compressed image.

Another advantage to digital above traditional photography is that some models of digital camera, for example the PowerShot by Canon, have a QTVR panorama function, where it's possible to align the separate images in the viewfinder. These digital cameras also come with their own stitching and panorama creation software. Although I prefer Apple's QuickTime VR Authoring Studio for stitching, this image capture technique definitely has my choice above other systems, especially where tripods aren't allowed or you have to be quick.

It's also possible to capture still images using a digital movie camera, or to produce still images from a QuickTime movie to produce the images necessary for the stitch, but I have found that this produces inconsistent results and a lot of post production fiddling. It was an option when digital cameras were rare but now it is not the ideal option.

Whatever happens, the images have to be digitized, and the best option isn't to use any compression (although high quality JPEG is fine) until after the QTVR movie has been produced. It's easier for a stitcher to blend a relatively high resolution image with more information than a low resolution image. My definition of high resolution for QTVR is 1000 pixels high by 800 pixels wide at 72dpi. A higher resolution than this will only take a long time for the stitcher to process. Remember that the resulting panorama "window" will never be much larger than 400 pixels. The panorama on the CD (Chapter8/pyrenees.mov) is made from images 800 pixels high by 600 pixels wide at 72dpi and its window is 300 wide by 800 wide. Use the zoom on this panorama check out the resolution. My workflow involves creating a high-resolution panorama, which I use as a "mother file". After this I can create other panoramas from this at a later date depending on my needs, for example, a low-resolution version for the web.

This aside, it's also possible to produce acceptable QTVR movies with a disposable camera that costs as much as a couple of hamburgers (with cheese, garnishing, and maybe some soft drinks). Food for thought for the photographer who wishes to produce top-notch professional work or the amateur just wishing to add some life to his home page.

It's important to note that QTVR movies are like images, they're available in all sizes and shapes which are easily produced by the free software such as MakeCubic, and products like Apple's QuickTime VR authoring studio or third party software and hardware solutions like IPix and PanoWorx. The resulting panorama or object movie can be customized to the platform and target of your choice.

Cylindrical panorama movies using photography

I once made a panorama from a gondola in Venice. This was of course asking for trouble. The boat rocked not only from side to side and up and down, but it also moved slowly forwards in the time it took me to make all sixteen images, making it very difficult to connect the first image up to the last. I had no tripod, completing the conditions that make the creating of a panorama extremely difficult, and don't get me started about the guy who was steering the boat, he had no intention of helping out at all. Not only that, but it was taken on the Grand Canal, one of the busiest waterways in Venice, as seen in the following image. Check out the other gondola on the canal – it's lost about three meters! The finished panorama is on the CD `Chapter8/gondola.mov`.

The result needed intensive reconstruction in an imaging program, but more of that technique later. The result wasn't what I would call acceptable photography, but it gives some kind of impression of what it's like to be in a gondola, as shown below.

I have also made panoramas with a small camera hidden in a shoebox. In this case, it was forbidden to take photographs too close to the Hall of Congresses in the Kremlin in Moscow. Not only was it a problem (especially with KGB guards walking around) but also it was so cold the batteries in the digital camera began to fade. I had to keep taking the batteries out and warming them up

underneath my armpit to get them to work again. It needed a steady eye to keep the series in a reasonable order and on line with the horizon (`Chapter8/kremlin.mov`).

The results of shooting by hand are at best acceptable but usually less than professional. Another example of forbidden photography was the panorama I took in the Russian underground during Gorbachev's regime. I had no idea if it was allowed; I was more concerned about the reaction of the Russians around me being photographed by a westerner with a bizarre looking digital camera.

Quickly does it – the paparazzi panorama

Lets take two examples, the "quick and dirty" approach, and the "anally-retentive" approach. Although I much prefer taking my time and giving the attention a good panorama deserves, a lot of times it's not possible, like when I was chased by the police while making a panorama of the back of 10 Downing Street, the British Prime Minister's house. Yes, the tripod does look like a rocket launcher! It's often not possible to place a tripod in a public place, not only because of the safety issue, which is given as the excuse. They don't want other people falling over the tripod legs, or you getting in the way and annoying other people. I was told by a policeman to stop making a panorama using a tripod near Buckingham Palace. I was however allowed to take the photograph using a hand camera. The policeman explained that they had had situations were, for example, someone from an advertising agency would drive up in a flashy car and park outside the Palace, a professional photographer would take a photograph, and they would drive off again. Later, the image would appear in magazines, giving the illusion that the Royal Family endorsed that make of car.

Another example of quick and dirty is the assignment in which I had to walk the GR10 trail across the Pyrenees from coast to coast (below).

The QTVR movies would be used to make a travel CD of the route. This meant carrying all my equipment in my backpack, including digital camera and laptop (which I stuck in my sleeping bag to protect it). I made about 470 panoramas across the trail, of which one of the most difficult ones was the Hourquette d'Arre, as shown here and on the CD (Chapter8/pyrenees.mov):

I was standing on a col (a saddle between two peaks, a place used to pass between two mountains) at about 2500 meters. There was a cold front coming from the west (I could see the clouds building up at 1500 meters ready to push up to were I was). Using the excellent stitch function in my Canon PowerShot digital camera, I was able to visually see the two images I needed to align up to make the next step in the panorama. The images could then be later downloaded from the camera straight into the computer, as shown here, so I can then use the stitch software to produce a panorama.

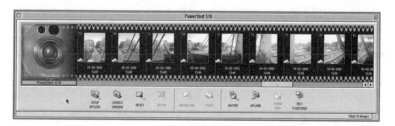

However, the wind was blowing so hard it was rocking me backwards and forwards, making it really difficult to keep the horizon consistent at the same level. This is the most important thing in making a panorama, to make sure that the chosen horizontal is consistent across all the photographs that have been taken, as is not the case shown in the following image:

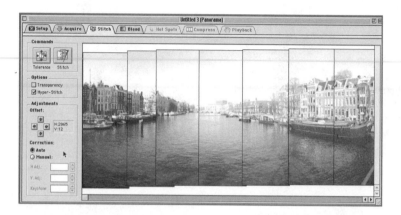

If the horizon is consistent then it makes the process of stitching the images together at a later date a lot easier. If some of the images are too high or too low the stitcher will crop them at a later date, losing a part of the image on the top or on the bottom, and that is a pity. As discussed in Chapter 3, it's important to avoid parallax, but with hand held cameras it's almost impossible to turn a camera on a focal point with such precision. In that case, if possible, it's best to avoid making panoramas where a close up object is in juxtaposition against a far way object, such as a tree that is close by against a mountain range in the distance. Make sure when you are making your panorama that you have sufficient overlap to allow the stitching software to blend the two images together. Also make sure if you're making a 360° panorama, that the images actually do complete a full circle and overlap each other at the end!

Slow and steady – tripods and other equipment

However, lets assume we wish to create quality panoramas, what is it that we need? Well, apart from the camera, a steady tripod is essential. There are several products available on the market (see Chapter 3) that specialize in tripod heads for QTVR panoramas. The sturdiest tripod is the best plan, as the less chance of it moving during the shoot the better. It's important that it doesn't move when you are rotating it. This can happen when you touch the camera, for example to change focus, advance or change film, or to press the shutter. Ideally you should keep away from the camera and tripod as much as possible - you can use a large memory module for digital cameras with shutter-release cable and automatic film advance for traditional cameras. A spirit or bubble level is also useful if you wish the panorama to follow the horizon perfectly, although this may not always be the case. There are spirit levels for sale that fit onto the flash socket of a camera. Some of the specialist tripod heads are calibrated to click when turned into equal sections (usually 12 to 16 sections), however it is possible to make do with a card that you can place under the camera that has been marked into the segments. The specialist tripod heads also have the advantage of positioning the camera's focal node (and not the film plane), above the point of rotation, thus avoiding parallax.

As already explained, in principle you can use any cheap camera or any video camera that takes stills. On the other hand you'll have more control with equipment that allows more manual settings for things like exposure and depth of field. Also the ability to change lenses adds to flexibility, helping you to adapt to every new session. The common 35mm single lens reflex (SLR) camera is a popular choice for making panoramas, but digital cameras have a greater advantage above traditional film. If you do wish to use traditional film then you'll either have to scan in your pictures after development, or have your film developed and then the images stored on a photo CD such as produced by companies like Kodak.

A rectilinear (non-distorting) lens is a better option, as then there is no need to adjust later on for fisheye or barrel distortion. The shorter the lens, the more expensive it becomes and it's hard to find a rectilinear lenses shorter than about 15 mm. Short lenses however give a wider field of view, which allows you to make a panorama using fewer images. It also allows for more overlap, which is essential when stitching the final panorama. A shorter lens also gives you a taller field of view, which can be important for interior views.

Let's take a look at the differences between punctilious and paparazzi methods. I have made two examples of a panorama from the Magere Brug in Amsterdam. I took the first just by hand.

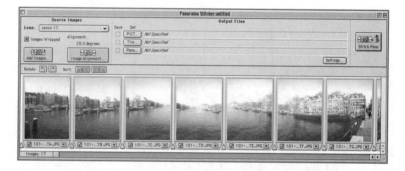

For the second I used the QTVR tripod head made by Kaidan. You can see the differences in the levels on the horizon, the consistency in taking the pictures vertically, and the uniformity in the overlap. This image shows the pictures taken with the tripod and imported into QuickTime VR Authoring studio. You can already see from the images that the horizon is consistent throughout the images. Compare this the first, where the images show slightly different horizons.

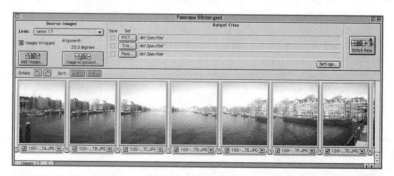

You can see that the 'paparazzi' panorama will have to be cropped more extensively that the panorama underneath, thus losing a part of the field of view and making for a less immersive image. You can also see that the overlap is inconsistent, making it more difficult to stitch.

It's a stitch up

Now we these images and put them through the stitcher. I used Apple's QuickTime VR authoring studio (Macintosh only) to stitch both images, but there are other products on the market, for example VR PanoWorx (www.vrtoolbox.com) This software tool is available for both Macintosh and PC.

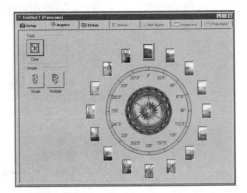

Another product is Photovista by MGIsoft, (Windows only – www.mgisoft.com). The stitching of the paparazzi panorama presented a lot more work than that created with the tripod. Although it's possible to manipulate the stitching, this takes extra time and the result can be uncertain. I once made a panorama by hand that needed to be re-stitched about twelve times before I managed to get the results I was looking for. In that example the levels of the horizon were so inconsistent that the stitcher had to crop the image a lot, slicing the top off a mountain.

Problems in widescreen

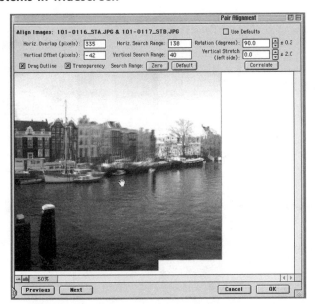

Here's another example of an Amsterdam panorama. The second image has to be directly manipulated to create a better stitch. In Apple's QuickTime VR Authoring Studio it's possible to give individual settings to each overlap in a panorama. However, creating a panorama with inconsistent overlaps creates its own problems when creating a perfect 360° image and the program will not always be able to do exactly what you want. This demands a lot of trial and experimentation, adding to the time it takes to make a good stitch. This is the toll you have to pay for not using a tripod.

If you can't use a tripod then keeping the horizon consistent needs a steady hand and a good memory for keeping the overlaps consistent. It's possible after practice to develop a routine and it's advisable to do a couple of experiments before hand to get used to the technique. Keeping the natural horizon exactly in the middle of the viewfinder is one trick. Placing the middle of the previous image taken at the left (or right) edge to get consistent overlaps is another.

Don't worry if you have taken the images in the wrong order, or taken the images upside down (when holding the camera in portrait mode – yes, I'm left handed). This can be easily rectified either in an image program like Photoshop, or as one of the options when importing into the stitching tool. It is however, advisable not to take the images in landscape mode as portrait mode gives more height (field of view) to the panorama. It's also possible to set the overlap in VR PanoWorx. If the images are inconsistent then they'll need a greater overlap. The images are "dancing", losing image detail at the top and bottom in relation to each other (the black areas). This reduces the field of vision of the final panorama.

Other examples of bad stitching are shown in the following screenshots. Here, the cables supporting the bridge are correctly aligned, but the buildings in the background are out of synch:

Here, the buildings are okay but the cables are now out of synch:

So what are the options available when stitching to create the perfect image? In Apple QuickTime Authoring Studio there are options to select the type of lens used. There are standard lens settings (for example for the 15mm lens, or the QuickTake 200 camera), which are customizable to the settings you used to make the images.

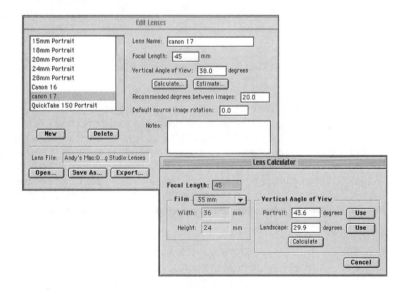

It's also possible to influence the stitching process using the image alignment settings. With these settings it is possible to incorporate the size of the lens of the camera that you used, and amount of images that you took. You can also specify the overlap between the images and the search range (that is, how far the stitcher will search between two images to find the best blend). This is especially handy when the images you have taken are by hand and the overlap is inconsistent. However, the higher the search range the longer it takes for the computer to make the calculations to complete the stitch, and may lead to incorrect stitches. This setting is not only for the horizontal axis but also for the vertical axis. The best way to get the ideal settings is to experiment, although the stitch programs often come with additional settings for standard cameras and lenses. These settings are also customizable to the settings on your camera.

> *In general, for panoramas of landscapes that are far way a 28mm lens is fine, while for closer work 15-18mm lenses work well.*

Sewing box

The options to influence the stitching process can be selected according to the quality of the original images and by if you intend to retouch the finished strip later in an imaging program. In total, six options can be selected from the Stitch Settings window.

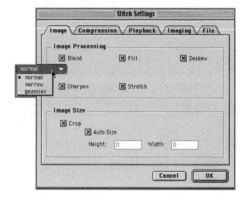

The options are:

■ **Blend:** Blend is the option to mix the two images together at the overlap to form a homogenous whole. This works very well, but sometimes it works to your disadvantage. For example, if an object is in one photograph (let's say a stray tourist), but not in the next photograph where it overlaps, the result is a ghost – a compromise between something (the tourist), and nothing (an empty space). Here are three different algorithms of blending, normal, narrow, and gaussian. I find normal works best but if you are having trouble with a blend you might try the different options. Whatever you chose, the blend is applied to the whole panorama and not to an individual blend between two images.

■ **Fill:** Fill is useful in filling in gaps that may appear between two images. The fill takes place either at the top or at the bottom and this usually involves filling in the holes with a pixel color that is equivalent to the pixels around it. This can involve the color of the sky, from example a sample of the blue pixels in that specific area. It also works in sampling the ground color and filling in with that color. It's seldom convincing but enough to cover small spots. It's however advantageous to have this option on and later to retouch in an imaging program (for example Photoshop or PaintShop Pro).

- **Deskew:** When stitching the panorama, especially images taken with the hand, the end photograph will tend to be significantly higher or lower in relation to the horizon than the start image. Deskew 'skews' the image so that these two images line up with each other. If the image is deskewed it will be slightly manipulated but because it occurs over the whole length of the image, it will probably have little effect on the whole panorama.

- **Sharpen:** When blending the images together it can have the effect of blurring the total image slightly, as the overlap is a compromise between two images. Sharpen brings a little life back into the image, sharpening the image, increasing the contrast. If you're not intending to correct the images later in an imaging program, you can try this to see if it improves you panorama. I personally prefer to sharpen the image later using Photoshop, as I feel that Photoshop not only has a better sharpen algorithm, but I can also try different settings for each panorama for the best effect.

- **Stretch:** QTVR movies work from a specific formula, and so the original panorama image has to be of particular dimensions. According to Apple, to be able to run on Macintosh and Windows computers, the width and length of the image has to be evenly divisible by 4, otherwise there may be 'unpredictable results' when viewing. Stretch simply stretches both the height and width of the final stitched image so that it fits within this category. Although purists may disagree, because this occurs over the entire length of the image it has little effect on the finished panorama.

- **Crop:** Crop has the effect of cutting down your image, missing out those bad bits that have not stitched well. It does this over the whole length of the panorama, so if you have used the Fill option, there may still be bits of fill left over from at places around the top and bottom. An example of this is the panorama I made by hand hanging out of the Campanile in Venice, as mentioned in Chapter 3 (see the CD `Chapter3/QTVR /Campanile.mov`). If you look at the panorama at the bottom (sky is less of a problem), you see attempts of fill by the stitcher. I usually crop my images in PhotoShop, as this gives me more control over the final result.

The resulting panorama from the stitch is an image file. QuickTime Authoring Studio stitcher produces a PICT file that is rotated 90°, so that it's standing on its side. This is done because a PICT file has a limit of how wide it can be and the length of an average panorama usually surpasses this. The image file can then be used for making the QTVR movie, but it can also be used for other things. On the CD (in the folder Chapter3/QTVR_demos) are examples of a screensaver I made with Macromedia Director that uses the panorama image (and not the QuickTimeVR) as artwork. The Director file (with comments in the Lingo code) is also on the CD (Chapter3/QTVR_demos/screensaver.dir). You can import the images as PICT files you wish and adapt the Lingo to your own needs.

Once the image is stitched, a TILE file is created that can be used later to recreate the movie with hotspots or another duplicate movie with different settings. However this file is actually not needed and can be deleted when finished.

Constraining zoom, pan, and tilt

Using the TILE file we just talked about, the QTVR movie is finally created. After the file has been created a window appears with the QTVR and its standard settings.

In this window it's possible to adapt the field of view, and to set the starting point of the movie. It's also possible to set the amount of tilt, that is, how far the user is looking up or down at the beginning of the run time. Also available is an option to set the zoom settings, so that the user can see the panorama fully zoomed into a few pixels if wished. These options can be set for each individual panorama.

The settings that you select are your choice and may depend on what the purpose of the QTVR is – for example a large FOV setting like 800x300 will be great for a CD-ROM, but will create a QTVR that is too large for the Web. However, its your choice, go ahead, knock yourself out.

Cylindrical panorama movies using 3D-software

Making a QTVR panorama in a 3D-drawing program is relatively easy (after all the difficult modeling has been done that is). You can either make several images and stitch them together as described above, or using a 3D drawing programs (like 3DS Max and Strata Studio Pro) create the panoramic strip as an export option. Because you're not being blown around in the wind or being chased by the police, you have full control over the quality of the images you create.

A standard setting for your camera could be a 15mm lens and images taken in 16 sections around 360°. However, you're free to experiment as the stitching software has a certain amount of flexibility. Depending on the software package you can save your ideal settings for other projects.

Creating CubicVR panorama movies by photography

Making CubicVR panoramas using traditional photography requires the right equipment. By taking two 180° photographs back to back using special fisheye lens, or even a single 360° image using specialist one-shot lenses, it's possible to create a CubicVR panorama. These solutions are, for example, the RemoteReality OneShot360, the "EyeSee360" sold by Kadian, the Be Here TotalView Photo, and the VRi Surroundphoto. It's beyond the scope of this book to go into all the details about the technical specifications of each lens, however it's important to be aware that making convincing CubicVR panoramas involves a lot of preparation. It's impossible to create a professional CubicVR movie without the right equipment. Although CubicVR is a cylindrical VR panorama on steroids, with a much more convincing "mmersive" experience, it will not replace it entirely in the near future because of the problems of creation. CubicVR is however the future, not only because of its extra immersive effect, but also as it's much more efficient with memory and disk space. Because CubicVR needs fewer images than cylindrical panoramas it is much more efficient than the cylindrical movies for images over 120 degrees VFOV (looking up and down).

Basically, you'll need to produce either six 90° square images, or two 180° hemispheric images, or, alternatively, an equi-rectangular image using a full frame fisheye lens. Well that's as easy as falling into a hole, you might think. So when does it start to get difficult? After that, actually it's all downhill, and free! By using the MakeCubicPPC (Mac only) software that's available from Apple's web site, or with a freeware PC version available from www.panoshow.com/panocube.htm, it's relatively easy to stitch the image into an excellent CubicVR. Remember. It's also possible to place hotspots in this QTVR, and that can also be done with the same software.

Other software solutions are also available for the Mac and PC from iPIX and Panoscan, but you will have to pay for this software, and in the case of iPIX you'll have to purchase a license for every panorama produced. iPIX has announced a component for QuickTime that allows iPIX images to be played inside the QuickTime player as well. More authoring applications for creating cubic movies are in the works from third party vendors as well.

Other vendors are Panoweaver (shown here, which uses 2 fisheye pictures just like iPIX), Realview 3D (again, 2 fisheye pictures) and ImmerVision (uses a proprietary ultra-wide angle lens that requires two shots)

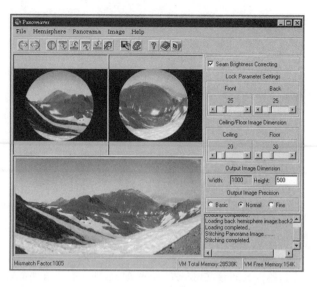

Once the equi-rectangular image has been converted to a cubic movie you can export the cube faces as PICT files from the Quicktime Pro movie player (export to image) for easy retouching in Photoshop. This isn't done automatically but has to be done frame by frame. Because the cube faces are 90° by 90°-plane views they look comparatively normal, unlike fish-eye images that appear distorted. This makes it a lot easier to make any changes to the images. It would be, for example, difficult to remove a tri-pod or camera from an equi-rectangular or fisheye image because of the extreme distortion at the edges, but as a flat cube face it's easy to edit the bottom face, which looks like a normal picture.

Creating CubicVR panorama movies with 3D software

Because all the conditions are under your control when using 3D-software, it's relatively easy to make CubicVR movies in this way. Simply place a 'camera' in the middle of the scene you wish to make a CubicVR movie of. The lens you use should be set to 90°. Make four images moving from left to right in 90° increments (numbered 1 to 4). Make an image looking directly above and one looking directly below, and number these 5 and 6. You can download the program MakeCubic from Apple's website (http://developer.apple.com/quic ktime/quicktimeintro/tools/index.html#qtvr). Simply load these images into the software and the CubicVR movie is then created. These are the settings that are available from MakeCubic

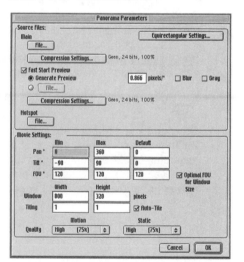

An example of this is the CubicVR created by Dan Roam for DeepCold (www.deepcold.com). The resulting movie can be found on the CD (Chapter8/deepcoldCubic.mov).

This is a scene from his upcoming CD-ROM about a cold war conflict in space. He simply placed his models around the camera, took six images, and produced the CubicVR. The CubicVR images opened up look like this.

Further examples of this work in QuickTime can be seen on the CD (Chapter8/deepcold.mov). There is a Strata Studio Pro file with the basics already set up on the CD (Chapter8/CubicVR.smd), this is Mac only unfortunately.

Making object movies using traditional photography

When creating an object movie you're going to make a series of images that need to be precisely at the same alignment with your object, while you rotate the object around its center. If you're shooting a multi-row object movie, that is, you can look not only around, but also above and/or below, then you're going to repeat the shoot with the camera at different vertical positions. This can be extremely difficult and time-consuming work, and unlike making cylindrical panoramas where you can wing it, here it really helps to have the right equipment and to take the time to get the quality you need.

Taking all kinds of precautions, like gluing your object to the stand (unless it's a fashion model, they don't like it when you do that), helps in creating a convincing object movie. The problem with object movies is that they need to be consistent in the angle at which each photograph is taken, otherwise when the user revolves the movie the object may appear to dance or jiggle about, creating a unconvincing effect.

You generally want to shoot against a clean backdrop, the best being black, but it will depend on the color of the object. You may wish to use a very definitive color that will help later in masking the images at a later date. Include a small marker object in the frame (but not on the turntable) in case you need to precisely align your images later. You can edit the marker out later in an image manipulation program like Photoshop.

Shooting an exposure every 10 degrees of rotation for a total of 36 images is the standard procedure. It's possible to make the movie smaller by shooting 24 exposures 15 degrees apart, but the motion of the object will be jerky. You don't have to shoot the object from every angle – maybe one side, like the back, isn't interesting – and four exposures 90 degrees apart provide a complete view.

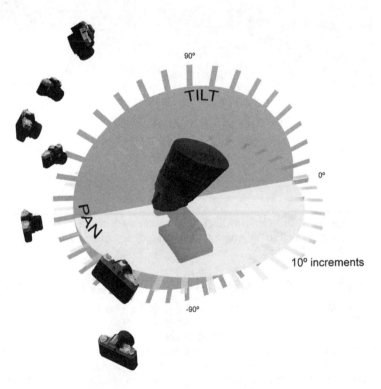

For a multi-row movie, you typically want to shoot at 10 degrees vertical increments as well. A full top-to-bottom shoot requires 18 rows, but a shoot from more than 10 degrees to 30 degrees underneath is really pushing the boat out. Shooting from directly underneath is extremely difficult.

Although this can be done with a glass turntable or by suspending the object, matching the rotation angles and camera registration with the rest of the shoot is laborious. Expect to spend many hours with an image manipulation program like PhotoShop trying to get it just right.

Look first at the object from every angle and rotation. Set up your lighting so the object is well lit at every angle and you don't get glare or lens flare. Don't change the lighting, exposure, or focus during the shoot, as this will create darker or lighter images within the object movie. Set your camera for fixed exposure, not auto-exposure.

Now you're ready to take some pictures. With the right camera and rig, you can automate the whole shoot and capture your images directly into QuickTime VR Authoring Studio, Widgetizer, or VR PanoWorx.

Making object movies using 3D software

If you're generating images directly from a 3D-modeling program, your task is much simpler, aside from creating the models in the first place. Generating a series of images of your chosen object is easy to achieve, and some 3D programs such as Strata Studio Pro even deliver a free set-up with the camera in place. This set-up is also on the CD (QTVR demos/object movie.smd). Simply create the images of your model at 10 degrees intervals of rotation.

> *If you're doing a multi-row movie, start from the highest point – normally 0 degrees or directly overhead – do a row, drop 10 degrees and do another, until you're as low as you want.*

Apple recommends that you save the images with sequential filenames, using a leading zero for numbers below 10 – for example, Row01shot01, Row01shot02..., Row01shot36, Row02shot01, and so on to Row18Shot36. As you become more experienced you'll be more inclined to produce complex multi-row object movies so you may be rendering as many as 648 images. Remember that this will demand a lot of time and disk space. It might be wise to render a series of images at 45 degrees (45 images) or 90 degrees (12 images) to make sure everything is perfect with your settings before you commit to a full series of 648. The amount and type of image preparation you need to do depends on how you created your images. If you shot with film, you need to develop to CD or scan-in prints, slides, or negatives. Again, this process would be eliminated if a digital camera had been used. The scanning process is also likely to introduce some jitters from frame to frame. When using traditional photography it's wise to shoot your images with a marker object in the frame and use it to precisely align and crop your images.

If you used a camera of any kind to generate your images (as opposed to using 3D modeling software), you probably need to retouch every image using Photoshop or a similar program. No, object movies aren't for the faint of heart.

The pedestal is another problem, as you'll probably want to eliminate this from the final object movie.

The best results are to reduce the background to a single color in every image. Differences in color, no matter how slight, may show up clearly in an object movie, especially after compression. Also, a solid color compresses better (3:1), and you can easily make a solid color transparent. It is common practice to matte a background image into each frame at this point. You can make it a lot easier for yourself, and due to the better compression, save a lot of bandwidth, by making the background transparent and compositing a background image into the movie later.

Retouching in an image program

After the images have been stitched, you may want to remove unwanted pieces form the final image before creating the movie. Obvious things like tripods and reflections in mirrors, exposure differences and artifacts (pixel noise that comes from nowhere). One of the most useful tools is cloning – selecting a piece of image from another spot in the image and pasting that over the spot to be retouched. This can be useful when, for example, eliminating a tripod using samples of the ground surrounding the tripod. There are no set procedures for this, you are only limited by the options available in your imaging program and your own creativity.

You *will* need special software to create an object movie. QuickTime VR Authoring Studio, VR PanoWorx, and Widgetizer are examples. Photovista 3D Objects is also another choice (www.mgisoft.com). Most of these software companies have demo software that you can download. These demos usually have limited functionality or are only valid for a trial period. The exact procedure for making an object movie will depend on the software package that you use. In general, you specify the number of rows, the degrees of rotation, and number of images per row, the initial view, and the folder that contains the images, and then the software creates the movie.

Compression issues

You have two opportunities for compressing the images. You can compress before the images are assembled into a movie or when you create the object movie. If you compress now you might find you get slight differences between the images due to the different compressions, which will show up later in the object movie. There is a benefit of the similarities between images, resulting in a smaller file, if you compress the whole movie at once. If you must compress beforehand it is advised that you compress the images using the same compressor for all the images – so, for example, don't use GIF compression on one and JPEG compression on another.

> *In general it's useful to keep a high resolution non-compressed version and use that as a source file for movies tailor made for different uses (for example for the Web).*

You can choose a compressor at any stage of the creation of the QTVR movie. Personally I prefer to compress at the very last stage, as this has the advantage of getting the highest quality for creating the main image, then utilizing the compression algorithms to create the file size/quality ratio that is necessary for the job. I always make a panorama that is of the highest quality I can achieve, then use this as the mother file to create the movies optimized for either web, CD or hard disk play back. Photo JPEG compression yields the sharpest images but it also has, in general, the largest files. Cinepak compression takes advantage of the likeness between images, and this results in a smaller file size, but it provides only average quality at low bandwidths. Sorenson is probably the best compressor for Web movies, as it gives high quality at low bandwidths, taking good advantage of image similarities. However, the best bet is to experiment with different types of compression to find the best for you. The final compression algorithm that you chose will depend on the payoff between quality and quantity.

You can compress QTVR from QuickTime Pro or from many of the authoring programs available for creating QTVR. From QuickTime Pro you can also export the movie with several options for fast starting and streaming over the Internet.

I personally use the export function in QuickTime Pro for compressing my QTVR movies, as this has several options for exporting your final movie with different compression techniques. It's important to appreciate that compression types compress using different methods and algorithms. And as each image is unique, what works fine with one QuickTimeVR movie, may produce less than perfect results in another. Experimentation is advisable, especially when producing content for the web.

When producing QTVR for the Web you might wish to chose the "Fast Start" export function. According to Apple, QTVR movies don't stream.

Special QTVR Effects

As already mentioned in Chapter 3, there are several special effects that can be added to the QTVR movies to enhance this immersive experience. Sound is an obvious example, and directional sound really brings the whole image to life.

Other effects can also be added. Digital Devil (www.digital-devil.com and click the SPECIAL FX tab), have created two creative QTVR movies with special effects. There's a fantastic little movie where there's a separate sprite layer that reacts to user input at run time. Click on the water to see the water ripple...

Another effect by Digital Devil is a QTVR movie moving through time. This object movie was created with images that have not been taken at different increments around an object, but from the same position over increments of time see the pictures in the following diagram:

Summary

The creation of special effects isn't only dependent on the techniques but also on your creativity, and with the progressive enhancements made to QuickTime by Apple and the continuing introduction of third party software. The process of creating panoramas is not complex, it can just take a bit of practice and effort to get the images in the first place, but the results can be spectacular. Hopefully this chapter has explained enough for you to want to, and be able to, try creating some of your own.

QTVR movies are going to be really big in the future of multi-media, but now we're going to get even more interactive!

9 Interactive Media: Assembly, Scripting, & Delivery

Flow charting, sketching, and planning your project isn't always necessary. If you just want to do some nicely designed play and stop buttons, designing and implementing is all you really need to do. If you're planning on anything more complex though, you should take some time to do some planning beforehand. Projects that involve modular structures, embedded timelines or 'complex' user interaction can become a bit chaotic if you haven't planned out your steps. I know it's hard to focus on organizing your project, when you just want to see the final results as soon as possible. But with a bit of organization, you'll get your project up and running faster and the performance should be better.

I'm going to use several real-world examples to show you the process I take to create a project. The main example I'm using is a project for Paraphonic.com, we're going to take a in depth look at this as a case study at the end of the chapter. Paraphonic.com is a site I've been working on with two musicians in Sweden. Our plans for the site were to release a virtual EP and video every couple of months. Before we started work on the final site, I wanted to do an interactive QuickTime project that would act as an introduction to our future plans and would try to entice people to come back at a later date.

Goals and objectives for the audience

Before I start working on a project, I like to jot down ideas and make some sketches. Most of the personal projects I do are directed at fellow designers, who are experienced users of interactive media. When I'm doing any kind of commercial project, I check what kind of audience it's directed at, and work from there.

If you're working solo on a project, often just globally planning out your ideas in your head is enough. But when you're working with others, it's a good idea to make sure that everyone knows what you're planning and can give feedback. I often just make a simple textual description of my plans, which I revise several times.

For example, after doing a lot of thinking, I wrote down the main idea I had for the Paraphonic.com project. The first project on Paraphonic.com will involve user interaction with a layered piece of music. By moving the mouse over a target area the audience will be able to direct the sound.

- The sound will first fade from the first track to the second

- The second soundtrack will fade to the third

- The third soundtrack will fade to the fourth

By interacting with the sound, an accompanying video loop will be played. When changing from track to track the video will transition from one loop to another.

Storyline articulation

At this point you want to start visualizing how your project will work and what the different steps of user interaction will be. This is especially important when you're working with several people on the same project, because they need to know exactly what's going to happen to the content you're planning on including in the project.

Describe the typical path a user will take through the project, as this will also help you discover any irregularities in your ideas, which you will then be able to adjust.

For the Paraphonic.com project, I made a couple of quick sketches showing the way I wanted the project to work. I wanted the musicians (who would be working on the four sound tracks) to understand exactly what the user would be able to do. At this point I had only thought of mixing four tracks with different instruments in each track. The musicians responded to the story-line sketches with the idea to let every track have the feeling of a part of a normal song, from intro to finish. If I hadn't done these sketches early on in the project, the musicians probably wouldn't have had enough information to base their feedback on.

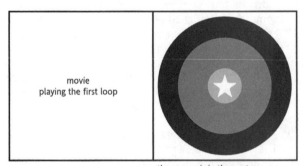

movie
playing the first loop

the mouse is in the center.
the video starts looping the first bit.
In this zone the first and second
soundtracks are mixed by the user.

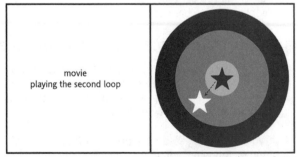

movie
playing the second loop

(star = mouse pointer)

the mouse moves to the second zone.
In this zone the user is mixing the
second and third soundtrack.
The video stops looping, and plays
on past the first fade.
When the video has reached the second
loop part, it starts looping the
selction of the second loop part.

Flowcharting the interactions

Now you can start sketching out the optimal placement of the different elements of your project. Making a temporary design will help when you're working on the flowchart, and you'll know which elements you'll have to include in the final design. Also, having a temporary design will make it easy to do interaction tests. The image below shows the temporary design I made for the Paraphonic.com project.

Again, sketch the path a user will take through the project, and how you need to organize your scripting to make this path possible. At every step, comment the sketches with pointers that will help you when you've reached the scripting stage.

If your project is going to be reused in the future, try to work out how you can adjust your interaction flow-chart to make re-purposing as easy as possible. Basically, you want your flow-chart to work in a way that when you come to the production stage, you have as few steps as possible when making the movies. Check all the things that may change in future content, for example, video dimensions, graphic titles, and text descriptions. Then, think about ways how you can minimize the time it will take to change these different elements.

I wanted the branded player for u2.com (shown below) to be as simple as possible. This was mostly for production reasons: I knew that the video sizes would vary a lot, and there wouldn't be a lot of time to alter the interface every time a new video arrived. I fitted all the controls into one sprite track. This way only the background image would need to be changed, if the movie dimensions were larger or smaller then normal.

Also, while organizing the flow of your project, you should think about ways of keeping it as user-friendly as possible. Think from the audience point of view, and take into account how experienced your audience is.

Connection speeds

If your project will need to cater for users with varying connection speeds (28k/56k/cable/adsl) you should think of ways of directing them to the right content. Often, the easiest thing is to make three (or more) different versions of your project that will support your audience's needs. If you want to make only one version that will be useable for different connection speeds, ask the audience to enter their connection speed as early on in the project as possible.

It's been my experience with content of high interest that people with a slow connection speed often want to see a higher-quality version and want to be able to choose to wait for it to load. If your content is purely of an informational nature, you may want to minimize the steps it will take for a user to get to the content. For this you may want to have the movie deliver the right version via a reference movie, based on the connection speed they entered when installing QuickTime.

The Paraphonic.com project was being directed at seasoned Internet users with higher than average connections. This didn't mean that I wasn't going to try to make the project as small as possible. But because the experience of the video and audio were the most important elements of the project, I didn't want to sacrifice the quality too much.

QuickTime Player version

Just because you made your project using the latest version of QuickTime, doesn't mean that your users will have it installed. For example, QuickTime 4 doesn't have support for technologies like Sorenson 3, Flash 4, and XML (to name but a few). So when you're using the latest version of QuickTime and its many new features to author your movie, it's recommended you check which version the user has installed. Using programs like LiveStage Professional, MakeRefMovie, and XMLtoRefMovie, you can have your project check which version of QuickTime the user has installed and request that those with an earlier version of QuickTime upgrade their software.

For the Paraphonic.com project, using LiveStage Professional, I made a QuickTime movie that resembled a button and embedded it into the Paraphonic web site. If the QuickTime version installed was lower than 5, I changed the button graphic to 'click here to upgrade to the latest version of QuickTime'. Otherwise the button stayed the same and said 'click here to enter'.

Interface feedback

Try to get under the user's skin; think of the kinds of feedback you would want to receive when going through the different steps of interaction. Refine your interface ideas to make every button click and mouse interaction seem natural and obvious.

The audience should always know what your buttons are going to do when clicked. When using icon-buttons, give simple textual feedback on what will happen when clicked. This is especially important when you're planning to use buttons that differ from the standard 'VCR' buttons (stop, pause, play, rewind, fast forward). For the Video Matrix project for id-t.com, I used a QuickTime text track to give information on every button rollover.

If you're planning on deploying your project on the Web, give as much information as possible about the loading state of your movie. When you're using progressive downloads, give some kind of feedback on how far the movie has loaded. When a user clicks on the play button, and the movie stops playing because it isn't loading fast enough to keep playing, you want them to know why it has stopped. For the u2.com branded player, I had the background of the navigation bar change color based on how far the movie had loaded. Also, I limited the drag region of the navigation thumb to the amount the movie had loaded. I did this so people wouldn't be able to drag it to the end of the timeline only to find out their video had stopped half way.

When you're using streaming tracks, tell the user when the stream is buffering, as shown below:

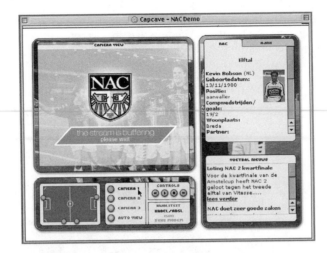

If your project demands that you can't let the audience play your content while it's loading, try to entertain/educate them while they wait. You can use Flash to make a small game to play while waiting, or you can explain to the audience what's going to happen (or what you want the audience to do) when the content has loaded. Any kind of extra communication with the audience will keep them interested and stop them from clicking away. Hopefully this will also keep them from opening any new windows and multitasking, which may make the download time longer and can impact the performance of the project when it's loaded.

When I did the Video Matrix for id-t.com, I wanted the video to load a bit before letting it play. While the content was loading, I showed a Flash animation describing how the user would need to interact with the project.

Testing the interactions

If your project involves any complex navigational scripting, or processor intensive direct interaction with content it's a good idea to use a temporary interface design to do some tests. Because the combination of video and interaction can be quite hard on the cpu, you want to know what the best combination of video codec, audio codec, and interaction technique will be. Also you want to know for sure that the performance will be good on as many different kinds of computers and OSs as possible. And you want to know all this *before* you've spent hours designing an interface that will have to be changed because the performance isn't good enough.

If you're going to be putting your project online, always check your tests on a web server. Performance of QuickTime projects can be dramatically different when viewed online. Interactive QuickTime usually involves a lot of tweaking, to get a good multi-platform result. The more tests you do early on, the less hassle you will have at the end of the ride. If you have any problems that really have you stumped, there are several places to consult:

- www.blueabuse.com – This site has loads of great tutorials and a forum, which is supervised by the makers of LiveStage Professional.

- www.totallyhip.com/lsdn – This site, which is also from the makers of Livestage Professional, contains downloadable behaviors, tutorials, and the searchable Livestage Pro mailing list archives.

For the Paraphonic project I did several test movies to get the volume switching through mouse interaction part working correctly. I tested a couple of different interaction techniques with several sorts of sample content to make sure that the CPU usage would stay as low as possible. I also checked different codecs to see which ones would work best in combination with the interaction. For the video I tried setting after setting using Sorenson 3. After numerous versions, I found one that was low on cpu usage and file size but still looked nice. For the audio, I was using 192kbit MP3s early on, but they inflated the file size too much. The Qdesign codec sounded great, and made the files very small, but performance on Windows compatible machines left a lot to be desired. In the end I compressed them as 96kbit MP3s. Even though the audio quality wasn't fantastic, the file size was one third of the earlier version and CPU usage was decreased.

Using Flash: for interaction and other purposes

There are quite a lot of reasons why you might want to choose Flash opposed to bitmaps for your interface, a few of which are listed below:

- Vector images can be a lot smaller then the bitmap equivalents.

- With Flash you're able to embed custom fonts in your design.

- You can use smooth vector animations in your interface.

- With Flash you can easily have transparencies in your interface, giving that extra 'wow' factor.

- If you want the user to be able to scale your interface, vectors will stay smooth. Bitmaps won't.

- You can easily have your buttons trigger sounds.

But there are a number of things you may want to look out for:

- Always check what version of Flash is supported by the version of QuickTime that you're creating your project for (for example, Flash 3 with QuickTime 4, Flash 4 with QuickTime 5).

- Using complex vector images, gradients, and animations can impact the performance of your project.

- QuickTime does have some problems drawing Flash tracks every now and again. So when creating your Flash work, don't forget to go back and forth between QuickTime and Flash to check and fix drawing issues.

Flash can be a good alternative to a QuickTime Sprite track. You can make your whole interface in Flash, and have it show pictures and display text. Using LiveStage you can then wire up your flash buttons to load video and audio. Also, if you want the user to be able to scale your movies or put them in full screen, a Flash interface will look better then the bitmap alternative.

Flash tracks can also be used for effective preloaders, allowing the user to play a game while waiting or just to show a smooth vector 'loading' animation. I've used Flash preloaders in the past for animated explanation screens that are shown while the movie is loading, as was shown earlier in the chapter.

If you're doing anything with your QuickTime movie that may already be quite CPU intensive (like changing the volume of several sound-tracks continuously, or playing several movies at once) you may want to choose to use bitmap buttons in the sprite track. These will be less processor intensive than the Flash equivalent.

For the Paraphonic.com project, I used Flash as a preloader, to give the user some tips on how the project would work, while the content was loading. For the interaction, I kept to QuickTime's Sprite track. Flash didn't offer me anything extra that would help the navigation, and the interaction load would already be quite heavy.

Collecting and developing media elements

If you're planning on developing media specifically for your project, I advise you to wait until you've tested your scripting ideas. Too often, I see QuickTime projects with content that looks great, but that suffers because of the scripting part having been an afterthought. If you've tested your scripting ideas well enough, you'll have more realistic ideas how your content will behave in the final product. And, at least you'll know that your content *will* work in the final product.

Often when content hasn't been specifically compressed (or sized) for your project, performance will suffer. You should always try to reach the perfect balance of performance versus bandwidth versus quality. Of course with every project this balance will be different. For example, projects that are purely of an informational nature will demand that you sacrifice quality over bandwidth. Also, the original media files should always be of the highest quality possible. When compressing a video or audio file, you want to give the codec as much information as possible to work from.

Making the final interface design

After having done a number of test movies, to make sure everything you're planning on doing is completely possible, and is working as smooth as you can get it, it's time to start work on the final design for the movie. When I'm designing the final design of an interface, I usually make the rough version in a vector application like Fireworks or Illustrator. This way I can easily move elements around and resize them. When I've finalized element placement, I move the design over to Photoshop, where I make everything look pretty. If you slice your image using Fireworks or ImageReady, you can simply note down the x/y values of the slices and use them to put the puzzle back together in LiveStage Pro.

Try to export your design in a way that your video (or flash) layers won't be on top of a picture or sprite track. Remember that whenever you put different kinds of content on top of each other, you're giving QuickTime a hard time when it comes to redrawing the screen, especially when you're placing any kind of content over a video track. Whenever these different types of content use alpha channels or transparencies, the slowdown will be worse. Sometimes you can get away with it without much trouble, but do some tests check to make sure.

One of the most important things to keep in mind when using QuickTime, is never to assume anything. With QuickTime, you can combine numerous media types, but each media type will have a different kind of performance. Some may, for example, work fine on their own, but become sluggish when combined with others.

Now that I knew which elements I would need to include in the final design, I was ready to make a final design for the Paraphonic.com project. I changed the first idea I had of using a kind of target interface to the idea of having an LP cover, with a record hanging out of it. This way the video would be part of the LP cover, and the audience would use the record to interact with the video and audio. Also, to make sure the audience would understand that they're the ones mixing the audio, I designed four volume bars on the top of the LP. Also, I exported the graphical elements of the design, in a way so that no media elements would be covering each other.

Implementing the final version of your interface

So, the interaction tests are out of the way, and you've finished the final version of your design. Now it's time to combine the interaction tests, which you did earlier on, with the final design. Again, this involves doing a lot of testing. At this point you'll also need to implement the feedback elements, which you planned out in your flowchart.

When doing small adjustments to see if you can improve performance, don't forget to write down the changes that you make. There's nothing worse then having to spend several hours back-tracking your steps after having made some kind of faulty adjustment to your project.

Compressing

Try to keep the final compression of your content as one of the very last steps of the production process. You should know by now what kind of compression is needed and you'll only need to tweak your settings to get the very best out of your content.

When compressing, always use an uncompressed source file. This way the video or audio codec will have more information at it's disposal to base the compression on. In the compression world there is a saying that makes it clear: 'garbage in – garbage out'.

Always save every compression setting that you use, and note down what kind of content you used it on. That way you'll be able to reuse it in the future for similar content.

Testing

When testing your work, check every button and every combination of every button. At this point you really want to give your project a hard time, to make sure it will stand up to any user interaction. I usually ask as many people as I can think of to check the final version of my project before launching it. This way I can make sure that people understand what the project is doing, and can make design adjustments if this isn't the case. Also, this way the project will be tested on many different kinds of computers with different kinds of Internet connections, which is always a good thing.

Case Study

Paraphonic.com is a web site, which is still in a pre launch stage. In the future we're planning on releasing an online EP with a video every couple of months. Before we started work on the final site, we wanted to do a project that would get us all involved in the site, and which would act as a teaser for the final version. We wanted to do something out of the ordinary and unique, so the idea of an interactive project involving audio and video was quickly born. We chose to create the project using QuickTime as opposed to other video technologies like Real or Windows Media, because it's the only video technology that has a truly interactive architecture.

The Paraphonic.com project involves:

- Andreas Pihlstrom (andreas@paraphonic.com), Stockholm, Sweden: Music and Flash.

- Linus Wahlstedt (linus@paraphonic.com), Stockholm, Sweden: Music, Illustration.

- Jonathan Puckey (jonathan@capcave.com), Amsterdam, The Netherlands: Video, Interactive QuickTime, and interface design.

Thinking, sketching, and storyboarding

I knew that I wanted to have the user interact with both the video and audio. As the site was going to mainly hinge on music, sound interaction was the most important factor in the equation. Due to technical limitations, the video would always be a visualization of the audio, not the other way round. If we had several soundtracks, all layered on top of each other, and they all had variations in sound, we could have the user direct and play around with the sound. After a lot of brainstorming, I wrote down roughly what I envisioned with the project:

- The first project on Paraphonic.com will involve user interaction with a layered piece of music.

- By moving the mouse over a target area the audience will be able to direct the sound.

    - The sound will first fade from the first track to the second

    - The second soundtrack will fade to the third

    - The third soundtrack will fade to the fourth

- By interacting with the sound, an accompanying video loop will be played. When changing from track to track the video will transition from one loop to another.

Next I made some sketches to visualize the kind of navigation I was thinking of, and made some images depicting the story line of the project, which I could send to the guys in Sweden who were going to be doing the audio.

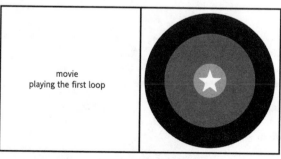

movie
playing the first loop

(star = mouse pointer)

The mouse starts in the center, and the video starts looping the first bit. In this zone the user mixes the first and second soundtracks.

As the mouse moves to the second zone the user is mixing the second and third soundtracks. The video stops playing the first loop, plays on past the transition, and when it reaches the second loop, it starts looping the second loop.

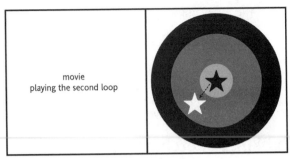

movie
playing the second loop

(star = mouse pointer)

I sent off the story line to the musicians, and they were very excited about the project. They had the idea of using each of the tracks that were going to be mixed, to illustrate a part of a song. So track one would be the intro, track two would be the main part, track three would be the crescendo, and track 4 would be the outro.

To prepare myself for the detailed process of scripting the project, I made a temporary design and used it to make a kind of flowchart. The following images represent the various stages of the project and the text explains what should be happening:

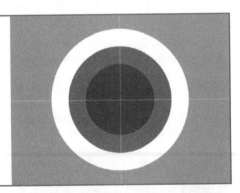

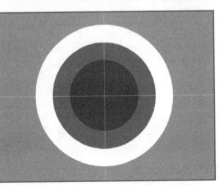

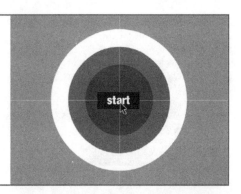

VIDEO

to make sure that the mouse is over the target when the sound starts playing have a 'start' button in the center of the target.

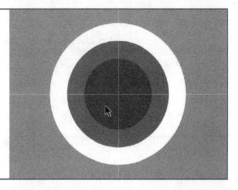

VIDEO

video playing first loop of video
sound track 1 = half volume
sound track 2 = half volume
because mouse is in between the center and the outside of the first circle

VIDEO

when the mouse is outside of the target a graphic pops up telling the user that to mix the sound the mouse needs to be inside the target area

I also drew the following technical sketch that I could look back on if I got confused during the process of scripting the interactions:

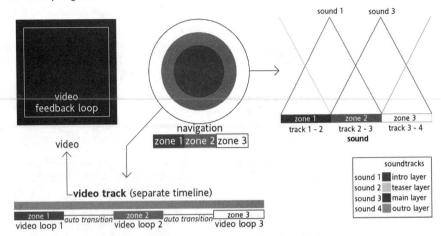

Testing the interactions

I used the design that I had used for the flowchart to start testing and preparing the complex scripting parts of the project. First of all I made a note of all the values (in pixels) in my design that would be needed in the scripting stage.

Center point of target	X = 160, y = 120
Size of first circle	50
Size of second circle	75
Size of third circle	100
Size zone one	Size of first circle > 50
Size zone two	Size of second circle – size of first circle = 25
Size zone three	Size of third circle – size of second circle = 25

I created the temporary interface in Macromedia Fireworks and exported it as a .gif image file. For the sound files, I used a couple of (totally legal) MP3s that I had lying around on my hard disk and cut them down to be the same length.

Scripting with LiveStage Pro

Now, let me explain how I did the scripting. We're not going to discuss all of the code, because some of it's used more then once with different values. Basically the scripting converts the position of the user's cursor on the navigation to the volume of the different audio tracks, and plays an accompanying video loop.

We're going to:

- Make a new project in LiveStage Professional

- Add the tracks into the timeline

- Create the sprite track (which handles the interactivity) and add the navigation images into it

- Script the sprites in the sprite track, to get the navigation working.

For all the scripting parts of the project, I used LiveStage Pro from the guys at TotallyHip. LiveStage is basically the Macromedia Director of interactive QuickTime.

1. First of all, we'll create a LiveStage project, and save it in the folder where we want the project and content to reside.

    LiveStage will create a folder called `library` in that folder, and this is the place that we'll need to keep all the files that will be used in the project. Now that we've put the files into the `library` folder, we'll first drag the four sound files onto the LiveStage timeline (the green lines).

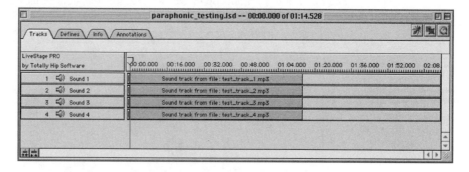

2. Next we're going to insert a sprite track. This is where all the interaction scripting will be done. In the menu go to Tracks > Create > Sprite.

3. By double-clicking on Untitled Sprite in the timeline, we get the following menu that allows us to change its duration to be the same as that of the soundtracks:

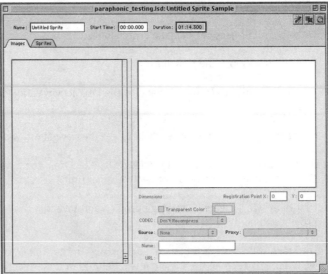

4. While we have this window open, we can drag the image files that we'll be using in the navigation to the Images tab:

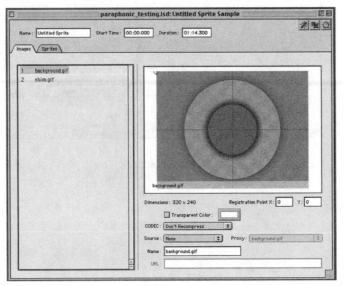

5. We can then click on the Sprites tab to create the sprites that will hold the interactivity and the images. Click on New Sprite, rename it, and select the image it will hold.

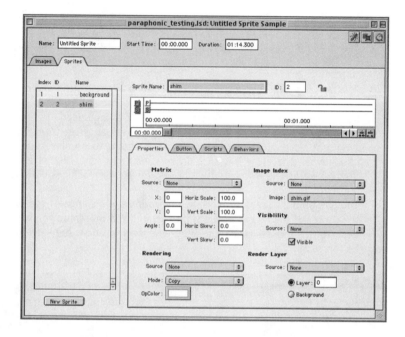

We need to make two sprites, one that will hold the background of our navigation, the target, and the other (that we'll be using for most of the interaction scripting) which I call a "shim", basically nothing more then a 1x1 pixel graphic. Imaginatively we'll call these sprites background and shim respectively.

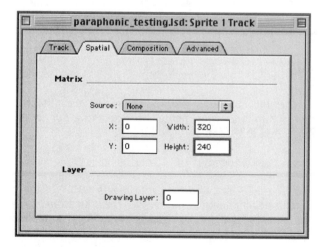

As the sprite track needs to be the same size as our navigation, we need to change its dimensions. In the LiveStage timeline, double-click on the name of the sprite track, and a window with track settings will appear:

Click on the Spatial tab, and change the dimensions.

Now that all the mundane tasks are complete, we can get to the fun part, which is scripting the interactions.

1. Double-click on Untitled Sprite in the timeline. Choose the Sprites tab in the Sprite Buttons Sample window.

2. Select the shim in the Sprites list. Then click on the Scripts tab and make sure it's active, and you'ill see a number of handlers for the sprite. A handler is essentially a trigger that causes a wired movie to execute a script. So for example, when you put some script in the "Mouse Click" handler, it will be executed when the sprite is clicked on.

   For the navigation, we're going to be scripting in the "Idle" handler. The "Idle" handler executes code over and over again, when no other handler is being executed. The frequency of this event is affected by the value you specify in the sprite track's idle-frequency setting. We're going to keep the frequency set to execute the code every $1/60^{th}$ of a second. All the code that we're going to be discussing next will be in the idle handler. Therefore it will ideally be executed every $1/60^{th}$ of a second (however, in the real world, the frequency will be less on slower machines that can't keep up).

   The navigation is going to work by measuring the distance of the mouse pointer from the center of the target. As we want the audio to mix smoothly, we need to build in a delay for the mouse navigation. Otherwise the transitions between the sound tracks will be too rough.

   > *By using the 1 pixel image file sprite to follow the mouse with a delay, the audio fading will be a lot smoother. Even if the user is moving the mouse around the navigation at top speed.*

3. Having the shim sprite follow the mouse with a slight delay is easily done. First we measure the distance between it and the mouse pointer and divide it by a number (here I used 10). Enter this code into the "Idle" handler:

   ```
   speedx = (mousehorizontal - boundsleft)/10
   speedy = (mousevertical - boundstop)/10
   ```

4. Remember that the higher the number is that you're dividing the distance by, the slower the sprite will move towards your mouse. Now we move our sprite by the amount calculated above. Add this script:

   ```
   thissprite.moveby(speedx,speedy)
   ```

   Therefore, every time this code is executed the sprite moves $1/10^{th}$ of the distance between it and the mouse pointer towards the mouse. The sounds are going to be mixed by measuring the distance from the shim (which is following the mouse pointer) to the center of the target.

5. `boundsleft` and `boundstop` are the x and y positions of the sprite, and `160` and `120` are the x and y positions of the center of the target. This makes the code to add:

```
height = 120 - spritenamed("shim").boundstop
width = 160 - spritenamed("shim").boundsleft
```

We first calculate the vertical and horizontal distances from the sprite to the center of the target, and then once we have the vertical and horizontal distances, we use Pythagoras' theorem for right-angled triangles to find out the distance. Meaning that the actual distance is the square root of the sum of squares of the horizontal and vertical distances.

This is shown in the following image. The diagonal line represents the actual distance from the shim to the center of the target, and the gray and black lines represent the horizontal and vertical distances:

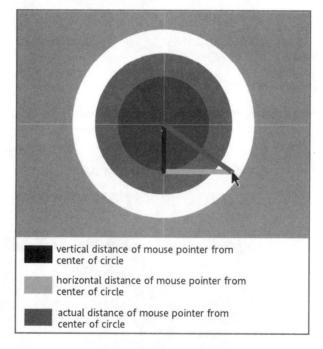

vertical distance of mouse pointer from center of circle

horizontal distance of mouse pointer from center of circle

actual distance of mouse pointer from center of circle

6. In our QuickTime script (abbreviated to QScript) we add:

```
distancefromcenter = sqr((height * height) + (width * width))
```

Using this distance, we can check which zone the sprite following the mouse is in. We need to know this, because we're mixing only two tracks per zone (and will be playing a different video loop in every zone).

If the distance is between 0 and 50 we're in zone 1.

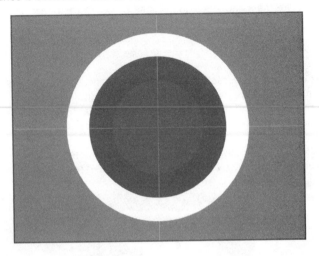

7. So we code:

```
if(distancefromcenter>0 and distancefromcenter<50)
    zone=1
endif
```

If the distance is between 50 and 75 we're in zone 2.

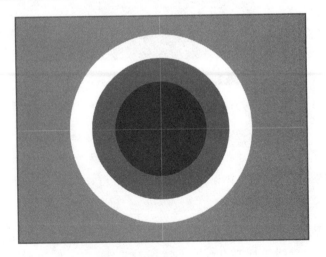

8. So we code:

```
if(distancefromcenter>50 and distancefromcenter<75)
    zone=3
endif
```

If the distance is between 75 and 100 we're in zone 3.

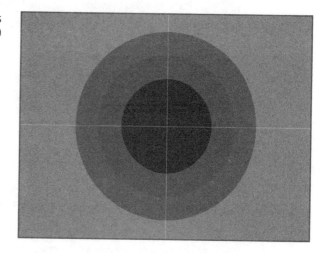

9. And in the script:

```
if(distancefromcenter>75 and distancefromcenter<100)
    zone=3
endif
```

Scripting the audio

Now that we know which zone the sprite's in, we can mix the right audio tracks. Check back to the technical diagram to see how the audio is mixed. When you're in Zone 1, and your mouse is dead center of the target, Soundtrack 1 will have full volume and Soundtrack 2 will be silent. When your mouse is close to the outer edge of Zone 1, Soundtrack 2 will have near full volume, and Soundtrack 1 will be nearly silent.

To change the volumes we need to write the following bit of script:

```
if(zone=1)
    tracknamed("sound 1").setvolumeto(255 - ((distancefromcenter -
➡0)/50 * 255))
    tracknamed("sound 2").setvolumeto((distancefromcenter - 0)/50 *
➡255)
    tracknamed("sound 3").setvolumeto(0)
    tracknamed("sound 4").setvolumeto(0)
endif
```

continues overleaf

```
if(zone=2)
    tracknamed("sound 2").setvolumeto(255 - ((distancefromcenter -
➥50)/25*256))
    tracknamed("sound 3").setvolumeto((distancefromcenter - 50)/25*
➥255)
    tracknamed("sound 1").setvolumeto(0)
    tracknamed("sound 4").setvolumeto(0)
endif
```

```
if(zone=3)
    tracknamed("sound 3").setvolumeto(255 - ((distancefromcenter -
➥75)/25*256))
    tracknamed("sound 4").setvolumeto((distancefromcenter - 75)/25
➥* 255)
    tracknamed("sound 1").setvolumeto(0)
    tracknamed("sound 2").setvolumeto(0)
endif
```

In every zone the formula has some different values, so I'll use the formula from zone 3 to explain. For the track that has to be near full volume when the mouse is near the lower border of one of the zones, we use the following formula:

```
tracknamed("sound 4").setvolumeto(((distancefromcenter -
➥75)/25*255))
```

To change the volume of the track named Sound 4, we first need to get a value between 0 and 1 based on the position of the shim sprite within the zone that it's in, and then multiply it by the maximum volume amount allowed in QuickTime, which is 255.

So if the sprite is in zone 3, first we subtract 75 from the mouse pointer distance, which gives us the position of the mouse pointer in zone 3 as 12.5. Second, we simply divide the distance of the mouse within zone 3 by the size of zone 3, which is 25. 12.5 divided by 25 gives 0.5 or half, which means the mouse pointer is in the center of zone 3.

We can then simply multiply this proportional distance of the sprite within the zone by 255 to get the correct volume.

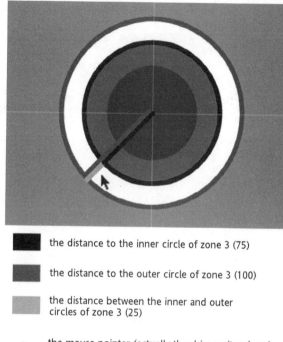

the distance to the inner circle of zone 3 (75)

the distance to the outer circle of zone 3 (100)

the distance between the inner and outer circles of zone 3 (25)

the mouse pointer (actually the shim sprite when it is given time to catch up) is a distance of 87.5 from the center of the target

For the track that has to be full volume when the mouse is at the outer border of one of the zones, we simply reverse the formula by subtracting the formula we just used from 255. This way, it's silent when the other track is full volume and vice versa.

Hurray! We have the track volumes mixing from zone to zone! Now let's get the video working.

Scripting the video

The video will play on a different timeline to the audio. This is because the audio will be playing normally, while the video will be playing a certain loop according to which zone the mouse is in. To have the video on a different timeline, we're going to play it in a movie track.

1. First we create a movie track by selecting Create Movie from the Tracks menu, and change it's dimensions to fit the video. We also need to change its length to be the same as that of the soundtrack; otherwise it will disappear half way through!

   For example, the following sequence of events will happen when the mouse moves from zone 3 to zone 2:

   - Video stops playing the loop of zone 3

- Video plays backwards to the loop of zone 2

- The video has entered the loop for zone 2

- The video starts looping zone 2

2. We only want to execute points 1 and 2 once, when the mouse has moved over to another zone, so we need to make a little structure that will only execute the code once This is the code that does this:

```
if(zone=1)
    if(thesame!=1)
        executeevent(6001)
    endif
endif

if(zone=2)
    if(thesame!=2)
        executeevent(6002)
    endif
endif

if(zone=3)
    if(thesame!=3)
        executeevent(6003)
    endif
endif
```

In the event that we execute, we change the value of the variable thesame to the number of the zone that the mouse has entered.

So let's say the user changes from zone 1 to 2, it will ignore the first if statement, because we're not in zone 1. Then it goes through and checks if we're in zone 2, which we are. It then checks the value of the thesame variable. If the value is something other than 2, it knows we haven't executed this code yet, and will go on to execute the custom event handler number 6002. In this event, the thesame variable will be given the value 2, making it impossible to execute the code again until the mouse has left the zone and entered it again.

3. It's the executeevent(600x) command, which executes the code that stops the current loop playing, and makes the video run in the right direction to reach the next loop. Let's keep to the example of moving from zone 1 to 2. This is the QScript:

```
globalvars thesame firstlooptime secondlooptime direction

thesame = 2
```

```
firstlooptime = 2360
secondlooptime = 3480

childmovietracknamed("Movie 1").SetLoopingFlags(knoloop)
childmovietracknamed("Movie 1").setplayselection(false)

childmovietracknamed("Movie 1").SetSelection(2360, 3480)

if(thesame=3)
   direction=-1
   else
   direction=1
endif

childmovietracknamed("Movie 1").stopplaying
childmovietracknamed("Movie 1").setrateto(1 * direction)
```

As we only want the video to start looping again when it has reached the right time, we need to define the two loop times, which we'll be checking in the idle handler. The loop times are defined using QuickTime's standard time scale of 600 ticks/second. Therefore, if the loop starts at 4 seconds and 28 frames, the script time will be:

$(4 * 600) + [(28/30) * 600] = 2960$

Next, we set the video to stop looping, stop playing the video selection, and set a new video selection that the movie will start looping when it's reached the right time.

Now we need to check which direction the video has to start playing to get to the right loop. If the last zone the mouse was in is 3, then we'll have to play backwards to get to the loop of zone 2. Otherwise the zone is 1, which means we'll have to play the video forwards to get to zone 2. To set the video in the right direction, we first stop the video. Next we use the value in the variable direction to play the movie in the right direction.

> I know it doesn't sound all too obvious to stop the video from playing and then start it straight away afterwards, but it seems to improve the performance a bit. Just one of those things!

4. Now that we have the video running in the right direction, it's time to go back to the idle handler to check if the video has entered the two looping times, so we can tell the movie to loop the selection:

```
if(childmovietracknamed("Movie 1").movietime>= firstlooptime and
➡  childmovietracknamed("Movie 1").movietime<=secondlooptime)
    if(childmovietracknamed("Movie 1").movieislooping = false)
        childmovietracknamed("Movie 1").stopplaying
        childmovietracknamed("Movie 1").SetPlaySelection(True)
        childmovietracknamed("Movie 1").SetLoopingFlags(kloop)
        childmovietracknamed("Movie 1").startplaying
    endif
endif
```

In the QScript code above, we're checking if the time of the movie is between the first loop time and the second loop time. If it is, we want the video to start looping between the selections that we set earlier on. As we only want to execute this event once, we'll check first to see if the movie has been set to loop yet. If it hasn't yet, we stop the movie, tell it to play only the selection, tell it to loop, and then we start playing it again. Now the video will start looping.

After I did some tests by checking the project from a web server, I saw that every now and again the video seemed to jump out of the loop and go back to the beginning of the movie and then stop playing. We can catch this little bug by checking if the movie has stopped playing, and if it has, then we need to:

- Set the selection to be looped again
- Tell the movie to loop
- Go to the first loop time
- Start playing the video again.

5. The script to handle this is:

```
if(childmovietracknamed("movie 1").movierate = 0)
    childmovietracknamed("Movie 1").SetSelection(firstlooptime,
➡secondlooptime)
    childmovietracknamed("Movie 1").SetPlaySelection(True)
    childmovietracknamed("Movie 1").SetLoopingFlags(kloop)
    childmovietracknamed("Movie 1").gototime(firstlooptime)
    childmovietracknamed("Movie 1").startplaying
endif
```

Keep your mouse inside the target

To put a warning graphic on screen, I first created a warning sprite and gave it an initial placement outside of the screen. If the distance of the mouse from the center of the target was greater then 100, the sprite is moved on screen. When the user moves the mouse back onto the target the sprite is moved off the screen again.

6. This is the script for the "Idle" handler:

```
if(distancefromcenter>100)
    if(warningmoved≠1)
        spritenamed("warning").moveto(65,131)
        warningmoved=1
    endif
    else
    if(warningmoved≠2)
        spritenamed("warning").moveto(800,600)
        warningmoved=2
    endif
endif
```

The following image shows the warning sprite in the center of the target that's appeared as the pointer has moved more than 100 from the center:

Scripting the Flash pre-loader

As all the content has to be downloaded before the user can start interacting with it, I needed to make a pre-loader. I chose to do the pre-loader in Flash, so that I could add some animation to it while the content would be loading. Basically the Flash pre-loader doesn't do anything but show a variable in a text field that's sent to it from an idle event in the sprite track. I put the text field and the loading animations in the first frame of the Flash file. In the second frame, I made a button that the user would have to click on to start using the project. The following is a screenshot of what the pre-loader looks like:

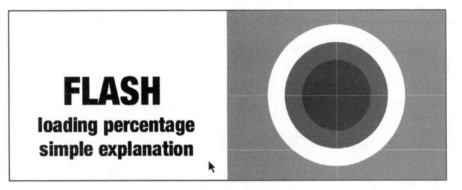

Frame one of the flash file

First of all, I made the loading animations. I used movie-clips for the animations, which gave them a separate timeline from the root timeline of the Flash movie. This way, QuickTime wouldn't have to be playing, for the Flash animations to play, because the movie-clips are on a different timeline.

To display the loading percentage, I created a text field, and turned it in to a variable field. Then, I entered percent in the variable field.

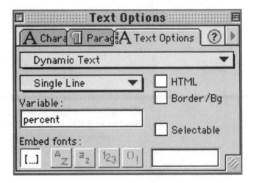

This makes it display the value of the variable called percent, which is sent to it from the sprite track in QuickTime.

Frame two of the Flash file

In the second frame of the Flash file, I made a button that said click here to enter and made keyframes in the "up", "over", "down", and "hit" handlers. Using LiveStage I added some scripting which is executed when the user clicks on the button, but let's leave that for a moment.

After having exported the flash file, I dragged it onto the LiveStage timeline. I offset all the soundtracks by one second, which is the time that we would be jumping to when the content had loaded. As I'd offset the soundtracks by one second, I made the other tracks one second longer. I didn't offset the movie track, because I wanted it to pre-load while the sound tracks were pre-loading.

To send the percentage value to the Flash track, I used the background sprite of the navigation. This saved me from having to make an extra sprite, just for this purpose. In the idle handler of the background sprite I entered the following code:

```
localvars percentage donethisalready
if(donethisalready≠1)
    if((MaxLoadedTimeInMovie / 45600)<1)
        percentage = (MaxLoadedTimeInMovie / 45600)/1.23 * 100
➡tracknamed("Flash  1").SetFlashVariable("","percent",percentage,
➡false)
        else
        percentage = ((MaxLoadedTimeInMovie / 45600)+
➡(childmovietracknamed("Movie 1").MaxLoadedTimeInMovie / 5120))/2 *
➡100
        tracknamed("Flash 1").SetFlashVariable("","percent",percentage,
➡false)
        if(percentage=100)
            gototime(20)
            donethisalready=1
        endif
    endif
endif
```

This code checks both the time that has loaded in the root movie, and the time that has loaded in the movie track (which is a separate timeline). When they've both loaded, we go to the second frame of the movie, and therefore display the second frame of the Flash track (the click here to enter button).

Let me simplify the code, to make it easier to understand:

```
percentage = (MaxLoadedTimeInMovie / 45600) * 100
```

`MaxLoadedTimeInMovie` is a property that returns the amount that the movie has loaded in 600 time units per second. By dividing `MaxLoadedTimeInMovie` by the length of the movie and multiplying it by 100, you get the percentage that the QuickTime movie has loaded.

```
tracknamed("Flash  1").SetFlashVariable("","percent",percentage,
➥false)
```

This sets the variable `percent` in the flash track to the percentage that the movie has loaded. This variable is then picked up by the text field, which I created earlier.

```
if(percentage=100)
gototime(20)
endif
```

When the movie has fully loaded, and the variable `percentage` has a value of `100`, the movie goes to the second frame. I used the value `20` to go to the second frame because we're talking in QuickTime ticks (30 frames in a second, 600 ticks in a second). Therefore, 600/30 = 20 ticks for one frame.

The script has now sent the QuickTime movie to the second frame, and the click here to enter button is displayed. To make the movie go to the time that we offset the other tracks to earlier, we simple double-click the flash track in the time line and enter gototime(600) in the Mouse Press handler of the flash button:

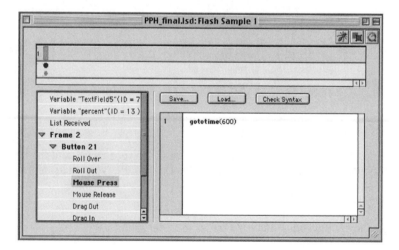

Before the video and audio started playing, I wanted to get the audience's cursor in the navigational area, as I sketched out in the flowchart:

I created the start sprite and had it execute the following code when clicked on, this is another of LiveStage's handlers:

```
globalvars start
MoveTo(800, 600)
setselection(600,45363)
SetPlaySelection(True)
setloopingflags(kLoop)
startplaying
start=true
```

At the end of the code you see that I changed the value of the variable called start to True. Basically I added an "if/endif" exception to the shim sprite, which would only start executing the code when the start variable is set to True.

Finalizing the design and finishing the scripting

So I'd finished testing my ideas, and was sure that the performance of the final project would be acceptable. I sent the test movie I had made over to the musicians, and they too were happy with the performance and feel of the project. While they worked on the audio tracks, I did the video in After Effects and then started work on the final design.

After playing around with the design for a bit, I saw how much the target area looked like a record and how the Flash/video area could be made to resemble a record cover. Also, I changed my ideas on giving feedback for the different soundtrack volumes. Instead of using text tracks to tell the user the percentage, I decided to make four colored bars in the top of the player. I thought they would perpetuate the playfulness of the project and also look rather nice as a design element. To create this design I decided to give the project a custom shape using QuickTime's skin track.

Making the QuickTime media skin

A QuickTime media skin consists of two black and white image files:

1. The skin-shape image, which uses pure black to define the visible part of the skin and pure white to describe the invisible part of the skin:

2. The drag area image, which uses black to define the draggable areas and white to define the non-draggable areas:

To create the skin in LiveStage, we create the skin track and adjust its duration to be the same as the other tracks in the project. Next we drag the two black and white image files into the corresponding Window Shape: and Drag Area: boxes as shown in the following screenshot:

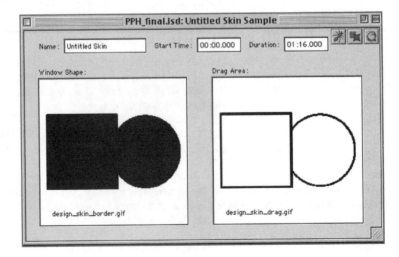

3. Don't forget to change the size of the sprite track; it must fit the project exactly.

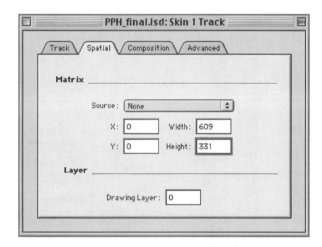

I also decided to add a close-window button (in the top right hand corner of the square section) to the design, as when using a skin you lose QuickTime's standard button to close the window.

The following image shows the completed skin with the graphics applied:

The grand unveiling

After all this, it's time to show you it working. The following screenshots are all taken from the project, but rather than just looking at screenshots, why don't you go to www.paraphonic.com and actually interact with the project yourself!

This following screenshot shows the current Paraphonic.com front page:

Clicking Enter opens QuickTime and displays the loading graphic in the square section, along with the loading percentage we mentioned earlier:

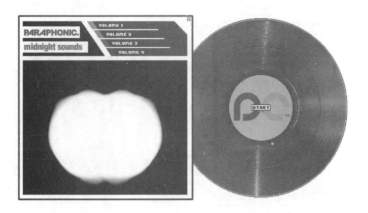

When it's finished loading, you are invited to click START.

The mouse starts off in zone 1, the video is playing the first loop, and soundtracks one and two are being mixed.

Now the mouse is in zone 2, the video is playing the second loop and soundtracks two and three are being mixed.

The mouse is now in zone 3, the video is playing the third loop, and soundtracks three and four are being mixed.

Finally, if you move the off the record, then you get this warning:

I hope you enjoy the experience of this project. It was a lot of fun to do, and hopefully a lot of fun for you to read about - and useful too of course! Feel free to drop by at www.quicktimers.com to see my future projects.

Summary

Developing interactive media for QuickTime has much in common with developing for any other platform. You need to plan, plan, then test, and test again. Whatever you design and whichever tools you decide are best to use in your project, keep in mind that it's the end result that matters.

The tools that you use to create your interactive QuickTime experience are important though, and the next chapter will help you to decide which.

10 Tools

One of QuickTime's most powerful features isn't really a feature at all – rather, it's a product of its intelligent design. QuickTime was designed as more than just a way to watch pretty pictures on your computer and share them with your friends. The QuickTime engineers envisioned a system-level component that would allow a myriad of different programs to use the same data, as part of a single, smooth workflow. In short: QuickTime is a broad, interoperable file format.

This means that we're not stuck using just one or two tools; the media project we're assembling can freely be moved from one tool to another, as the situation warrants. Since there's no need to make just one tool that solves every problem, developers are free to write tools that do a few things really, really well. And there are a lot of tools! I picked a handful of them for this chapter, and I'll give you a quick tour of them, including how to use them with QuickTime.

QuickTime has created an ecosystem of programs that wouldn't even exist without it. They range from huge programs costing thousands of dollars to small, indispensable utilities that can be downloaded for free. By the end of this chapter, you'll know what some of these tools do, and a little bit about how they do it. Along the way, I'll create a couple of projects to show how some sample workflows might go.

I'll say again: this isn't in any way an exhaustive list. If I were to write about every QuickTime aware application, this chapter would be even bigger than the book is. If there's something you need to do in QuickTime that can't be done with some combination of the tools in this chapter, then there are lots of really great online resources that will be able to help you. The following URLs are just a few, you'll find plenty more dotted around the book plus a whole list in Appendix A:

- www.blueabuse.com/

- www.apple.com/quicktime/

- www.judyandrobert.com/quicktime/

- http://lists.apple.com/mailman/listinfo/quicktime-talk

Linear Media

Let's start with the obvious ones, video editing tools. Enter Apple Final Cut Pro, Adobe Premiere, and Apple iMovie. QuickTime is hard at work in these programs, capturing and displaying video, adding SMPTE effects (sometimes in real time), compressing video, and saving it for use in other programs.

Final Cut Pro

Final Cut Pro is the new kid on the video editing block, and it's gaining a lot of respect very quickly. It was designed to work in the same way that traditional editing suites work, so people who are used to using dedicated editing systems will feel at home using Final Cut. With the new version, version 3, it includes Apple's ColorSync technology to maintain accurate color from the camera to the consumer. It can also render effects (like the color correction and several SMPTE effects) in real time, and is the first desktop video editing program that can do this completely in software. Previously, in order to do real time effects you would need some kind of hardware processor – either a card in your desktop computer, or a specialized system. Having this functionality in software allows work to be done on a laptop in the field, for example. It also really annoys the hardware manufacturers!

Of course, all of Final Cut's muscle is thanks to its QuickTime underpinnings. The new OfflineRT format in Final Cut Pro 3 is essentially QuickTime's motion JPEG codec at work, allowing the storage of about 40 minutes of footage in 1GB of hard drive space. Final Cut can import and export everything that QuickTime can understand, and provides some good presets for media delivery once you're done with it in Final Cut. If you're serious about compression, it would be better to pick up Discreet's Cleaner 5, which is a great help when you're looking to do some commercial-grade compression of QuickTime (or any other) media.

Premiere

Adobe Premiere is the grand old dame of video editing. It's been around since the days when a 1GB drive was considered enormous. Since DV wasn't around when Premiere was released, it's always been able to capture video from pretty much anything. Professional-level or consumer capture board, it doesn't care. Also, Premiere runs on both MacOS and Windows, unlike iMovie and Final Cut Pro, which both run exclusively on Macintosh.

Premiere, having been around awhile, is also a more mature program. As is typical with Adobe applications, Premiere features excellent integration with other Adobe tools, and makes use of Adobe's increasingly standardized cross-application user interface.

The theory here is that if you already know Photoshop or Illustrator, you'll pick up Premiere more quickly. You can see the familiar Navigator, Info, and History palettes here. They work the same way as they do in other Adobe applications, which is a great feature, if your workflow already includes Adobe tools.

In addition, its ability to import and export just about anything is very powerful.

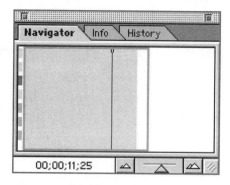

Since Premiere can import a different variety of file types to QuickTime, it can be a very handy way to translate an Autodesk animation to a QuickTime file, for example. Simply import the file to Premiere, and then export as a QuickTime movie.

✓ **All Readable Documents**

Previous Drive
Next Drive

AVI Movie
Adobe Illustrator Art
Audio CD Track
Audio Interchange
AutoDesk Animation
Bitmap
CompuServe GIF
DV
Encapsulated PostScript
Film Strip
JPEG file
MP3 Audio
PICT file
Photoshop File
Premiere Bin
Premiere Storyboard
Premiere Title
QuickTime Movie
Sound Designer II
Sound Edit
Sound Edit Pro
Tiff File
Truevision Targa file
Windows Waveform

The QuickTime export feature of Premiere is excellent, giving you a lot of options, presets, and (potentially) confusion.

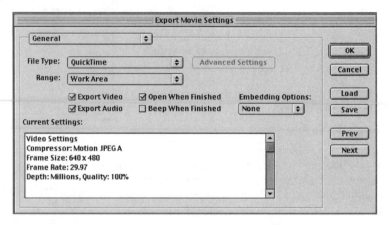

To make this easier, Premiere comes bundled with Cleaner EZ, a dramatically scaled down version of Discreet's video compression tool. It works fine, but for the best results export your video with very little compression, and do any serious compression work in Discreet's full professional version of Cleaner. A good lossless export codec to use for this is PNG. "But it's for still images!" I hear you saying. While it's true that PNG is most famous for compressing still images for delivery over the Web, it's also a relatively quick and small lossless video codec as well.

iMovie

For the sake of new users (its intended audience) iMovie is a bit elitist. It really only knows how to deal with DV formatted streams. Other than that, it's pretty much a very simple version of Final Cut Pro. Don't scoff though – it provides very high-quality output to DV tape, and lots of easy-to-understand file export options.

In fact, if you don't understand (or don't want to understand) Cleaner, or some of Final Cut's more advanced options, you can use iMovie's presets with media from another application. So, do all your editing in Final Cut Pro or Premiere, export as DV, and compress it for the Web using iMovie! That's QuickTime's interoperability at work.

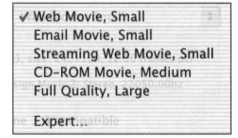

There's nothing better for quick and dirty editing, or to simply capture a DV stream to work on in another application – an older version of Premiere, for example, that doesn't capture very well from DV. Another big plus for iMovie is that it's free, and you probably already have it: it comes with every Mac sold, and is available on Apple's website (www.apple.com/imovie/).

Remember a few paragraphs ago, when I said that iMovie only knows how to deal with DV? There is a way to fool it into importing just about any QuickTime-compatible media. Unless it's extremely high quality media to begin with, it won't look as good as "real" DV format media, but if you're stuck, here's how to get it going. All you need is QuickTime Player Pro:

1. Open the offending, non-DV, non iMovie-happy bit of media in QuickTime Player Pro.

2. Select File > Export.

3. In the Save exported file as... dialog box, choose the Movie to DV Stream option from the Export: drop-down menu, and save the file with a .dv extension. This might take a while, depending on the length of your media.

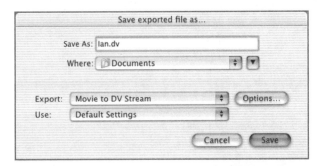

4. Go back to iMovie and select File > Import File and, just like magic, your media will show up.

5. Your file will import, and iMovie will be able to use it like any other DV stream.

Also, Apple has provided a free tool called HackTV that accomplishes much the same thing. You can download it from http://developer.apple.com/quicktime/quicktimeintro/tools/index.html.

QuickTime Player Pro and AppleScript

On the topic of getting the most out of cheap tools, I want to talk a little about the amazing things that can be done with QuickTime Player Pro and AppleScript. QuickTime Player Pro is an incredible steal at $29.99 from the Apple website (www.apple.com/quicktime/). AppleScript, and the tools I'm going to show you are all free, and can't get much cheaper than free. Go to the AppleScript and QuickTime website at www.apple.com/applescript/qtas.html (http://www.apple.com/applescript/scripts/scripts.00.html for OS 9 scripts) and download everything you see there. I'm going to show you a couple in particular in OS X, but they're all incredible.

By way of introduction, AppleScript is one of the Mac OS's hidden jewels. Much of what you see and do on the Mac can be automated using AppleScript and, as you'll see, much of what you can't see can also be automated. Generally, scripts fall into two categories: free-standing scripts, called Applets that operate like little programs, complete with icons; and embedded scripts that show up in an existing application's script menu.

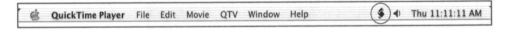

I'm going to show you one of each. The best thing about these scripts from Apple is that you can open them up, and see how the programmer wrote the script, then learn from that code and use it in your own scripts! If you're at all interested in making your life easier with scripting, pick up one of the many AppleScript books available today.

I'm not going to cover the installation procedure here, since it's all covered in the ReadMe file that comes with the script collection, and it may change over time. Please read the ReadMe file carefully for complete installation instructions. Once the QuickTime scripts are installed, you'll see a new item under the Script menu called QuickTime Player Scripts (you may have to log out and log back in for this to appear). Take a look through some of these yourself – there are some very powerful QuickTime features exposed through AppleScript. Without AppleScript, in order to access some of these features, you'd have to buy a full-featured authoring program like GoLive or LiveStage (we'll talk about those later on in the chapter).

As a quick and impressive thing to show off, let's add some chapters to a movie. Previously, it involved text files, timecode, and some really goofy syntax. Now, all it takes is a few menu commands.

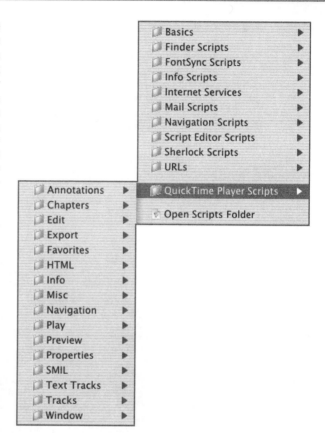

Adding chapters to a movie via AppleScript

1. Open some video in QuickTime Player Pro. It was a beautiful sunny day outside, so I pointed my camera out of my apartment window and took some shots of downtown Vancouver. I'm going to make chapter stops when different buildings are in the frame.

2. Create a new chapter track (click the "script" button on the toolbar followed by: QuickTime Player Scripts > Chapters > Create Chapter Track). It will ask you which track the chapter will describe. This is more important with interactive movies that have multiple tracks in them. For now, just pick the Video Track.

3. Using the time slider, go to a frame where you'd like to start a new chapter. Add a new chapter (Script > QuickTime Player Scripts > Chapters > Add Chapter at Current Time) and give it a name when prompted.

4. Note the new popup menu (BC Place) in the previous screenshot. Selecting items from that menu will send the viewer to different parts of the movie – much like bookmarks. You've got a couple of chapters now! Repeat as often as you like. Don't forget to save your movie.

> *The OS X script should work under 9 as well (even though Apple says it won't).*

AppleScript and media skins

Let's take a look at media skins. There's nothing that says a QuickTime movie, when played in the player, has to look like QuickTime Player. You don't have to have all those buttons, drawers, and other user interface gadgets that you normally see in QuickTime player. Normally, making a media skin involves many steps of cutting, pasting, creating tracks, etc. In QuickTime player this is no more, it can all be done with one simple AppleScript.

Inside the folder you downloaded from Apple, go to `QT 5.0 Applets-Droplets/ Media Skin Droplets`:

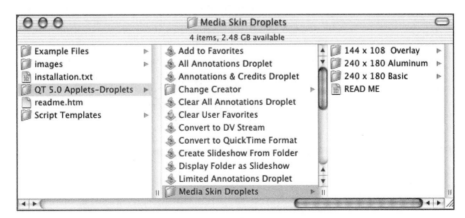

Pick one of the choices and open that folder. Inside that folder, you'll see a "droplet" (which is a special kind of applet) called Apply Media Skin Droplet. Droplets are designed to accept files or folders "dropped" on them. So, help it be true to its nature by taking your movie and dropping it on there. Choose a location to put the results. Sit back, relax, and watch the blinking lights. At the end of it all, you'll get a perfectly skinned movie.

Notice that the movie shown in this screen shot has none of the standard QuickTime interface elements on it.

If you take a look through the folder where the Apply Media Skin Droplet lives, you'll see all the pieces the script used to put it together. The frame is merely a Photoshop file that you can edit if you like. It could be anything you like. In fact, one of the included scripts creates a movie that plays inside of a QuickTime logo "Q". I'll leave that one as an exercise for you.

These scripts serve two purposes. One is to make your life easier (and give me some good demos to show you) and the other is your education. Open these scripts up in Apple's Script Editor and find out what makes them tick. AppleScript is a very simple language to understand; it was designed to look like English. To make your life much easier, you can copy and paste useful chunks into your own scripts.

Special FX

The next group of applications I'm going to talk about are ones that can do bizarre, unusual, and even useful things to your video. Oddly enough, they're also all based around QuickTime. The applications are Discreet combustion and Pinnacle Systems Commotion Pro, and Adobe After Effects. Generally, you can think of them as Photoshop for the moving image.

After Effects

Again, we find Adobe has been around the longest. They purchased After Effects from the original authors, and have somewhat replaced their quirky interface with something more Adobe-like. As a result, some of the familiar Adobe palettes are in attendance, but there are some still missing, so the Adobe experience isn't fully realized, making this program somewhat more difficult to learn. That said, once it's learnt, After Effects is capable of some very impressive effects, like this "shattering glass" video effect.

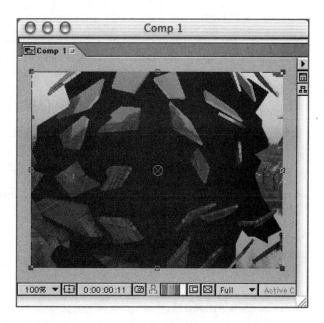

Taking a cue from Photoshop and Premiere, After Effects can read dozens of different file formats in addition to the ones that QuickTime can read natively.

combustion

Compared to After Effects, combustion (yes, it's in lowercase) is fresh and clean. There is no clutter in the interface – in fact, there barely seems to be an interface at all. They've really gone their own way on the interface. Because Discreet had its beginnings in the very high-end of the video editing, compositing, and correcting business, the features of this package are ported down from their video workstation products. This also means that there is good vertical integration. Someone could move their files from combustion on their Mac or Windows machine and be familiar with the tools and interface on the larger dedicated systems.

The combustion package includes real 3D tools, meaning that video can "fly" around a 3D space, complete with shadows cast on other "objects" in the 3D space. Some stunning effects are possible with this feature alone.

All Files
✓ All Acceptable Files
All Footage Files

AE Project
BMP
Cineon
ElectricImage IMAGE
Filmstrip
FLC/FLI
Generic EPS
IFF
JPEG
PCX
Photoshop
PICT
Pixar
PNG
QuickTime Movie
RLA/RPF
SGI
Softimage PIC
Targa
TIFF

Everything it does is non-destructive, meaning that you can always go back to whatever you were doing before, mostly because the requisite parts are still separate. Think of it as a very large and granular "undo" function.

To present this more simply, combustion includes a flowchart feature. In this simple example, the QuickTime movie I was using earlier has been turned and tilted, resulting in a strangely lopsided video.

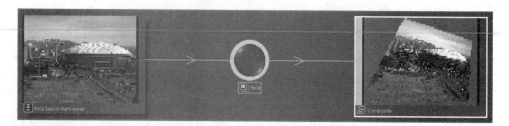

Just like all the other programs here, combustion can output its work to QuickTime, so that any other QuickTime-compatible programs can read the file with no changes.

Commotion Pro

Rounding off our survey of QuickTime's special effects crew is Commotion, by Pinnacle Systems. As the name might suggest, it's a very good rotoscoping tool. Rotoscoping (or roto for those who have been typing far too much lately) is a process where a special effect is added to a moving scene. The movie *Who Framed Roger Rabbit* features very obvious roto: the addition of a goofy animated rabbit to live-action scenes. Roto can also be used to remove things that you don't want to see in a sequence.

I need to emphasize here that roto is an art and a skill – it's still very difficult to do well. Commotion's designers worked hard to make it a very fluid and artistic process though. In fact, the tool palette looks more like Adobe Photoshop's than the palette of Adobe After Effects does.

I'm going to track the motion of a pair of white shorts. Once their motion is tracked, any number of different visual effects can be run on them. In the olden days, each frame had to be individually edited, but no more. I start by creating a new motion tracker from the Motion Trackers window.

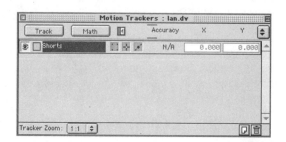

A green double-box appears in the movie, which we then resize to cover the shorts.

Then simply click the Track button (in the Motion Trackers window). The subject of this example provides a particularly good demonstration as the hand-held camera was bouncing all over the place, and the shorts themselves were moving around quite a bit.

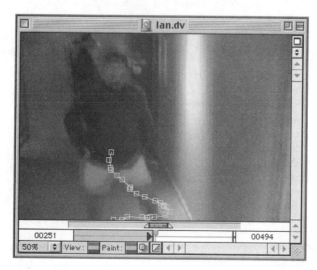

Commotion accurately tracks the motion of the shorts over the short sample time that I selected, and provides the path they followed. If I were so inclined, I could take that path and use it to apply effects like changing the color of the shorts, or adding an animated rabbit, for example.

LiveSlideShow

What does QuickTime have to do with still pictures? LiveSlideShow is a program that will take a collection of any QuickTime-readable images, and make an interactive QuickTime slideshow out of them, complete with fades, wipes, sound effects, and control buttons.

While you could do this with pretty much any of the programs I've talked about so far, LiveSlideShow does this with one very important difference. If you were to put together a slide show in Premiere, for example, you would drag images onto the timeline, and set the length of each to eight seconds or so. When this is saved to QuickTime format, it creates a movie of still images. Picture a film of a plate of whiskey-cured salmon going through a movie projector: 24 times every second, a new and identical picture of whiskey-cured salmon shows up. Why send a bunch of identical pictures, when QuickTime is programmable? We can send one image, tell QuickTime to wait a while (or even do an effect), and then continue on with the next slide (in our case, a tasty mackerel tart).

Being a consumer application, LiveSlideShow is very easy to use. Simply drag the pictures you want to use into the timeline, select some effects, and add captions. Totally Hip Software include some good templates with more to download from their web site at www.liveslideshow.com. You can also create your own if you like. The resulting QuickTime file can be sent to friends and family, or brought into another QuickTime program to do some more work on.

This is one of Totally Hip's pre-made templates, complete with a gently curving skin. The slide show picture and description are set to change every few seconds.

This is Canada Place at sunset.

The next two programs are somewhat different from the ones we've been looking at so far. Instead of saving captured QuickTime movies to disk for use elsewhere, these two QuickTime streaming programs send QuickTime movies through a network to be seen live. It's a tricky business because everything has to happen in real-time: the capture (including digitization, if necessary), the compression, filters, and encapsulation for streaming. Normally, this is a process that can take up to 10x real-time or more.

Sorenson Broadcaster

The first live-broadcasting program to be released for QuickTime was Sorenson Broadcaster. It's a good, basic broadcasting application. The version publicly available from www.sorenson.com (at the time of writing) hasn't been updated in quite a while, and requires the use of QuickTime 4 – it won't work at all with QuickTime 5 or 6 on the Mac, although the Windows version does work with QuickTime 5. Its age is a bit of a blessing though as it works on even the lowest end G3 computers – they were the state of the art when Sorenson Broadcaster was released!

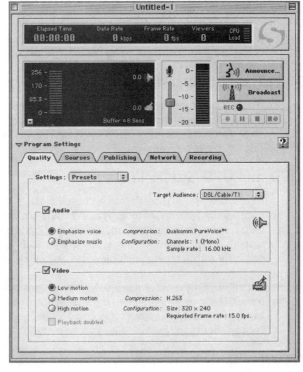

An important thing to know here is that for most operations, Sorenson Broadcaster requires a separate QuickTime Streaming Server running on another computer. Broadcaster handles the acquisition and compression of the audio and video, and then passes the actual distribution to the streaming server. The streaming server is free, however, and since it's open source, it's been ported to several platforms. There are also streaming service providers available that will set you up with an account on their streaming servers. Unless you have your own industrial-grade connection to the Internet, contracting out the distribution of your media is generally the way to go.

Channel Storm Live Channel

Live Channel, a Mac-only broadcaster from Channel Storm Software ends up doing much the same job as Sorenson Broadcaster, except they've thrown in all kinds of bells and whistles – including QuickTime 5 compatibility. Live Channel includes an integrated switcher. This means the operator

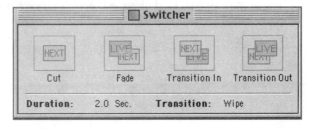

can switch between live video feeds, live audio feeds, and pre-recorded segments (which can include anything that QuickTime natively understands).

Titles and alpha-channeled overlay graphics are also supported, as well as any of the SMPTE transition effects that are built in to QuickTime. All this means that Live Channel is a complete software-based broadcasting studio.

It also includes a built-in streaming server, so you can do everything in one package. All this power comes at a price though: Live Channel is Mac only and requires a very fast G4 in order to work properly.

QuickTime Broadcaster

There is one other broadcasting tool: Apple's QuickTime Broadcaster. Apple has announced that this product will ship simultaneously with QuickTime 6. It runs on OS X only, and is a simple broadcasting application, somewhat like Sorenson Broadcaster. Unfortunately, at the time of writing, it has not yet shipped.

iDVD and DVD Studio Pro

As we draw the first section to a close, I want to quickly mention two other pieces of software, both from Apple. DVD Studio Pro and iDVD are the most full-featured and the simplest desktop DVD creation programs around. DVD Studio Pro is worthy of its own book, so I'll suffice with saying that it's a very powerful, professional-level DVD creation tool. You can make interactive DVDs, complete with scripting, multiple video angles, chapters, and animated menus – everything.

With iDVD, on the other hand, using Apple's pre-built templates, you can build a DVD project and have it ready to go in an afternoon. Using iDVD and iMovie with a digital camcorder, it's possible to make a short DVD from scratch in an afternoon. Next time you're sitting at home on a rainy Sunday afternoon, you could be making a DVD!

QTVR

QuickTime's ability to go beyond audio and video has created some excellent niches where developers are doing some incredible things. Entire web sites have been created within QuickTime VR environments, complete with directional sounds and interactivity. Just because it's called "Virtual Reality" doesn't mean that it has to look real.

Apple QTVR Authoring Studio

I'm going to start by showing you Apple's QTVR Authoring Studio (QTVRAS). It was released back in 1998, as a tool people could use to create panoramas quickly and easily. It hasn't been updated since, and it doesn't allow for the creation of "cubic" VR movies that were introduced with QuickTime 5. There are five different environments within this program:

- **Object Maker**: An environment to make VR object movies. These are basically pictures taken of an object from different angles and presented to the user as a virtual object that can be "picked up" and "rotated".

- **Panorama Stitcher**: This module takes a handful of pictures and "stitches" them together to make one long, thin panorama picture of an environment. Read on for a short demo of this.

- **Panorama Maker**: Takes long thin panorama pictures and turns them into looped panoramas that users can pan through and zoom in and out of.

- **Scene Maker**: If you've got more than one panorama of an area, and want to join them using "hotspots", this is the module you'd use.

- **Project Manager**: Keeps all your files and links organized for you.

Using the QTVRAS

1. Take some photos, I took some pictures in a nearby park, for example.

2. Drag and drop the images into the application in the correct order, and rotate where needed. This kind of thing would be simple if that's where it ended, but in our case, we've got to align these images to make sure that buildings line up properly.

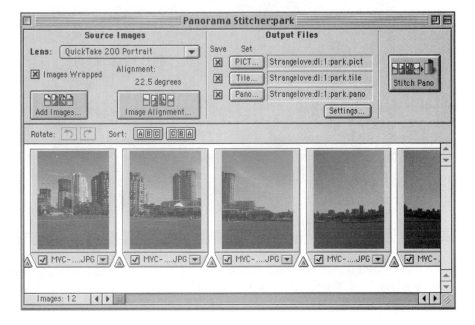

3. Click on the triangle between two of the images to open a new window showing the two images slightly overlapping and transparent.

4. Slide the images around until they match up and repeat for every picture seam. The more steady and even the source pictures are, the easier this part will be.

> *I should also mention that if you're taking the images by hand, it's best to leave a 10% (or more) overlap. This makes it much easier to line the pictures up in a stitching application.*

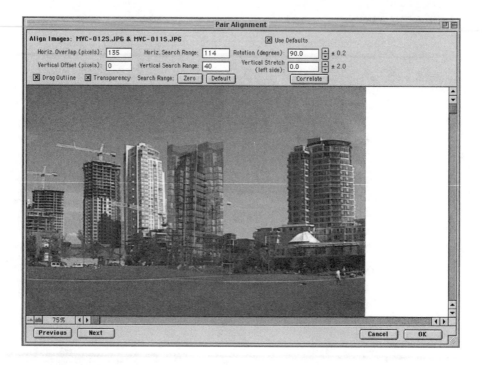

I didn't even use a tripod here (very bad practice!), so as you can see, my buildings don't line up very well at all. Some better equipment is needed, and we'll be taking a look at some later on in this section.

VR Worx

For now, let's move on to another full-featured VR authoring package, VR Worx from VR Toolbox. From when you first open the application, it's obviously a much more mature program than QTVRAS. The tabbed interface walks you through the steps required to make a panorama (and in my case, fix a poorly made panorama). Among the many features is the ability to grab from a live video input source – a FireWire camera, for example. I'm just using the same pictures from earlier.

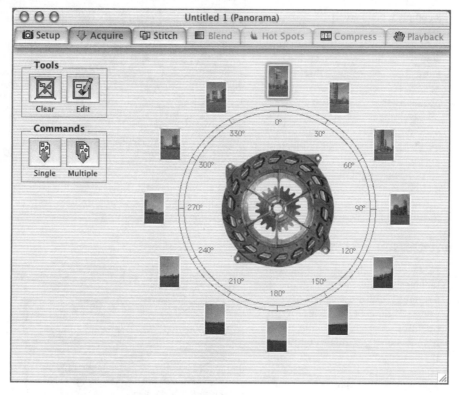

The automatic stitching in VR Worx is quite intelligent, and allows for very detailed manual adjustments after the automatic process. It's easy to simply step through the tabs one at a time, make the necessary adjustments, and end up with a VR movie at the end of it all. Like QTVRAS, VR Worx can create both object and panorama movies, both with the same intelligent and easy to use interface. As a nice bonus, VR Worx can be controlled via AppleScript, so it can be added to the automatic workflow system you're setting up after reading the AppleScript section.

Managing, stitching, and aligning images for 3D panoramas is a serious business, and there's a small handful of programs that do stitching and nothing else. Since they only do one thing, they tend to do it very well, with lots of options to fine-tune the output. I'm going to look at three of them: RealViz Stitcher, Helmut Dersch's PTStitcher, and Autolycus SpinImage DV next.

RealViz Stitcher

RealViz Stitcher is just what it says: a stitching program. It's available online from www.realviz.com. Simply load in all your images, and then using the onionskin overlay technique, line them up, so that they appear to make a complete panorama.

It has some nice tools built-in that would ordinarily be done in Photoshop or some other image editor. For example, one of the problems that could happen when taking images for use in a VR panorama is that the camera might be trying to make some intelligent decisions about what to do with color and light. For ordinary pictures that's fine, as you want each picture to look its best. However, if the pictures need to be stitched together, you don't want them to be different colors and brightness's. Stitcher can equalize the color and light values across your entire panorama, saving you several steps in Photoshop.

Helmut Dersch's PTStitcher

PTStitcher is the most raw and technical of the three programs. It assumes quite a bit of VR understanding on the part of the operator. However, at the same time it exposes a huge number of the options available in a VR scene. For example, the stitching environment happens inside a giant sphere. You can import images into the sphere one at a time, and position them wherever you like against the background grid.

It's also free, and unlike the other applications we've looked at so far in this section, it has split every function into a separate program. Through scripts, this collection of programs gives you complete, granular control over exactly what happens with your VR. Think of these programs as creating web pages in a text editor. You can get exact control, but you've really got to know what you're doing before even looking at them.

Autolycus SpinImage DV

In this chapter full of complex and tricky tools that do lots of different things, Autolycus SpinImage DV is a breath of fresh air. It makes object movies from a DV source, that's it. SpinImage DV gives you the bare minimum of options, so it's not a professional tool. It's the easiest program to use in the entire chapter, with just two little catches. One, you need a DV camera, which is less of a problem now than it once was, as you may already have one. The other catch is that you need a turntable that rotates at 4rpm (or a very steady hand and a good sense of timing). A 4rpm turntable isn't something that the average person would find lying around their house, but if you've got that and a camera, there is no easier way to make a good object movie. (If you don't have that stuff, read on and I'll tell you about some interesting VR hardware.)

Making an object movie using SpinImage DV

1. Position the object (in this case, a licorice candy) and click the Capture button.

2. When the capture is done (see below), render to QuickTime VR.

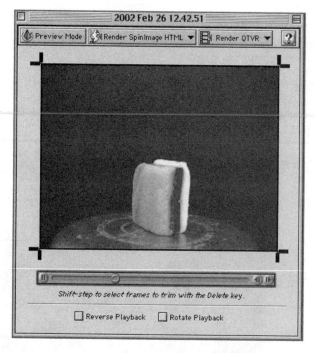

That's it! It can even create a little web page for you if you like.

Adobe Photoshop

This would be a good time to talk about Adobe Photoshop. I've mentioned it in passing throughout the chapter, and I will again before it's over. This fact alone shows how pervasive it's become as a general-purpose visual tool. It's come a long way from its roots as a utility to open, view, and save images in a multitude of formats. Entire companies have been founded and survive on making plug-ins for Photoshop.

Now that I've been through telling you about all kinds of programs that will stitch panoramas together for you, I'm going to take it all back and say that you don't need any of those programs – you can stitch everything together and do your color correction manually in Photoshop. It will take you longer, and the results might not be as good, but it's possible. To make this a bit easier, Panorama Tools also provides a free plug-in for PhotoShop that can map from various projections to other ones (for example, from fisheye to equi-rectangular etc.). It can also smooth the colors in panoramic images and a few other handy tricks. Create your panorama file in Photoshop, export as an uncompressed TIFF or JPEG and use any of the tools we covered to convert it into a panorama movie.

You can also use Photoshop to 'hijack' and touch up a panorama file before it becomes a VR movie. Take the stitched file, open it in Photoshop, and edit to your heart's content. Add people, remove buildings, do some color correction, add your corporate logo – whatever you like. Even better, Photoshop has excellent AppleScript support too, so you can add it to that enormous workflow system you're writing. Again, the Panorama Tools plug-in for PhotoShop can help a great deal here. The panoramic image has a non-Cartesian projection and can't be edited easily by hand. That plug-in can spit out many normal images (shots) out of a panoramic image. This is very helpful as the panoramic image is "curved" because it shows both front and back in one image: it's the inside of a cylinder de-wrapped to a flat surface, somewhat like the distortion that happens when a map of the Earth is shown on a flat piece of paper.

VR Hardware

Before we leave this section, and I get on with a tour of the programs you can use to put it all together, I want to talk about some hardware that will make this whole precision job of VR so much easier. A mistake in the picture-taking phase of assembling a VR movie is difficult to correct once you're stitching it all together. You saw the problems I had with buildings not lining up at the beginning of this section. It's really all about math. The purer and more exact the numbers coming in are, the easier your job will be when it comes time to turn all these images into a single VR experience. Human bodies are notoriously bad at being exact about anything, especially when it comes to holding cameras steady. Machines, on the other hand, especially the ones I'm going to show you, make precision their middle names.

- **Kaidan**: (www.kaidan.com) make all kinds of hardware to make panoramas and object movies easier to create. Everything from rigs that look a bit like deconstructed dentist's chairs to those revolving turntables that would have been really handy a few pages ago, to tripod mounts that swing your camera around a number of predefined "stops", so that you can manually take pictures of a panorama.

- **Panoscan**: (www.panoscan.com) takes that a step further, and makes the camera rotate automatically. Mount one of their cameras on a tripod, push the button, then duck and get out of the way. The camera rotates quickly, and outputs a panorama file. No stitching required, simply bring it into one of the utilities mentioned earlier, and convert this long thin file into a QuickTime VR movie. The main advantage here is resolution. The higher the resolution of your source image, the crisper, and more lifelike your scene will look. The cameras are very high-resolution capture devices (up to 5400 pixels vertical resolution), and since they're automatic, there's little chance of a clumsy human jiggling the tripod, causing problems in the stitching phase later on. As one might imagine, these are the most expensive of the capture solutions.

Not exactly a machine, more of a clever mirrored lens, Kaidan's 360 rig allows digital cameras to take an entire 360 degree panorama in one shot. It looks a bit like a hollow candlestick with a cone-shaped mirror on the end, and it gets attached to the front of the camera. The operator points the camera up, and takes a picture. The resulting image is processed in one of the VR programs we looked at earlier, and is turned into a panorama. The big benefit of this method over the camera-rotation ones is that this method takes just a fraction of a second to complete, making it possible to capture scenes in which there would be motion. The trade-off here is detail. Current cameras don't have high enough resolution to match the Panoscan units – but for situations where resolution isn't that big a deal, this is an excellent solution.

Interactive media

QuickTime is good at audio, video, 3D, virtual reality, and effects, but if you want to see what it does best, put all of these different media types into one file, and add a bit of interactivity. That's where the really cool stuff happens. I'm just going to scratch the surface of five different programs that can be used to bring all of QuickTime's strengths together. Anything you make with those other programs can be put together in one of these programs. In one special case, its output can be embedded within QuickTime.

Macromedia Flash

We'll start with that special case: Macromedia Flash. You can take any Flash animation and embed it in QuickTime. The basic interactivity you design in Flash will work in QuickTime and the end user doesn't even have to have Flash installed. I'm using Flash 4 in this example, since QuickTime 5 understands Flash 4 files. If you've got Flash 5 installed, just make sure you don't use any of the advanced Flash 5 features, save your file as a Flash 4 file, and import it into QuickTime. QuickTime 6, release pending, promises to support Flash 5.

I whipped up a beautiful animation in Flash, consisting of a red square that moves across a white background. I gave it an action of "stop", meaning that if someone were to click on the red square as it passes by, it would stop the movie.

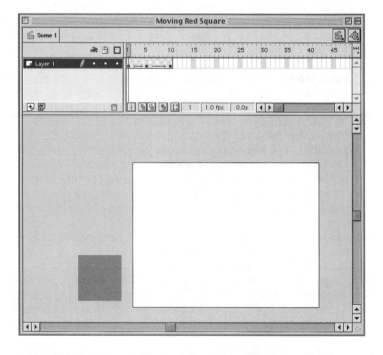

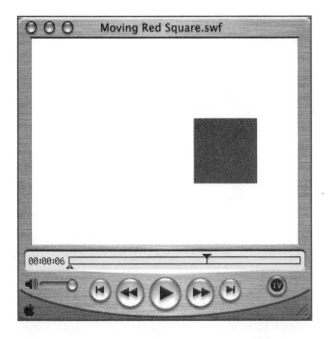

Then, to prove a point, I opened the SWF player file in QuickTime Player on the OS X machine with no Flash installed. It's as beautiful as it was in Flash on the OS 9 machine, and more importantly, when I click on the red square, it stops playing, even in QuickTime Player.

Now comes the fun part. Select the entire Flash movie, open another QuickTime movie and select Edit > Add. This adds the Flash movie as a special Flash track to the QuickTime movie. It also gives us a bit of a problem, since the Flash movie is obscuring the first bit of the QuickTime movie. See the selected area of the timeline, that's where the Flash movie overlaps the video.

This is simple to fix. In the Movie Properties window, we now have a Flash Track listed.

Select the Flash Track, then in the graphics mode popup select straight alpha from the list and voila! The red box now floats ominously over the city, and can stop the video when clicked!

Unless your Flash work is like mine (used to show something for part of the movie only) it's generally a good idea to make the Flash movie as long as the QuickTime movie. You wouldn't want your Flash-made navigation buttons to disappear halfway through your masterpiece!

That was just a simple example of using Flash to control QuickTime. It's quite common to build entire interfaces from Flash. As I said earlier, in the AppleScript section, there's no reason why your movie has to take on the appearance of Apple's QuickTime Player. If you combine a QuickTime movie with an interface built in Flash and a skin you create in Photoshop and assemble with AppleScript, it won't even look like QuickTime anymore!

Macromedia Director

The next program we'll be looking at is Macromedia Director. From the very beginning, it has treated QuickTime media as equal citizens, along with the other objects that Director can work with. Movies can be controlled, moved, animated, and programmed along with everything else in Director.

Here's what a QuickTime movie looks like in Director.

What's more, Director can truly understand the internals of QuickTime, allowing control of positioning and volume, as well as the ability to specify what happens when the user clicks on a certain point in a VR movie.

To make matters even stranger, you can export a Director movie as a QuickTime movie. This probably won't give you the output you're looking for though.

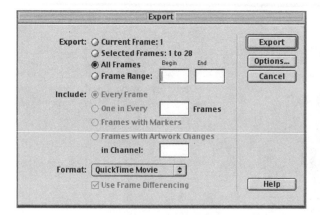

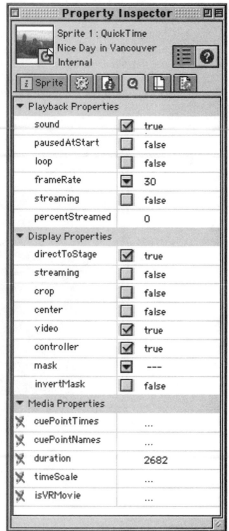

This exporter merely takes an image of each frame in the Director movie and saves it as a frame in a QuickTime movie. All Director's interactivity is lost, and the file generally becomes much larger. This feature is handy though for creating cross-platform slide shows from Director content, as Director players need to be custom-made for each platform they need to run on.

Tribeworks iShell

Tribeworks iShell is quite similar to Director, in that it can create multimedia applications, designed to be portable across operating systems. iShell uses QuickTime for all of its media handling activities. The interface takes a little bit of getting used to, but it's quite logical. Everything in the program is handled by something above it. The object hierarchy explains this nicely:

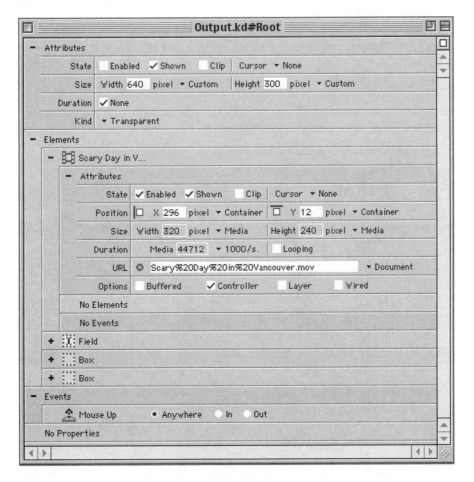

The QuickTime movie is an element, and the element has certain attributes. Using this methodology, it's quite simple to make a basic interactive movie wrapper. Every piece of media (including QuickTime movies) used in iShell has an associated URL. The URL might be local to the user's computer, or (and this is cool) it can be anywhere on the Internet. Using this feature, and a bit of thought, entire interfaces can change, depending on what files get sent from a server. Taking this one step further, different copies of iShell can communicate with each other through the Internet. This kind of functionality is present in Director too, but not nearly as easy to use as iShell.

Adobe GoLive

Adobe GoLive's inclusion in this list of QuickTime programs might seem a little strange to some of you. However, this QuickTime editor has been around for a good many years now, and even comes with a web page editing package! All kidding aside, there's much more to GoLive than just the web page editing part. Since the very beginning, they've included a very respectable QuickTime editor as a module within the program. You can add and edit different kinds of tracks and basic interactivity to movies from within GoLive.

I'll be adding a text track to our QuickTime movie, and embedding it into a web page, all from within GoLive.

Adding text to a movie using GoLive

1. Open a new, blank web page, and drag your movie onto it. Then, to open the movie in the QuickTime editor, just double-click on the movie on the page within GoLive.

2. Using the timeline button on the toolbar, open the Timeline Editor window.

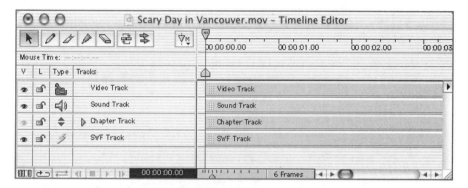

3. Notice that GoLive sees the Flash track (shown above as SWF Track). Drag a text track from the Objects palette into the timeline.

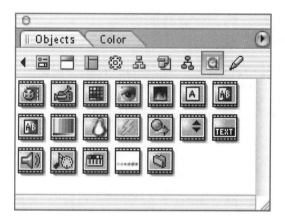

The "samples" area (the right two-thirds of the timeline) shows the duration of each instance of the text track. Simply resizing them and adding more samples can make the text change throughout the movie. We can then continue editing the web page, or take that movie and embed it somewhere else.

Totally Hip LiveStage Pro

I'm ending things with Totally Hip's LiveStage Pro. It's considered the premiere QuickTime interactivity editor. In concept, it's very simple. The programmers at Totally Hip have simply exposed the interactivity that QuickTime already has built into it. They gave it an interface to do what it always could. This software has sparked an explosion in QuickTime creativity. People have built everything from custom players to spreadsheet programs in QuickTime, using LiveStage. All we're going to do is set the town on fire!

LiveStage's Tracks tab should look familiar to you, we've seen something very similar already in GoLive, and it's the same basic idea behind timelines in Premiere, Final Cut, and even iMovie. You'll also recognize the chapter track (Chapter Track) we added with AppleScript, the Flash track (Flash 1) we added in Flash, and the text track (Text Track) from GoLive. To all these tracks, we're going to add an effect track.

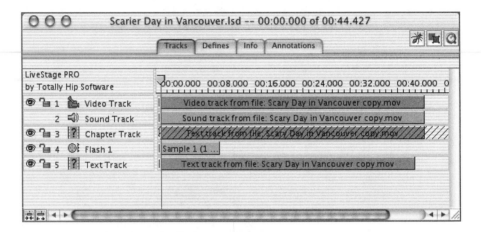

Remember when I said that QuickTime can create effects in real time? We're going to set something on fire, but we'll do it in a very clever way. Rather than doing some fancy video effects in After Effects, for example, we'll simply tell QuickTime to place an effect track showing a mathematical representation of fire. On playback, QuickTime will render the fire from the math in real time.

Setting Vancouver on fire with QuickTime effects

1. Make a new effect track, and position it around the time in the video where we want the fire to appear.

2. Double-click on the effect track to get the sample information dialog. From there, go into the settings area and set the fire parameters.

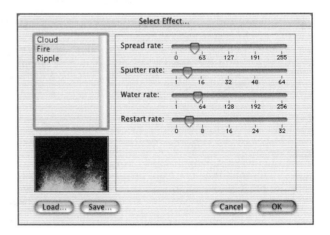

3. Since we've already positioned the effect where in time we want it, we need to put it in the right position on the movie.

Click on the effect in the timeline, and go to Window > Show Stage Window. Move the box around until it's positioned properly.

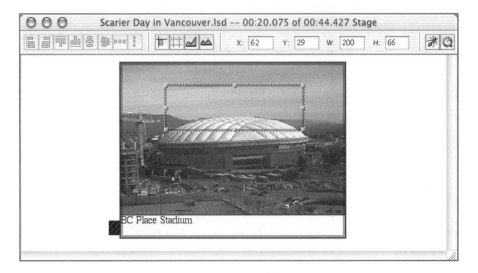

4. The only thing left to do is to export this project as a QuickTime movie (File > Export Wired Movie). Going full circle, we can open it in QuickTime Player, and admire the handiwork.

I should also mention here that there's a great LiveStage tutorial in Chapter 4. If you missed it, stick your finger in this page, and flip back.

Summary

QuickTime media can be as simple as a still JPG, or as complex as an entire web site built as a QVTR movie. It's possible to create astonishing QuickTime movies with free tools and scripts, it's limited only by your ideas. When working on more professional projects though, you may feel it's worth the time and money you need to invest in some of the tools and products we've investigated in this chapter. Many are available as time-limited, but fully featured, trial versions from the web sites listed in this book – so you can decide for yourself just how useful they'll be to you.

Like everything when working with QuickTime, it really is up to you!

11 Authoring DV for Film and DVD

Making movies at the dawn of the Third Millennium has been made a lot easier with the help of technology. After more then a century of a movie-making monopoly, everybody can become a filmmaker. Please note that we said become a filmmaker and not be a filmmaker. Only the tools have changed, you still need to have the gift for making films.

By looking at today's trends in filmmaking, we can conclude that filmmakers have embraced the idea of "going digital". This began more then 10 years ago, when non-linear editing systems began to show-up on the market at some astronomic prices. A few years later and an NLE (non-linear editing) system can be purchased at a fraction of the cost, which is many times better and faster.

Besides editing, there are other processes involved in filmmaking; acquisition and distribution. We can shoot our footage on 16mm, or Super16, 35mm, or even 70mm film and distribute on film. Or, we can shoot with a digital video camera and distribute on film. It is less expensive and gives almost the same "look". How close can we get to that look of a film if we shoot on digital? We shall try to answer this question and find out more on this subject in this chapter.

Capture

The process of video capture includes several sub-processes that we'll look into here. The first one is the process of digitizing the analog signal into a digital one. After doing this, the video and audio signals will be in the digital world. If the video and audio signals were already digital (shot on a digital format camera and transferred via a digital interface onto the computer), this part of the capture process can be skipped.

The information after digitizing will be too large to be handled by a mid-level computer. Because *all* the information in every frame is redundant, some of this redundancy could be eliminated via compression. Why would somebody need to discard the redundant information contained in the digital signal? One, because it occupies a lot of space and two, because the speed of the data stored on hard disk is tremendous (a lot of information per second means more data to be streamed). There are computers capable of sustaining huge data-streams and capable of storing a large amount of data, but the prices of those super-computers are beyond imagining. So, compression is a good option. For more information on bitstream and compression, please see the MPEG-2 coding section.

This is the second step of the capture, **encoding**. Along with the elimination of the redundant information, an algorithm may discard important or useful information, not in all cases though. The process of encoding may be lossless or can generate some degradation of the picture quality. These mathematic algorithms have the generic name of **codecs**, the big difference between the codecs is: some are hardware-codecs, software algorithms inside micro-chips residing on the video-capture device, and others are software-codecs, in which case the software algorithms reside in a computer program, that uses the computer's own processor. Nowadays, all hardware codecs are real time, which means the process of capture of one second of video and audio takes exactly one second. Several software codecs are real time, too, but only on fast processor-computers. There's more on real time later in the chapter.

The next step of the video capture is storing the information onto disks so we'll discuss the various types of storage next.

Dealing with Native DV compression

Being a cross-platform media, QuickTime is made to be the exact solution for the digital filmmakers. This means all the files generated on a platform can be used on any platform, whether a Mac or Wintel (Windows OS + Intel-compatible architecture) with the only condition that the machine which is playing the video files should have the appropriate codec in order to decode the information. The media is also a very versatile one, supporting a lot of codecs, whether they are hardware or software codecs. The main codec that we usually deal with when it comes to editing is the DV codec, also known as **Native DV**. It's the most suitable codec for DV editing; it combines a good quality picture with a pretty tight compression. But the most important feature is real time compression, mandatory for an editing system. It comes bundled with the consumer and prosumer-level digital cameras, so the cameras have a hardware codec and record the video and audio signals onto the tape in this format. The majority of editing and post-production software comes bundled with the software codec, so they can capture the video and audio information in its original native format.

From the technical point of view, the algorithm used is Motion-JPEG, meaning that every frame is compressed regardless of the content of the neighboring frames. The advantage is that it allows for accurate frame editing, meaning you can insert video and audio at any point you want without the need to decode anything but the frame you are currently in. Plus it offers real timecode support, which means the exact timecode of the tape can be stored along with the movie (the information on video and audio channels, to be more correct).

Exact timecode serves a lot of purposes. One is off-line editing, when editing is done into the computer using low-resolution video files and then taken back to the on-line editing system. It's like virtual editing, not using the real video footage but a working copy. This is similar to the days when the movies were edited using the cutting machines (they were physically cutting the film) using a working-copy. Using the exact timecode from the master tape is also useful if a rough edit is to be made, using a lot of low-resolution footage and then, you need to recapture only the material used in your actual edited sequence at a higher resolution.

Also, very important, when it comes to compressions and digital video/audio files is the loss of quality you might get. With the DV format, there's no loss of quality when you copy video between your DV device and computer. When you capture video to your computer, edit it, then export it back to tape, you retain the quality of the original footage.

Selecting DV hardware

The boom of technology of the last five years brought to light a wide range of hardware for digital video capture. For this purpose we need a capture device, also known as, capture board. We shall stick with the term "device" because there are a lot of computers today using their own capture devices, so there is no need for an actual card. As we mentioned, the cameras are analog or digital, so the capture devices should allow analog and/or digital video and audio capture.

The analog inputs/outputs can be:

- Composite Video: the most common interface hence, the less accurate due to the small bandwidth of the video signal.

- S-Video, or "Y/C": with a better quality because of the separation of the luminance (Y) and the chrominance (C) signals.

- Component Video: very good picture quality due to the separation of the video signals in luminance (Y) and color-difference signals (B-Y and R-Y).

- RGB interface: pretty similar to the Composite Video.

Analog interfaces don't allow timecode capture. This has to be done via serial data interfaces, the most common being RS-232 and RS-422. In this way we can capture the video material with the original timecode information existing on the tape.

Digital video captures are more versatile. For instance, the so-called IEEE 1394, FireWire (Apple Computers' terminology, the actual inventor of the IEEE 1394 protocol) or iLink (Sony), supports Native DV video and audio transfers plus timecode and controls. It's one of the revolutionary inventions of the last century. It's rapidly gaining ground with all new computers nowadays. Apple ships all its products with this interface on-board and many other PC-systems manufacturers are including it as a "must have" option.

Another digital capture option is the Serial Digital Interface, or SDI. This is more "professional" then FireWire. Basically, the signal is still digital, but is separated on its Components (Y, R-Y, and B-Y). It's the digital counterpart of the Component Video from the analog world. The picture quality is much better, but its price makes it prohibitive for the prosumer market, therefore is to be found only on professional equipment and, still, as an option.

So, what do we actually need after we've got our video and audio on the tape? We need to get the material into the computer. This is done via the capture device, be it analog or digital.

Film-to-DV transfer

Some of us might shoot on film, edit in a non-linear environment and then want to go back to film again. The process of "blowing-up" (DV-to-film transfer) is explained later on in this chapter so here we'll discuss the concept of film-to-DV transfer. There are two main issues involved: the **frame rate** and the **aspect ratio**. These two factors are very different in the film and video worlds.

Frame rate in television is 30 frames-per-second (fps) in NTSC and 25fps in PAL. Each frame is interlaced and consists of two fields. So, we can speak of 60 fields-per-second (NTSC) or 50 fields-per-second (PAL). Frame rate on modern film is 24fps. What happens when we want to transfer film frames to video? In PAL, as we can see, there should be no big problem, because the frame rates are pretty close. Actually, each and every frame of film is transferred to two fields of video (one frame). In this case, the movie plays 4% faster and the all the sounds are halftone higher. This makes a movie two minutes and 24 seconds shorter then the film copy. It's annoying if want to transfer music from film to DV, but the majority of our audience won't notice anything.

If we want to transfer film-to-video in the 60 fields-per-second world (NTSC) things get a bit more complicated. Engineers noticed that five fields of NTSC have the exact duration of two frames of film. So, if we manage to record two frames of film on five fields of video, the sync problem isn't a problem anymore. The workout is to take a film frame and record it on three NTSC fields. The very next film frame we take it is to be recorded on two fields of NTSC video and so on. This means that every other film frame is shown for 1/20 second while the others are shown for 1/30 second.

The name of the process is **3:2 Pulldown**. There is a downside of this workout though, imagine the film has pans and zooms. After the transfer to video they don't look as smooth anymore as they did on the film. Another disadvantage comes from the fact that in real world, the NTSC's frame rate isn't 60, but 59.94 fields-per-second (or 29.97 fps), "drop-frame mode". The difference is very slight though, of only 3.6 seconds per hour.

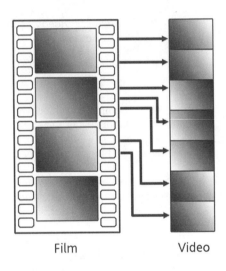

Film   Video

There are some pieces of software that support 3:2 Pulldown in order to work with DV files originated on film (After Effects, combustion for example).

The aspect ratio is what we get if we divide the width of the picture by the picture's height. The traditional television aspect ratio is 4:3 (or 1.33:1). Film aspect ratio could be different; there are 1.33:1 film aspect ratio, or 1.78:1 (16:9), or 2.35:1.

Storyboarding

What is storyboarding? Interesting question, because it means slightly different things to different people in the movie business. For instance, for the Director of the film, it's a series of small drawings with the dialog next to them, each and every scene of the movie drawn on paper to help the Director have a wider vision of the whole project. For the D.P. (Director of Photography), a storyboard is something more complicated with every shot drawn with its corresponding lighting-scheme and camera movements, so much for the dialogs. And we can go on with the editor's storyboard, which isn't much different from the director's one, with the exception that's even more complex.

So, basically, storyboarding means working with some sketches that help the user to visualize the workflow of the movie from that person's point of view. The storyboard can contain pictures, small or more complex drawings, text, be it the actual dialogs and/or indications such as the movement of the camera, lighting-schemes, cutting-points for the editor, etc. Combinations or parts of all of these things make up the constituents of the storyboard. A good example of a famous storyboarder is director Terry Gilliam ('Brazil', 'Twelve Monkeys'). In his interviews he explains how he first "draws the movie", almost every scene and shot in order to see it mentally and then proceeds to the actual filmmaking.

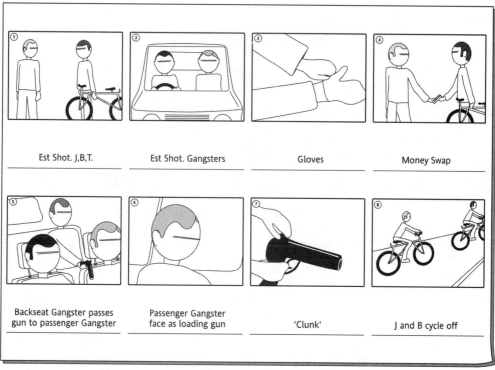

| Est Shot. J,B,T. | Est Shot. Gangsters | Gloves | Money Swap |

| Backseat Gangster passes gun to passenger Gangster | Passenger Gangster face as loading gun | 'Clunk' | J and B cycle off |

Time management

But storyboarding isn't only used to visualize the movie before it's done. It also serves a very deep concept in filmmaking, of **time management**. What does time management mean? Have you ever watched a boring movie with endless shots that were saying nothing? Of course you have. On the other hand, have you ever watched a fast-paced action movie with rapid cuts from many angles that was carrying you along with the story? Yes again, of course you have.

Amongst many things, time management is one of the important factors that leads to a well-paced movie. Be it a melodrama or a "shoot 'em all" style film. Time management is counting the seconds of every scene, of every shot that composes any scene, in order to have a rough idea of how long each scene will be. A good director can answer this question before the slate goes "clack!". Time is everything: for the producer, time means money; for the director, time means the duration of dialog, or of a silent scene; for the DP, time means the length of pan-shot, tilt, zoom, etc.; for the audience/viewers, time is the unperceived dimension of the movie. Except they'll know when something feels wrong.

But, nobody is perfect, so if you don't know how many seconds this scene or shot should be, don't worry! Just be sure you have a storyboard with you and, during the shooting of the images, make sure you do different takes, with different timings and write them down by the drawings of your storyboard. Remember, you're shooting on DV, so it's cheaper than the film, you can afford the luxury of doing so!

Content coherency

As we already saw, all the people of the crew use storyboarding. The director, DP, editor, and the continuity person all have one. In this chapter we'll discuss the last two people involved in the process of filmmaking. First, we'll explain the concept of content coherency and then how the participants get involved in the process.

The story should flow, without glitches, should carry away the viewer, shouldn't be confusing. Differently said, the content of the action should be as natural as possible. Or, in fewer words, we should respect the content coherency. Of course, lapses of time are allowed and flashbacks are very nice in a movie. But, still, it should respect the coherence.

The content coherency is achieved by editing. The editor has one idea of how the movie should look thanks to the storyboard. The storyboard tells the editor the flow of the shots in the scene and the flow of the scenes. It's also very important to have logical cuts from one scene to another, such as in a dialog scene, for example, there are two people, A and B, talking to each other. A is on the left side of the shot and B on the right side. During the whole dialog, the people should remain in the same spatial positions, unless they are moving while talking to each other, no matter how many cuts the editor wants to make.

Otherwise, a jump in continuity is made. In 99% of the cases, a jump in continuity is not desirable. But this isn't up to the editor, if the shots went bad and the A and B are the other way around in one shot. This is the job of the continuity person. This key person stays by the director and the DP and keeps track of all the camera angles and the position of the characters on the set. How does this person keep track of all that? You guessed it, with the help of a storyboard.

DVD interactivity

Storyboarding for DVD is different than storyboarding for film. DVD storyboards are more like a flowchart, a map of the DVD interactivity. We all know that DVDs have a certain degree of interactivity: from skipping one scene to another, through changing from one chapter to another, to changing the viewing angle of the camera of one video track, choosing the language of the audio track and the subtitling language as well, etc.

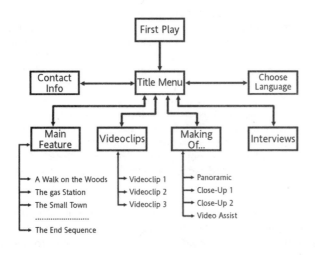

Let's look at a possible flowchart of a DVD that has a main feature film, with lots of scenes, some pop-videos with three of the soundtrack's songs, a making of the movie, and interviews with the actors and the crew.

First Play is a piece of video with audio, an introduction, or just some graphics, it can be the main menu as well. Contact Info can be the movie distributor's contact information. Choose Language menu is meant to choose both the language of the audio version as well as the subtitling language (if necessary). Main Feature is the actual film and is divided into scenes numbered and named by the action depicted. Videoclips is the chapter with the pop-promos. The Making of … are scenes showing how the movie was made, shot with several cameras, giving the viewer the choice of interactively changing the camera angle. Then the chapter with the Interviews follows.

Edit

Editing is the process where we tell the story, take our viewer with us, and walk him/her through the ideas we want to communicate in the first pace. Through the process of editing we can communicate moods, we can influence the audience, we can make our audience remember our movie because we used a very nice piece of music in an appropriate moment, etc.

Organization issues for complex projects

From the editor's point of view, a film is made out of scenes, which are made out of a series of shots, edited all together. The action of the movie can be linear, like the car we have mentioned before, or can be non-linear, like a person telling the story of somebody driving a car and not beginning "with the beginning". A good example of a linear action movie is *Die Hard*. The action of the movie is following the real-life flow of the actual action. An example of a non-linear action film is Tarantino's *Pulp Fiction*. Can anybody tell how the action goes and "who's on first base"? Pretty hard, but not impossible.

In complex projects it's difficult to follow the action, so it's the editor's duty to organize the material so the crew can stay focused on this stage of the film. The shots are identified by **scene** and **take** marked on the slate, at the beginning of every shot. A take is a duplicate of a shot, so if the director decides to make three different shots with the same action, **actually, there's only one** shot with three different takes.

The assistant editor or, in many cases of a low budget film, the editor, starts ingesting the material into the computer and organizing the information of video and audio stored into the computer as QuickTime movie files. The editing software often refers to these files as **clips**. Clips are organized in folders inside the editing software, often called **bins**. On the computer's hard disks, the QuickTime files can be stored in a different manner; the bins and clips exist only inside the editing software's world. So, a bin can contain one or several clips, according to the takes of every shot. The bin's name can be the name of the shot, consequently the clip's name could be the name of the take. It is a way of organizing clips, not a "must-be" way. In complicated projects, like non-linear action movies, there are actually more actions interlaced with each other and interacting from time to time. In order to keep track of every action, it's better if each action is edited separately and then, parts of the action might be copied, to give the actual "look" of the movie. It's easier this way to make duplicates of an edited sequence, with slight changes and then decide which one serves the subject the best.

At this point of our presentation, we should mention, for those who aren't familiar with the process of computer editing, or non-linear editing, that after the process of capturing the material onto the computer, no copy of the actual QuickTime movie files are made. Only links to the original files are made through the editing software. The process of non-linear editing is usually non-destructive and reversible, meaning that any change in the sequence being currently edited doesn't affect the original clips unless specified by the manufacturer of the software.

Real time or render

Everything that happens inside the computer, in our case the manipulation of QuickTime files, has to pass through the computer's processor. Inside the processor there's nothing but math processes. Depending on the complexity of the math operations and the processing capability of the processor, the time spent on the calculations may be different. Now, video and audio represented inside the computer as QuickTime files have their own intrinsic time. We know that a 10 second videoclip takes 10 seconds to be played in normal speed. In this case we say the video runs in **real time**. What happens if the calculations that take place inside the processor are too slow and the computer cannot keep the pace with the actual time of the video? Nothing much, the video files are stored on the hard disks, so they don't go anywhere, only the process is slowed-down. So, the video won't playback in real time.

What makes computers not play the video files in real time? QuickTime files are stored on hard disks and hard disks are characterized by a certain transfer-rate, which is translated into the speed the device can play the video file. When a transition between two video files is added, there are actually two video streams playing on the whole duration of the transition. This doubles the actual transfer rate needed to play the files from the hard disk and can exceed the physical hard-disk's transfer rate. Also, if we were to apply a bunch of video effects on a video file, as we stated before, the video file is not modified but the processor needs to calculate the changes. It's at this point the video stream might get non-real time. So, what's to do? Create new files (editing is a non-destructive process) that merge all the properties and all the streams in only one video file, so the computer can play that stream in real time. This is called **rendering**, because we can actually get to see that the computer is making those calculations. Don't get carried away! Real time means that the processor is still making calculations, only it does them really fast and that 10 seconds of action actually happen in 10 seconds.

A lot of capture card manufacturers advertise amongst their features "real time editing and effects", offering various options and prices for the "goodies" the cards can do. Instead of using the computer's processor when it comes to do the calculations on those QuickTime files, it is easier to transfer the hard task to one or two or several processors residing on the capture card. So, more features and real time processing. Of course, one has to pay for these features. Luckily enough, prices go down day by day, as the competition is harsh in this market.

Pre-visualization editing

When non-linear editing systems showed-up, there was almost nothing in real time. The terms, at that time, were **offline** and **online.** Some might say it's the same as render and real time. Well, it isn't. The process of editing was practically the same, but working with QuickTime files was different. First, a low resolution version was stored in the computer. Analog video was digitized with a high compression, sometimes 10:1 or even as low as 20:1. At this low resolution, the stream of video was kept low and the existing hardware could cope with it, so actually, the editing was done in real time. But, because the video quality was too low (high compression = low quality), one couldn't use the edited sequence to print, film, or broadcast. This was offline editing, with an offline video quality.

To be online, meaning at least broadcast quality, the non-linear editing system generated an EDL (Edit Decision List) interpreted by a linear, complicated, and expensive edit controller and mixer. Practically, it was a tape-to-tape editing, but without any operating editor. At that time it was a breakthrough in technology. Later, online machines showed up, meaning that first, an offline was to be made and then, everything was to be re-digitized for an online version, where the operator had to wait for hours for a long render. But, fortunately those times are over now and technology has made possible pure online machines, whether they're real time or not.

What can we do if, due to complicated effects or composites, our editing system doesn't allow us to visualize our sequence in real time? There are systems that support a low resolution preview in real time, even if the QuickTime files are high-res inside the computer. But these machines are expensive and hard to find. A good decision could be to do what is called a rough-cut, a sequence edited only with cuts. No transition effects, no color correction, nothing. Just to give us an idea of how the story goes, to time the scenes, to edit the music, to trim the cuts. Everything is in real time. After the director gives the OK, we can start building-up our complicated project and transitions, color-corrections or any other video effect including compositing, masking, rotoscoping, titles, and graphics. In most of the cases, we'll end-up rendering.

Transfer

So, we've finished editing our film, we've finished the title sequence and the end credits, we're done with the color correction and other special effects, and we're ready to deliver the movie. Remember, it is still inside the computer as DV format, so how do we get it out and in what format? In this section we'll cover the transfer-to-tape and the transfer-to-film issues.

Transfer to tape

It's easy and everybody is doing it. Using the same capture card, we should be able to transfer our movie to tape. We can use the same Native DV format through FireWire to output or we can use any other output option, depending on the format we want to record. It's good to have a master tape, international version, if needed, in digital format.

Transfer to film

This is one of the most difficult issues in the process of digital filmmaking. There are a lot of differences between digital video and film. Resolution, frame rate, and frame size are only some of the issues we'll discuss.

Video, in our case digital video (DV) is shot at a 30 frames-per-second (NTSC) or 25fps (PAL and SECAM). Every frame is interlaced, meaning it consists of 2 static fields combined all together to form the frame. So, we can talk about 60 (NTSC) or 50 (PAL) fields per second. Film, on the other hand, is always shot at 24fps (non-interlaced), be it 8mm, 16mm, 35mm, or 70mm film format.

So, what's the difference between fields and frames? The film camera captures a film image in the same way a still-picture camera does: the entire frame is captured all at once using only chemical processes. The shutter opens in front of the film letting the light from the lens make it's way to the film. This happens 24 times in a second. Video records half of the image every 1/60th (NTSC) or 1/50th (PAL) of a second, this is called a field and two fields form a frame. This is due to historical reasons: when video first showed-up in the twenties, the chemical materials forming the TV sets' screen, called phosphors, were too slow to respond to a full frame of a video every 1/30th (1/25th) of a second. A technological problem that was sorted-out due to a compromise, the alternating scan-line method. We still have to use interlaced scanning today, because of compatibility reasons, even if technology made TV sets with higher quality and with higher refresh rates (like computer monitors).

Earlier we mentioned the term "resolution". Video cameras capture the image in discrete steps, or **pixels**. Once again, depending on the video system, standard resolutions are: 720x480 in NTSC and 720x576 in PAL. Film resolution is higher and depends on the size of the film: 8mm, 16mm, 35mm, or 70mm. It also depends on the density of the photosensitive particles present on the film's emulsion. An average resolution for a 35mm film is 2000x2000 pixels, or 2k, and it's used in most of today's movies.

After seeing what the major differences are, we still want to output our movie to film. Well, good news is about to come; it's possible to do a DV-to-film transfer (film blow-up) with the help of sophisticated software and hardware equipment. From the technological point of view, there are three types of DV-to-film transfer devices:

- **Film Recorders** are high-resolution DV-to-film transfer devices. We can achieve a high quality on the film, up to 2k, or even 4k, of pixel resolution. There are two techniques available: shooting with a special camera, a high resolution CRT monochrome monitor, through special red, green, and blue filters; or more effective and more expensive, projecting the digital image directly from the QuickTime file with three micro-lasers (one for each color component, red, green, blue) scanning the film's surface without the use of other optic devices.

> *None of the above processes are in real time. The device is sending one frame at a time to film.*

- The **kinescope** is a real time DV-to-film transfer device that uses a high-resolution monitor and a special film camera. The trick is that the camera's shutter has been modified to be synchronized with the video frame rate, dropping some selected fields from the video image in order to produce a 24fps image recorded on the film.

- The top of the line of the DV-to-film transfer devices is the **Electron Beam Recorder** (or EBR). The film is held in a vacuum box while electrons are beamed directly onto it. The process is black and white because the electron beam has no color, only intensity, so the device is interpreting the DV files, separating the color components, and projecting each and every one onto a film. The three films are then composed using red, green, and blue filters to generate the color copy. The three "component" films are generated in real time. This method of transfer is the most expensive one, but the most accurate with the best picture quality.

Even if the price for the video-to-film transfer is a bit prohibitive, there's still an excellent option that we have to deliver our movie in a reliable, modern, and good quality medium. We'll look at this in the next section on DVD.

DVD

DVD stands for **D**igital **V**ersatile **D**isk. There are a lot of DVD formats, for audio, for video, or plain data, etc. We shall talk about DVD-Video here. A DVD-Video is composed of MPEG-2 video files, graphics, interactive menus, and music.

So, what do we need to have in mind when authoring a DVD? We need to structure our project in chapters and subchapters, like a book. Then, we have to decide the languages available for the film, prepare the subtitles, and create the menu's background, buttons, and the navigation flowchart. Last, but not least, prepare our video files, meaning, convert them from QuickTime movie files into **MPEG-2** files, the video file format widely accepted for a DVD-Video title.

MPEG-2 format

After finishing editing our sequence(s), the special effects, the introduction, all the animations, we're ready to export our project for DVD Authoring. MPEG-2 is a standard for video file encoding and compression. MPEG is an encoding and compression system for multimedia content defined by the **M**otion-**P**icture **E**xpert **G**roup. MPEG-2 provides compression support for broadcast quality video.

A particularity of the MPEG-2 compression process is that we can use a wide variety of MPEG-2 encoders, whether they're software codecs or hardware ones, and still be able to decode the MPEG-2 coded files on any computer or stand-alone player. So, the algorithm of compression can be different but the final result is universally playable.

Any compression algorithm exploits the redundancy information in video. MPEG-2 removes both the temporal and spatial redundancy that are present in motion video. **Temporal redundancy**, or **interframe** redundancy, arises when successive frames of video display images of the same scene. It's common for the content of the scene to remain fixed or to change only slightly between successive frames. **Spatial redundancy,** or **intraframe** redundancy, occurs because parts of the picture are often repeated, with minor changes, within a single frame of video.

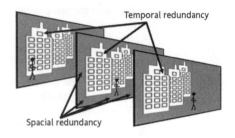

Obviously, not all segments of a video have the same temporal and spatial redundancy. An example of low spatial redundancy is a video with complex picture content, while a low temporal redundancy example is a video with fast moving sequences. So, there are segments on a video that can be highly compressed (high redundancy) and there are segments where the compression is pretty low.

Hence the content of an entire movie doesn't have the same redundancy all along the duration of it. Sometimes, a higher compression is possible, sometimes not. Higher compression means fewer bits of data to be transmitted and vice-versa, lower compression means more bits to be encoded. Therefore, a variable bitrate compression algorithm is desirable. MPEG-2 is one of these. The purpose of the compression is to eliminate both redundancies. An ideal codec analyzes each frame, filters-out the redundant information and preserves the detail.

Why should we compress at all? As we've already mentioned when talking about capturing, there are two main reasons.

The bitstream of uncompressed digital video is too high to be sustained by normal computer devices and the uncompressed files occupy too much disk space.

Terminology

Before seeing how to convert our DV projects (made out of our QuickTime movie files) into MPEG-2 files for distribution, let's first walk-through MPEG terminology.

MPEG is developed for a certain set of profiles and levels. **Profile** describes the quality of the video. **Level** describes the resolution of the video. The basic system, used in the common DVD-Videos is known as **Main Profile Main Level** (MP@ML).

A picture in DV format is a matrix of pixels, 720x480 in NTSC or 720x576 in PAL. A pixel is a sample of the original image at a point in the matrix. Each pixel contains the information of the intensity of the three primary colors (RGB) in a byte of data per each color. A byte has 8 bits, hence the term 24-bit RGB image. Another term used in the digital video world is YUV color-space, denominating the Luminance (Y), and Chrominance (U and V) components of the image. MPEG uses the YUV-space to encode the information contained in the picture. The human eye is more sensitive to luminance (brightness) than to color, so during the process of compression we can discard more information on color and keep the information on brightness. MPEG-1 algorithm uses the 4:1 compression for chrominance, while MPEG-2 algorithm uses 4:1 or 2:1 compression. The most used chrominance compression in MPEG-2 is 2:1. Everything depends on the codec, though.

When compressing in MPEG, the data within a frame is organized in small atoms of an 8x8 matrix of values, called **blocks**, so, there are luminance blocks and chrominance blocks. Because the information on chrominance can be compressed, the block of chrominance is bigger than the luminance one. In a 2:1 compression standard, the block of chrominance is 8x16 pixels, while in a 4:1 compression the block of chrominance is 16x16 pixels. One block of luminance and the corresponding block of chrominance together form a **macroblock**. A macroblock can have a size of 8x16 or 16x16 pixels, depending on the chrominance compression.

Because the MPEG compression is based on both spatial and temporal redundancy, there are two types of encoding that combined, form the MPEG-2 algorithm. **I**-type compression stands for **Intraframe** and it eliminates the spatial redundancy. It's actually the compression that takes place within each macroblock and depends on how much the chrominance information is compressed. An **I-frame** can be recreated (decoded) without reference to any neighboring frames.

P-type refers to **Predictive**. In P-type compression, every macroblock from one frame is compared with the corresponding macroblock from the previous frame (the most recent past reference frame) and the difference is used for the encryption of the compression algorithm.

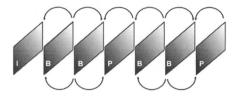

B-type refers to **Bi-directional** and works the same as P type but in both directions. Every macroblock from one frame is compared with the corresponding macroblock from the previous and the next frames and the difference is used for the encryption. We say the information is relative to the most recent past reference frame and nearest next reference frame, as well.

P and B-types eliminate temporal redundancy. Hence MPEG-2's nickname as a temporal prediction algorithm. Due to the P and B coding types, MPEG-2 can use backward and forward prediction.

A sequence of I, P, and B-frames in a pattern form a **Group of Pictures** (GOP). The frames contained in a GOP are related and always begin with an I-frame, followed by P and B frames. An example of fixed pattern for a GOP is: `IBBPBBPBBPBBPBB`, one of the most commonly used patterns nowadays. Other options are `IBPBPBPBPBPBPBP` or `IPPPPPPPPPPPPPP`.

As we were mentioning at the beginning of this section, MPEG-2 is a variable bitrate algorithm. A very important parameter is the bitrate. We can use **Constant Bitrate** (CBR) or **Variable Bitrate** (VBR) encoding.

CBR encoding uses the same rate over the whole video, disregarding the high temporal or spatial redundancy that might occur within the picture content of the movie. VBR on the other hand allows for 'smarter' encoding, meaning that the bits that aren't used for encoding high-redundancy scenes are allocated for encoding less redundant scenes, improving the picture quality of the complex scenes. Whether we use VBR or CBR, we still need to assign a value to the maximum data rate attribute.

Too high a bitrate, and the file size hits the roof, it won't fit on our DVD media or it won't play correctly from our media. Too low a bitrate and we'll see compression artifacts, in another words, we experience picture quality loss due to a higher compression. So, according to our DV's redundancy, we can fix a bitrate that better fits our video. Some tests are advisable to be made first, before exporting our whole DV project to MPEG-2.

Creating MPEG-2 files

If you're still with us, you'll be happy to know we're now going to leave the theory behind and get on with some practice.

Let's create those MPEG-2 files. As we previously stated, a project for the DVD-Video media can consist of one video source file or several of them. We need to export our project from DV to MPEG-2. We can export one file at the time or, with some pieces of software, do a batch export, meaning exporting multiple files one after another, in the same process. The result will be the same: one or several MPEG-2 format files, ready to be imported into the DVD Authoring software.

The main parameters involved into the MPEG-2 encoding are:

- **Bitrate Type**: CBR is faster, but produces large files. VBR can be of two types: one-pass VBR or two-pass VBR. With one-pass VBR, I and P types of conversion are generally used. The two pass-VBR uses I, P, B conversion types but usually it's slower, due to the fact the algorithm has to analyze the picture content to estimate the temporal redundancy and make the temporal predictions, store the information in a temporary memory (**buffer**), and then do the actual compression, based on the estimations.

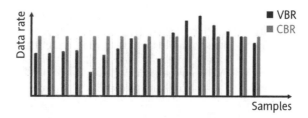

- **Maximum Bitrate**: The maximum bitrate is a very important parameter. The majority of the encoders allow users to modify it and it has a visible and dramatic influence on MPEG-2's file picture quality. Depending on the quality we would like to achieve and the size of our project, the maximum bitrate can be somewhere between 2Mbps and 9.4Mbps. Beware, Mbps means Mega-**bits** per second and is 8 times **less** than Mega-**bytes** per second! Some manufacturers express their bitrate in bytes or bits and both expressions are accepted as a standard. The majority of the encoders have the maximum bitrate associated with the video stream encoding section. Please, be aware of the fact that along with the stream of video, the audio stream is encoded too. The sum of the audio and video stream should never exceed 9.8Mbps in order for the DVD to play back properly, even though MPEG encoders allow us practically to set whatever bitrate we please.

- **GOP structure**: Some encoders let the users choose the GOP's structure from standard patterns. Some encoders don't even mention this parameter at all. Giving the users the possibility to change the GOP's structure can be a very powerful option for an experienced user and can prove to be a disaster for someone who doesn't understand the concept.

- **GOP length:** The GOP's length can be another parameter to be modified, depending on manufacturer. The standard length of a GOP is 15 frames. The GOP's pattern is also referred to as **P-Frame distance**. Logically, the GOP length must be an integer multiple of the P-Frame distance.

- **Sequence header**: The DVD specification also requires a sequence header before each GOP (the sequence header contains information about the MPEG stream, such as aspect ratio, GOP size, and bitrate). Sometimes, encoders have the option to include this sequence header or not. Be sure to check the checkbox for this option.

- **Frame rate**: The standard DVD frame rate is 29.97 fps in NTSC and 25 fps in PAL.

- **Image size**: The standard DVD image size is 720x480 in NTSC and 720x576 in PAL.

- **Audio sample rate**: Usually there are three sample-rates available: 32.000 KHz, 44.100 KHz (Audio CD quality), and 48.100 KHz. The last two are the most suitable for present-day DVD use.

- **Audio data rate**: We can choose between 224, 256, 320, and 384 Kbps for good DVD audio quality. The most common used audio data rates are 256 and 320 Kbps.

There are manufacturers that offer more parameters, depending on the codec. The noise over the video information can be taken as useful information therefore making the compression process very difficult and time-consuming, affecting the overall picture quality, too. Some codecs offer filters, used for a pre-encoding noise reduction. Please check the specifications and the manuals for a good understanding of the parameters provided.

Choose your codec

There are many popular software codecs available for both Mac and PC platforms, I've used Heuris Logic's. They're present in four flavors: Heuris MPEG Power Pro 1 (CBR MPEG-1 only), Heuris MPEG Power Pro 2 (CBR and VBR MPEG-1 and MPEG-2), Heuris MPEG Power Pro DVD, and Heuris MPEG Power Pro Transport. All Heuris codecs can read QuickTime, AVI, Avid OMFI, and Media100 QuickTime files, can apply filters to cut-out noise over the video, controls frame-rate, crop source, frame size, reference frames, filter parameters, etc. (for more information, see www.heuris.com).

The choice of hardware codecs really is a jungle. There are hardware codecs present on the video capture cards used for real time editing (we can capture directly in MPEG format or, more often, we need to export the project in MPEG format, real time or non-real time). Please check the specification of the cards if you want to purchase a video capture card for real time editing with a MPEG hardware codec on it; usually this is a well advertised feature.

There are special MPEG-1 and MPEG-2 cards that can capture the incoming video signal and encode it in real time to a MPEG file in a heartbeat. Just to give an example of such cards, Optibase (www.optibase.com) could be the most appropriate one. The card's generic name is MPEG MovieMaker 200S and it comes in several versions. The ones that can be used for DVD authoring purposes are M200S Basic FD1 VBR (supporting VBR coding) and M200S Publisher FD1.

Authoring DVDs

To cook a good meal, besides a good pan, we need good ingredients. These ingredients are our video and audio files in MPEG-2 format, graphics for the backgrounds, and the menu buttons. In the DVD world they are generically called **assets**. We can create these assets using common graphics and video software, export properly, and then importing them into the DVD Authoring software.

DVDs basically consist of video and audio clips that are linked together using menus, complete with subtitles and alternative language or soundtracks. Menus are graphical interfaces that give the users a certain level of interactivity by letting them watch the videoclips of their choice by selecting buttons on their screen. DVD Authoring consists of actually assembling the look of the DVD, programming the navigational links, and previewing our DVD in real time as we go. At this point we need the DVD storyboard we have previously created. It will help us to stay focused on what we want to achieve.

In this section we shall give only two examples of DVD Authoring software: DVD Studio Pro ($999) and iDVD (both from Apple, www.apple.com). We should mention that the workflow is practically the same in any DVD Authoring software, with the exception of some details and particularities.

1. When first opening a new project, we have to specify the preferences for the current project. We have to specify what will be the final destination: a CD, a DVD, a DVD volume on a hard disk, etc., so a progress bar can alert us to how much space remains free as we work. Also, we can choose the type of the video format files, whether they're MPEG-1 or MPEG-2.

2. The next step is importing our assets into the Container and organizing them in folders and subfolders. This is done by simply dragging and dropping the files or using the Import dialog menu. Then we begin to accommodate our video and audio files, according to the DVD storyboard we have previously created. As we go, we just might build up our menu. The menus can be still menus and motion menus. Still menus are made out of Photoshop files imported into DVD Studio Pro. To control the visibility of the layers created in Photoshop, we can use DVD Studio pro layers palette.

3. According to our flowchart or DVD storyboard, we might have several chapters and subchapters within our project. For every chapter and subchapter we need a cue-point to jump to when a corresponding button is pressed. These cue-points are actually markers on particular frames within a video stream.

    A higher level of interactivity can be achieved with DVD Studio Pro by adding to our project: slide shows (sequences of still images or video clips with or without audio), **scripts** (enabling us to create playlists of chapters and random playback of the DVD title amongst other things), web links (available only when the DVD is played-back on a computer, enabling us to launch web URLs), a **start-up action** (which determines what we can see and hear when the DVD disk is inserted in the DVD player), region coding, etc.

    At any moment of the authoring we can preview our project as it goes. When we think we've finished our work, we need to test our DVD title.

4. If everything is all right, we can then proceed to the final step of the DVD creation: building the DVD volume. The DVD volume consists of two folder that contain the audio and the video files, named accordingly: AUDIO_TS and VIDEO_TS. After creating the DVD volume on the hard disk, we're ready to record it on a DVD disk (burning the disk).

As we've already mentioned, there are a lot of manufacturers and a lot of DVD Authoring software. Depending on the version (light versions – for the beginners, to full professional versions for the advanced users) we can have different features available.

DVD Studio Pro

Apple's DVD Studio Pro provides us a huge wealth of features, from setting up to nine different angles.

iDVD

iDVD is DVD Studio Pro's little brother. It's rather drag-and-drop oriented, intended to be used to create 90 minute-long DVD-Videos or slide shows. Rather, it's an interface to build a homemade DVD than a DVD Authoring software. But, well, let's take it this way: it makes the complicated process of authoring DVD interfaces very easy. Why? Because, it's easy to use and very intuitive. It's very easy to get our DV files to work with iDVD. Actually, at this price level, I think it's the only DVD software that accepts DV files. We just drag-and-drop our DV files into the iDVD interface and they're ready to be played with.

Another option would be to export the DV file directly from iMovie, the complementary software used for editing. Since version 2.0.3 of iMovie, there is an Export to iDVD command. It's like exporting in any other format, the only exception is that it's the correct format and ready for iDVD import already. In iDVD we're able to make folders and group the DV files and still pictures.

A button similar to the play button of Apple's QuickTime player, the Preview button, switches the view from the DVD creation window to a simulated DVD player environment, with a remote-control floating item on the screen, simulating a real DVD remote-control unit. The preview action is available at any point of the DVD creation process.

One may say that the Burn DVD button burns the DVD. True, but something else is happening, too, a conversion from QuickTime format of the movies into the MPEG-2 format, for 100% DVD playback compatibility. This is a background process that can happen while we are performing any other task on our computer.

The DVD-Videos created with iDVD are compatible with the majority of the DVD Players available on the market. If you are not sure about that, please check out the Players Compatibility list by Apple at: www.apple.com/dvd/compatibility/.

DVD formats

So, we're ready to burn. But what should we burn? Opening a catalog of a DVD manufacturer we can find, at least, some codes and letters. Let's take them one by one. The standard diameter of a DVD is 12cm, the same diameter as a standard Audio-CD. There are 8cm DVDs too.

A DVD can be recorded as a single layer of data or as two layers. In this second case this means that the laser beam that reads the disc can reach both layers without turning it over. The codes for the layers are: SL = Single Layer, DL = Double Layer. Then, there are double-sided DVDs (DS), that record data on both sides, or single-sided, that record data on only one side (SS).

So these are the DVD standard formats:

- *DVD-5* = 12cm, SS/SL, 4.7 GB of data, over 2 hours of video

- *DVD-9* = 12cm, SS/DL, 8.5 GB, about 4 hours

- *DVD-10* = 12cm, DS/SL, 9.4 GB about 4.5 hours

- *DVD-18* = 12cm, DS/DL, 17 GB, over 8 hours

- *DVD-R* = 12cm, SS/SL, 3.95 GB

- *DVD-R* = 12cm, DS/SL, 7.9 GB

- *DVD-R* = 8cm, SS/SL, 1.23 GB

- *DVD-R* = 8cm, DS/SL, 2.46 GB

> *Of course, the length of movie available on every format can differ, depending on the compression we use for MPEG-2 encoding.*

Archiving

After finishing a project, when everybody's happy, we still have one more thing to do: archiving our work. We may need to make a little change in the future. Archiving is also important if we produce international versions of the movie. We'll surely need to go back and modify the audio, inserting the new language, change the titles, etc.

What does archiving mean? It depends on the type of the project. If it is a very small project (30 seconds to several minutes) we can burn a DVD-ROM with all the files we used in the project: the edited sequence, the source files, the rendered files, the graphics, the project files, everything. Before the DVD-era, people in the industry were using Digital Linear Tapes (DLT) for the same purpose. DLTs are pretty obsolete nowadays and, if still used, they're about to disappear from the market.

If we're talking about big projects, we cannot archive all the source files we used in the project. We don't even need to back them up, if we captured the video and audio with the corresponding timecode, later on we can do a batch digitize process, meaning the clip's information is kept in the editing software's project so we can re-capture the exact DV files we used in the first place. This is the advantage of using timecode capture. So, in larger projects, we only back-up our project's files, graphics, audio edits, things that are not too big, that can go on one or two CDs.

Tools

If you're looking for a buyer's guide of filmmaking hardware and software, well, you won't find it in here, just some examples and a few pointers. Discussions in this area can get outdated very quickly, especially if they favor one particular product over another, and in any case each one of your projects will have different requirements.

Hardware

The hardware involved in the digital film and DVD business is constantly changing, the quality is improving, the prices are dropping, it's evolution. The pieces of hardware that we look into when it comes to choose our gear are: cameras, editing, transfer, and distribution equipment. Let's take them one by one and see what features we should have in mind when we look for our equipment.

Cameras

The format is very important, whether digital or analog. Digital formats are preferred, but analog still can do the work. With digital formats, picture quality is expressed in number of pixels (thousands of pixels). The more pixels, the better the quality of the image.

Resolution is expressed in lines of horizontal resolution, the higher the number of lines, the better the resolution is. Inside the digital cameras, generally, compression is being made, exactly as the process described in the video capture section. The compression is usually described as a rate of 2:1, 3.5:1, 5:1, and so on. DV compression is 5:1, considered broadcast quality. The CCD's (Charged Couple Device) dimensions influence the sensibility and the image quality of the camera. Good cameras have three CCDs. 1/3", 1/2", 2/3" are standard dimensions for the CCDs.

Editing equipment

In the digital world, we don't talk about tape-to-tape editing anymore. It's the non-linear editing era. Such non-linear editing equipment comprises of: computer, video capture card, and storage devices. A computer can be a dedicated, proprietary one (such as Quantel's) or a common PC or Mac. Video capture boards are the key-issue for a good editing system. The capture board (card) is needed to capture the video and audio signals, convert them into QuickTime files, speed-up the rendering process, for real time editing capabilities, output the final project back to tape, etc.

Some specs for a capture card we should look into when buying our DV gear should be: video connection types (BNC or RCA) or audio (XLR or RCA), video input/output types (Composite Video, S-Video, Component Video, FireWire, SDI, etc.), how many layers it supports in real time, what video compression is provided (DV native or any other codec), the connection type (AGP, ISA, PCI), and the storage device connection (IDE, SCSI, FiberChannel).

Just to give some guidelines for the digital filmmakers looking for their gear, we'll mention that a good capture card needs to have BNC video connectors, or S-Video, Component, and S-Video input/output, XLR audio connectors. It has to support at least two video layers and one graphic layer with alpha channel in real time, several transition effects, and some video effects in real time, too, should be PCI based and definitely support the native DV compression.

Let's have a look at the major players on the market at the time of writing:

Matrox
Their product line (www.matrox.com/videoweb) is huge and are famous for making good picture quality video capture and signal processing cards. The applications of their products overpass the non-linear editing solutions. But let's see what we've got for our area of interest!

Matrox DigiSuite is their top-of-the line broadcast-quality analog video and audio Input/Output (I/O), as well as optional SDI I/O. DigiSuite comes in four versions:

- DigiSuite Full was the first one on the market, uses a compression algorithm named mathematically lossless compression which is, as Matrox anounces, uncompressed-quality video and is the only one supporting three layers of real time DVE and YUV color correction. ($4,220)

- DigiSuite LE is a two layers real time card, it uses M-JPEG compression format, offering good picture quality video at a data rate above 15MB/sec per stream. ($3,795)

- DigiSuite DTV is the only one to provide native DV, DV50, and MPEG-2 multiformat editing, actually allowing for combining DV and DV50 sources on the same timeline. It also can capture uncompressed-quality and MPEG-2 video for instant DVD authoring. ($5,995)

- DigiSuite LX is DTV's little brother, dealing only with DV and MPEG-2 compressions. ($3,995)

There are two options for entry-level video capture cards: one for PC, Matrox RT2500, and one for Mac, Matrox MacRT.

Pinnacle Systems
We shall mention only some of the representative members of the Pinnacle's big family (www.pinnaclesys.com):

- CineWave is a capture card in it's bare-meaning of the word, not having support for two layers real time editing. It can be used to capture in almost all QuickTime formats and for moving editing projects between multiple real time editing workstations, such as Avid, Media 100, Finish, and Adobe Premiere-run stations.

- Targa 3000 is the top-of-the-shelf card from Pinnacle. It supports up to three real time video layers and six real time graphic layers, real time transitions and video effects, DV25 and MPEG-2 codecs, and uncompressed RGB and YUV video streams. It also supports the following software: Adobe Premiere 6, Targa FX Chooser and FX Factory, TitleDeko RT, Hollywood FX, Commotion Pro, and Impression DVD Pro.

- ProOne is the entry-level card from Pinnacle. It supports DV, DVCam, and DVCPRO25 formats, two real time video layers editing, Composite, S-Video and IEEE 1394 I/O.

- Fast Blue: Their motto: "Everything in-anything out". It supports DV, DVCAM, DVCPRO 25, DVCPRO50, and MPEG IMX in their native formats, being the first system to support

MPEG IMX and Native DVCPRO editing. Blue can output in all the above formats, plus MPEG-2 and uncompressed making a native crossover between formats and playback in real time.

- Fast Silver is a native MPEG-2 real time editing card, with support for QuickTime export and QuickTime MPEG-2 or YUV uncompressed file formats.

- Fast Purple is the non-linear version of the old-timer Fast's VideoMachine. It supports DV/DVCAM and DVCPRO codecs and imports VideoMachine projects, QuickTime file format, and exports QuickTime and OMFI (Avid's Standard file format).

Storage considerations

The time when the cost for hard disk storage for video was thousands and thousands of dollars ended years ago. Yet, it depends on the image quality, the number of layers in real time, the compression, and some other factors that can make us decide to go for a cheap or for an expensive storage solution.

The storage should be in consonance with the bitrate of the data streamed from and onto the video capture card. The storage solutions range from internal IDE hard disks to internal SCSI disks and external raid arrays. The bitstream ranges from 66MB/s to some 160MB/s (Mega Bytes per second, which is 8 times bigger then Mega Bits per second). IDE hard drives are cheap and pretty reliable for low-speed ranges, providing 66 MB/s transfer rate at some 7200rpm (rotations per minute). 10000rpm SCSI disks can reach a higher transfer rate. The SCSI interface supports 160MB/s, but there's no disk alone that can supply such a speed.

Late reports indicate that 15000rpm SCSI disks are available. If we need a transfer rate around 160MB/s, we need an external RAID array. A RAID array hosts several SCSI disks which record data necessary for one stream on different drives. Imagine that we record a stream of data on two 80MB bitrate each SCSI hard disks and play it back from both disks at the same time, in parallel. We can obtain a 160MB/s datastream even if, physically, each and every disk isn't capable of such a speed. A third possibility is to use external, FireWire connected, hard disks.

Transfer and distribution equipment

If we output the final movie to videotape, we shall probably use the same VTR we used for loading the material into the computer to record back to tape.

If we decide to output to DVD, we need an internal DVD recorder or an external stand-alone DVD recorder. Nowadays an internal DVD recorder ranges from $600 to $2,000 in price. Usually, the speed of such burners is 2x to 4x (two or four times the real time, meaning it burns twice or four time faster the normal playback speed). The stand-alone DVD recorders cost above $1,500 and the speed is generally 1x or 2x. Some stand-alone recorders don't support PC connections, so we cannot output the movie with the DVD authoring made on a PC.

One of the most popular DVD burners is Apple's SuperDrive. We can find it on two of the three new Power Mac G4 models at the moment and it comes bundled with iDVD2 for DVD Authoring.

The SuperDrive can be used to burn and playback CDs and DVDs. It reads DVDs at 6x (7.8 MB/sec) and writes DVDs at 2x (2.6 MB/sec).

Other DVD burners available on the market are Pioneer's *A03* (approx. $700), APS Tech's (some $900), CD CyClone's *DVD Revo* (some $1,050), LaCie's (approx. $800), and QPS's QueFire DVDBurner Pro (approx. $750).

Software

We shall be talking about post-production software here, the ones that use QuickTime files and the QuickTime engine. The filmmaking software can be broken down into a few categories: editing software, compositing and 2-D effects software, and 3-D animation and compositing software. The categories actually define the term **post-production**, as it is the operations that are done in the computer over the QuickTime movie files. First we have to edit the video and the audio, then some effects are to be added, some nice titles and graphics and some 3-D animation and compositing, and the movie is ready to be published (or transferred).

Editing

The basic functions of non-linear editing software is to edit the digital video and audio, keeping in sync the video with the audio, add some transitions, correct colors, and, as far as possible, do this in real time.

Avid

Avid Technology is the pioneer of the non-linear editing systems. They practically invented the concept and rediscovered the process of editing. Since they hit the market, they've received a lot of Oscars for technology and innovations in the industry.

They have a large product list, we cannot make a run-down of everything, and we'll just mention the most poplar equipment nowadays. Media Composer is the pioneer of the group and one of the most popular. MC 1000, 8000, and 9000 are available, with same hardware but different software-activated features. It features unlimited video and audio layers, with two uncompressed video streams in real time, and different compressions. Multi-camera editing is a very powerful feature used in pop-promos and multiple-camera live recordings, allowing more than one stream of video to be previewed in real time.

Media Composer is famous for its project and media management features, improving the speed of editing through fast clip-search, Script-based editing, advanced user settings, multilevel sort functions, etc. It supports Dupe Detection, marking in small colors lines if a clip has been used more than once. In a few words, Media Composer is very easy to use and very fast. The Avid Xpress line is very similar, only less glamorous. A similar interface to Media Composer but it uses different hardware and compressions, hence, different picture quality.

Avid Xpress DVit is a software-only based product from Avid, targeted at entry-level users. We can add our own IEEE 1394 capture card and we're ready to edit, in Avid's personal style of environment. The top-of-the-line products from Avid are Avid DS (SoftImage Digital Studio) and Avid Symphony, both high-end finishing tools, combining editing with powerful compositing and color-correction.

Premiere 6

Is Adobe's editing software, it's been on the market for quite a while. Unfortunately, over the past years it has lost some of the market, mostly because of new comers. It's still one of the most popular, having versions for both PC and Mac. It comes as a software bundle with a lot of capture cards, such as the Matrox line and Pinnacle's entry and mid-level products.

It allows for three-points editing, insert and assemble-style editing, it has instant real time play, transition effects, video effects (like blurs, color corrections, mosaics, etc.), multichannel audio mixer, and very tight integration with all video post-production software from Adobe (including Photoshop and After Effects, see below). The interface is very friendly, user configurable, all windows are re-scalable and "drag-and-droppable". It provides direct support for IEEE 1394 interface (FireWire or iLink) on both platforms, Mac and PC. We can capture directly into the computer from our DV camera and output our movie back to tape using the FireWire integrated port, if available or any additional IEEE 1394 PCI card. A storyboard window allows for increased productivity, even though it's not as strong as the storyboard editing concept from Avid's. It allows for timecode based capture used for batch digitize processes.

A drawback is that it doesn't allow multiple timelines, which can prove to be very useful when a large project is to be edited, allowing for several versions to be made without affecting the main sequence. If you'd like further information DVision from friends of ED publish the book *Revolutionary Premiere 6 (ISBN: 1903450497)*.

Final Cut Pro 3

Everybody is talking superlatives about the latest Apple's editing software. It's actually the first one on the market that supports two layers real time editing with some real time effects, and color correction without any additional accelerating hardware. It's 100% designed for G4 processor computers (desktop or portable) and it takes advantage of all the newest inventions in technology from Apple and Motorola, such as Velocity Engine.

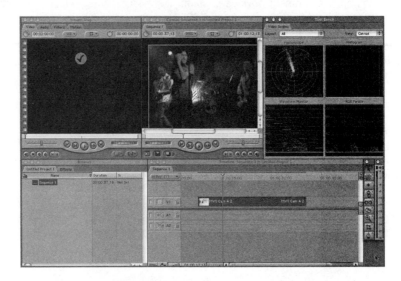

It allows direct-to-timeline capture in Apple's proprietary format, QuickTime movie, directly from any IEEE 1394 DV camera, allows multiple resolutions and transcoding options, timecode based batch capture, three-point editing, has an easy to use interface, built-in audio filters, including reverb, equalizer, echo, and noise gate, software built-in vectorscope and waveform monitor, and high-precision color correction tools with real time preview.

FCP3 has some interesting features that brings it closer into the compositing software category, too. It supports Bezier curves with movable motion paths. For more accurate picture resolution effects, it allows sub-pixel interpolation rendering. It uses Photoshop-like transfer modes, such as multiply and lighten for multiple layer compositing. It gives the editor more flexibility, allowing several sequences in the same project to be completed with the insertion of fully editable nested sequences. For non-real time effects, it allows real time wireframe preview. For those who want to create their own FXScript plug-in effects (filters and transitions), FXBuilder is an elegant and a powerful option.

Video effects can be applied on time range base, not just clip-base, which means you can apply a filter on several clips at once, without needing to apply the same effect several times on every clip with the benefit of instant parameter changes on all clips at once. It uses a powerful and easy to understand Media Management tool, with multi-item sorts, sifts, and Boolean searches for clips.

Previewing is made easy with the help of a low-res render option for a fast review, with each of the four render quality settings having a separate render cache. Unfortunately there is no PC version. If you'd like further information DVision from friends of ED publish the book *Revolutionary Final Cut Pro 3: Digital Post Production (ISBN: 1903450810)*.

iMovie
Final Cut Pro's little brother from Apple, is easy to use, drag-and-drop and cut-and-paste oriented for entry-level videographers. Actually, it's so easy to use, a professional user can get confused with the simplicity of iMovie. It comes bundled with every Macintosh DV (be it iMac or iBook).

Other tools

There are a number of other software tools that you may wish to use to polish your movie, for special effects or for those tasks that your editing system is not suitable for.

After Effects 5.5

Adobe After Effects is definitely, one of the most known compositing and motion graphics software's on the market. Everybody is using it and everybody is discovering its potential day-by-day, everyday. Every new release is a fiesta-time for the world-wide community. It's, maybe, one of the software's that has the most plug-ins available, due to its large acceptance. Since its version 5, it isn't a 2D compositing software anymore. It entered the 3D world through the front door. The newest version supports 3D space layer movements, 3D lights and cameras, changing angles, and animating into three-dimensional space. It also supports hardcore programming, via its expressions and parenting tools. After Effects is a true resolution independent software, supporting from thumbnail-size files up to 3k pixel-frames.

We don't have enough space to write about After Effects as we wish, so, we'll run through the specifications, highlighting only some of the really impressive features.

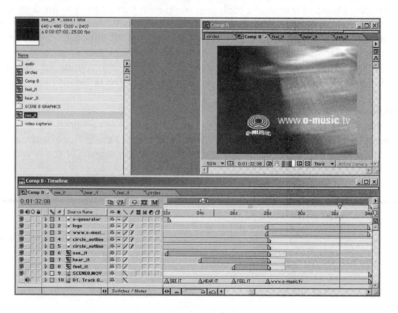

It composites and animates an unlimited number of layers in 2D and 3D space, with animation of multiple cameras and 3D lights, casting realistic soft shadows. It adds perspective to the composition through its new and realistic camera's depth-of-field. It allows for 2D and 3D multiple views. As we already mentioned, we can create procedural animations without using keyframes by defining live relationships between properties with expressions. The programming language is JavaScript, very popular and easy to learn/use. A brand new feature is also time remapping and frame blending, allowing us to create effects like variable speed (in slang, vary-speed), frame shuttering, playback delay, and hold frames. It supports powerful masking, combining multiple masks through Boolean operations, mask shapes can be animated and keyframeable.

A very powerful feature is the smart RAM Preview or Intelligent caching (Adobe's terminology), which allows us to render and store the temporary file in the computer's RAM and play it back at full frame-rate at the desired resolution. We said it's "smart" because once rendered, if we modify a part of the segment, we don't have to re-render the whole segment, but just the portion we've changed. Also, the RAM Preview temporary file can be saved as any QuickTime file, since it's already resident in the volatile memory. It's just a transfer from RAM to hard disk. Also, it allows for multiple compositions and nesting composition. To help the user with the nesting, a powerful flowchart is available, so we can easily keep track of our composition. It would be great to actually have control of nesting and compositing via a flowchart, not just another view option.

After Effects comes in two versions: Standard version and Production Bundle. The last one mentioned is completed with some more features such as: more visual effects, more plug-ins, motion tools, 3D channel effects, vector paint tools, and a render engine, making network rendering available.

Due to the fact that is 100% software based, After Effects is not real time. There's a solution that makes it faster, called ICE (Integrated Computer Engine), which is a PCI card including 8 parallel processors that can render up to 50 times faster then a normal computer processor. After Effects is a cross-platform application, working on both Mac and PC, if you'd like further information DVision from friends of ED have published the book *Revolutionary After Effects 5.5 (ISBN: 1903450780)*.

combustion 2

At the beginning there was a 2D compositing and paint software, named Illuminaire Studio, produced by Denim Software. In 1997, after Discreet acquired the package, they have split the paint and the compositing to create paint* and effect*. Don't look for a foot-note, the asterisk used to be a Discreet family personal identification. paint* and effect* merged again to form **combustion**, now in its second version.

It is Adobe's first competitor in the low-end niche of the market. It is a 2D and 3D compositing and effects package, featuring an intuitive and visual flowchart for visualizing and organizing multi-effected composites. The main difference from After Effects is that the flowchart doesn't serve only for viewing purposes, but it serves very well for organizing and editing effects. From this point of view, it brings it closer to an Avid DS flowchart compositing style. The package is also resolution independent, so the user is able to mix small resolution graphic elements with film scans and integrate them seamlessly in the same project. It has a great color correction tools, that work fine with 16bits/channel depth. The film tools provide powerful grain and color management features that are fully compatible with Discreet's top of the line packages flame and inferno. A brand new feature of combustion 2 is its integrated 2D particle system, providing a real time interactive visualization of smoke, fire, rain, and snowstorm effects. It also features a powerful character generator combined with sophisticated effects and textures for text layers. combustion also provides very powerful garbage masking with special vector shapes that are particularly used in advanced rotoscoping, fully compatible with top of the line flint, flame, and inferno.

combustion's interface isn't very intuitive for an editor/composition artist used to a timeline-based GUI, but Discreet users should be familiar with it, as it resembles other Discreet product's interfaces.

Commotion

It's the third in a line of compositing cross platform softwares on the market. It is resolution independent, and very powerful in managing traveling mattes. It has very good paint tools, which are easy to use and intuitive, and allows painting directly on the clip or on the timeline. Paint tools can retouch the alpha channel of a layer or can be used in conjunction with the SuperClone brush, for easily cleaning-up the footage or wire removal. There's a very interesting feature that switches between field and frame based operations at the click of a button.

Commotion has always been famous for its MotionTracker, a very powerful and precise tool, available only in the Pro version. This feature serves automatic masking, introducing new graphic elements with camera-moves precision, applying any effect to a moving object, cleaning-up footage through image stabilization, automating difficult to obtain precision paint-jobs combining the motion-tracking information with painting tools. The Pro version comes bundled with powerful plug-ins that improve the chromakeying process (Primate Keyer), image integration of new elements and elimination of unwanted elements (Composite Wizard), and introduction of new particles and graphic elements (Image Lounge).

Summary

Did we answer the question we have raised at the beginning: "How close can we get to that look of a film if we shoot on digital?" Not directly. There are many tutorials telling you how to obtain "that film look" if you shoot on DV. We cannot cover all that in this section. Just some common sense advice and the rest is... practice.

Let's run through some of the differences between the film and video. Motion Artifacts are something that film has and video doesn't. Why? Because the film recorded the image at 24 fps speed and video at 30 fps (25 fps) all interlaced (each frame is made out of two fields interlaced). A video frame can be de-interlaced, by eliminating one field and substituting the missing field (by doubling the lines from the remaining field). Because of the mechanic shutter of the camera, film has a natural motion blur, also influenced by the amount of light and the speed of the film. Grain is definitely a film's attribute. Film grain comes from the crystallization of the particles forming the light-sensitive side of the film during the process of developing an image. Colors and contrast are two more factors that make the difference, too. Film has a wider color palette then video and less contrast. Video tries to accurately reproduce the colors of the subjects to be shot and has a higher contrast then film. Film also has more defects then video. What does this mean? Film can have scratches, dust, trapped hair, random changes of luminance (flicker), etc. Film can be overexposed giving to the image a special white glow very hard to obtain with electronic devices.

Some of the differences can be eliminated or just attenuated, so we can make our movie on video actually look like film. The techniques apply in both production processes (shooting the movie) as well as in post-production (editing and/or special effects). We can alter the color, the contrast, and the level of the image. We can tweak the gamma, add grain, and some other "defects" to the picture using popular plug-ins. We can de-interlace the video frame and add motion blur to the image.

What this means is that the digital filmmaker has no need to feel inferior to their traditional-format counterparts. Why with all our advantages and our newly acquired knowledge of DVD creation – there's no reason why we can't create something in many ways superior and QuickTime is a major tool in that process.

12 Workflow Issues in QuickTime

The inception, creation, and deployment of QuickTime content presents many opportunities for avoiding the unnecessary expenditure of time and other scarce resources. As well as opportunities to achieve the greatest impact for the resources that are expended. These are workflow issues and they have to do with two main themes: pursuing a project in such a way as to reach as many members of the intended audience as possible, while maximizing the quality of their experience. And pursuing a project in as efficient a manner as possible consistent with those quality standards. In other words, our goal is reaching and moving an audience as cost-effectively as we can. Efficiency and deliverability are the key words.

The challenge is that we must aim at these lofty goals in an environment that can be wildly inconsistent and difficult to predict, especially on the Web. We need to look at the entire process from the inception of the project to the point where the audience experiences it. What follows are some key concepts and strategies with which to pursue these goals.

Efficiency

The pursuit of efficiency is best served by finding effective ways to minimize human involvement in mindless repetition, misunderstandings, and faulty communication, saving that precious resource for creative work. Computers offer excellent potential in this area, enabling us to attempt things that would be difficult or impossible without them but human relations skills are needed as well. We have to tap into that potential by being aware of the options available for project management, automation, application settings reuse, media archiving and repurposing, and becoming aware of and even expert with these subjects.

Project management

Unless a project is, by, and for a single individual, its inception and design will involve more than one person. Getting those several minds to work in concert and agree on project specifications or deliverables, costs, and timeframes as well as to consensually adjust those agreements during the life of the project is what project management is all about.

Project management, of course, is the subject of many an entire book so we can only touch on a few key points here and then entreat you to pursue the matter further with books such as: Siegel, David *Secrets of Successful Web Sites: Project Management on the World Wide Web*, Hayden Books, 1997 (ISBN: 1-56830-382-3).

"Secrets..." is a delightfully written book that uses case studies of real-world projects and producers to examine how best to manage the creative process. While its focus is on the Web, the principles developed apply equally well to all other areas of QuickTime deployment and even beyond that.

The essence of that process is educating clients and oneself to the point where the task can be conceptualized and consensually understood in terms of goals and ways to achieve those goals. Finalizing the design must respect all who are involved and, finally, the contract and its execution must be amicable and faithful to that agreement. There are procedures that one can employ to assure these outcomes. Those procedures can be learned and incorporated into your workflow.

Automation

Many applications automate repetitive actions as a matter of course. Video applications such as Cleaner 5 (Discreet), HipFlicks (Totally Hip), Squeeze (Sorenson), and After Effects (Adobe) perform multiple operations on thousands of frames just to render an effect or compress a few minutes of video. To this we add the capability of batch processing which enables one to queue-up hundreds or even thousands of video clips to be compressed with various effects and filters being applied concurrently. Since batch processing can tie-up a high-end machine for days at a time, it's very important to make sure that batch settings will produce the desired effect. Doing test runs on small samples first can save days of processing.

These automated operations are usually modifiable, savable as settings, and can be combined with other actions either by the application itself or with the help of system-level scripting such as AppleScript on the Macintosh. As well, there are applications such as QuickKeys (CE Software) that create "macros" with which one can automate almost anything that can be done manually. Scripts and macros for common operations are often publicly shared such as the AppleScript collection for the QuickTime Player available from Apple Computer at www.apple.com/applescript/qtas.html. These scripts require Mac OS X but can be adapted to Mac OS 9 and earlier in most cases.

To illustrate the enormous amount of time that can be saved, let's cite just one example. Imagine that you're processing hundreds of video clips for web or CD deployment and want to make sure that copyright and other information is included. Just drop the icon of the folder containing these hundreds of files on the AppleScript "All Annotations Droplet" and the work will be done in a tiny fraction of the time it would have taken to do this manually. Here's a brief description from the URI cited above:

- All Annotations Droplet – This droplet can be used to set the value of all or some of the available for QuickTime files. If an annotation does not exist, the script will create it.

To access the preferences dialog and set the value for specific annotations, double-click the droplet, and then click the Set Prefs button in the main dialog window.

- The following are the names of the available annotations: "Album", "Artist", "Author", "Comment", "Copyright", "Creation Date", "Description", "Director", "Disclaimer", "Full Name", "Host Computer", "Information", "Make", "Model", "Original Format", "Original Source", "Performers", "Producer", "Product", "Software", "Special Playback Requirements", "Warning", "Writer".

There are a good many other pre-made scripts described at the same URL and we invite you to spend some time looking these over and downloading the ones you think that you may want to play around with first.

Scripts, macros, and application settings files received from others may not fit your needs exactly but they do provide a head start. Learning how to take a script that does almost what you want it to, for example, and modify it to do exactly what you want is an excellent investment of your time. Careful attention to understanding how these tools and application attributes work will prepare the content developer to take advantage of future opportunities to automate, save time, and enhance creative potential as a result.

Archiving

Many projects require experimentation to find the best way to combine various elements, discover optimal compression settings, etc. or they require multiple versions that are identical in all respects except file size for multi-venue delivery. Thus, archiving original source files is a critical part of ensuring that workflow isn't interrupted by the need to reacquire source media or re-create graphic elements because the originals were modified or not saved. It's also a good idea to archive projects at logical points (milestones) in their development. This kind of archiving enables one to take a new direction in a project without starting over or to develop multiple versions of a project that are different from one another but use the same source and, lastly, it enables one to pursue multiple work paths to find optimal solutions.

Another compelling reason for archiving is saving project files to be used in successive projects. Even if used only for reference, the time saved can justify the effort and resources required to archive. Beyond that, it's often possible to re-use scripts, macros, settings files, or even use an old project file as a shell for a new project simply by including new media.

Archiving digital media, however, is neither easy nor cheap. As media (Zip, Jaz, CD-R, CD-R/W, DAT tape, optical disk, hard disk, and analog formats such as film and BetaSP tape), compression options (proprietary formats such as Dantz Retrospect and more open formats such as *.sit, *.zip, *.gzip,) and data formats (Motion JPEG, JPEG, MNG, PNG, etc.) are evolving with greater speed and diversity than the paper protocols before them. It is incumbent upon the media developer to think long and hard about the format and the media used to archive data. Uncompressed digital video, for example, can consume vast amounts of media space so compression of some sort is almost mandatory. What lossless compression formats will enable us to work with this source in the future without unacceptable limitations? How long will the media used last? How do I recover from lost, damaged, or suddenly dysfunctional media? How easily must this media be accessible in order to be useful?

Reliable and useful archives are also dependent upon budget. Ideally, one should archive data in multiple formats and at multiple locations both for redundancy and for accessibility. These archives should be well catalogued, possibly with a media database, and reviewed periodically. The good news about digital media is that it can be replicated without generational loss. The bad news is that it's so easily damaged or destroyed and there is so much of it. A CD-R or CD-RW disc, for example, does have a finite life span. Not all CD-R and CD-RW media is alike in this respect. Archival quality media claims to have a life span in the 100 year range but the average is around 18 years. Bargain basement media may not last more than 2-3 years. If the media recorded on it doesn't get transferred to another CD-R or CD-R/W or other media before the end of that life span, the media recorded on it is lost. If that is the only copy of your media, that media is lost to posterity. It's also important to attend to format and file type issues. If the equipment and software available to you won't read the disk format or cannot comprehend the file type, it's useless to you. Transcoding from one lossless format to another before obsolescence is a better strategy than trying to maintain ancient hardware and software. This generalization also applies to both analog and digital archives.

Think twice, delete once. You must back-up in order to be able to go forward.

Assembling a good toolbox

The QuickTime architecture enables a wide variety of creative work. Mastering all of it at any significant depth would be an astonishing feat. Most QuickTime authors have a good grasp of one or two major facets and a lesser grasp of others. Some areas of QuickTime may even seem like foreign territory. The QuickTime landscape is that vast.

Thus, the contents and use of one's toolbox will vary depending upon the range and depth of your involvement with QuickTime. The videographers, VR photographers, multimedia developers, and compressionists may have some overlapping interests and involvement but they will likely develop different toolboxes. Even where they may use the same application, their involvement with that tool will be quite different. Others will trade depth for breadth or interoperate with other developers to assemble a sufficient range of QuickTime expertise. As well, the target audience will have a profound effect on tool choice as the focus shifts from film to disk-based video to web-based delivery formats.

Assembling a good toolbox, one that is appropriate to the range and depth of your QuickTime work, and learning how to use it effectively, has a great impact upon workflow. A search on the keyword "QuickTime" at http://guide.apple.com, which is a catalogue of over 19,000 products for the Macintosh, returned 528 references.

Selecting the right tool

As the search results quoted above reveal, there are many tools to choose from and there's overlap between and among them. Choosing QuickTime software to capture and edit digital video can range from the free iMovie through FinalCut Pro and Premiere to exotic and expensive hardware plus software NLE suites from Avid and Media 100. The old adage, "Horsepower costs money, how fast do you want to go?" applies quite well in this area of QuickTime. In other areas, the choice is less a matter of money and more to do with learning curves or feature sets. For many, all of these factors must be weighed very carefully.

Being aware of what others in your field are using is one important part of an effective tool selection strategy. Being a subscriber to the lists, newsgroups, and discussion boards frequented by those folks is imperative. Lurking (reading but not posting) may be your preference but contributing with questions and comments wherever possible will yield better results. Most professional lists are composed of civil people so fear of being flamed or embarrassed isn't something that should hinder you. Sometimes, the very act of putting a question into words will suggest a solution or bring heretofore-unrecognized insights to the surface.

The other part of selecting tools to work with is scanning the environment and being on the lookout for freeware, shareware, and commercial products that can be tried out before buying (the predominant business model for QuickTime-based software). Beta testing is an excellent variation on this theme. The reason that this kind of activity is necessary in addition to listening to your colleagues in the field is that their experience and opinions are only partially congruent with the demands of your work. There are still a great many things that you will have to figure out for yourself because of the uniqueness of your approach to the creation of digital media. This is R&D and may seem like something that can be put off to a more convenient time. Here's a thought to help stave off that debilitating urge: Today's R&D is tomorrow's air supply.

All of these efficiency techniques will combine to do two critically important things:

1. Maximize the time and energy available for the creative work that only you can do. Computers can be a great help in executing your vision but if you are too worn out to be creative and responsive to your audience, the end product will not command an audience.

2. Reducing the cost of creating digital media. Regardless of how your work is supported financially, if the cost of creating it is prohibitive, it simply won't get done. If your project management is poor, if you don't have the right tools or if you aren't using those tools to their fullest capacity, vast amounts of time and energy will be drawn away from the creative enterprise, possibly to unacceptable levels.

Of course, a great product is not enough. The old saying about the world beating a path to your doorstep if only you will build a better mousetrap is an illusion in today's market. Unless you are developing for yourself, you will need to be able to bring your hard-wrought media experience to an audience with great fidelity to your vision. In other words, it has to be deliverable.

Deliverability

What does a person need in order to experience a book? What does a person need in order to experience computer-rendered media? The answer to the first question will cite far fewer barriers than the answer to the second question. Experiencing digital media is inherently more demanding. We need to reduce or eliminate as many of those barriers as we can, just to come close to being as accessible as a book. Delivering QuickTime media requires the presence of an appropriate configuration of QuickTime on a supportive computer and certain other things that we need to have in place so as to assure the highest level of accessibility possible. This section deals with those things that the author can influence most: detecting and responding to the absence or inadequacy of the version of QuickTime that is available on audience computers, delivering the right version of your media, and embedding QuickTime content in HTML pages both on the Internet, on CD ROM, and via their local hard drive.

Detecting QuickTime and responding accordingly

The power of QuickTime doesn't come into play unless and until it is available on audience computer systems. The primary exceptions to this rule include film and DVD because these media don't require a computer to be experienced, even though QuickTime may have been involved in their production at some point.

For all the rest of QuickTime content (web, removable media such as CD, and local hard disk), we need to consider the issue of detecting and responding appropriately to the status of QuickTime on the host system. This is much more than a simple matter of "present" versus "absent."

QuickTime is now more than ten years old (see www.friendsoftime.org) yet the current version of QuickTime will play everything that was created in previous versions of QuickTime all the way back to version one. This level of backward compatibility is an amazing feat of engineering. Unfortunately, no team of software engineers anywhere has yet figured out how to do forward compatibility. Thus, we not only have to detect the presence of QuickTime, we also have to detect the version as well unless our media production avoids all of the wonderful enhancements to QuickTime that have been made available since 1991.

There is one more variable. Even if your audience has the latest version of QuickTime, they may not have all of the components needed to successfully play back your media. There are several possible reasons for this state of affairs. Most commonly, the audience hasn't downloaded a full version of QuickTime because they have a modem, the QuickTime installer provides the option to do a "Minimum Install" and they want to avoid a lengthy download. Detecting this condition in versions of QuickTime prior to version 5 is complicated and directing the audience on how to download a specific necessary component can be challenging as well. Fortunately, QuickTime version 5 introduced a feature called "component download." This feature solves the problem elegantly and works as described in the following scenario:

With a minimum install of QuickTime 5, the audience approaches your media. Let's assume that your media requires the lens flare effect, which isn't a part of the minimum install. As soon as they invoke your media, QuickTime 5 or later detects this deficiency, offers to download the missing component and, if permitted, installs it "hot" so that no restart is required. The audience is then able to experience your movie as you intended it with minimum delay. This system also extends to third party components that may not have even been available when QuickTime was last installed or updated. So, even if your audience is modem-bound and has only a minimum QuickTime installation to start with, they will eventually build up their systems in small, comfortable increments as they encounter more and more QuickTime movies with higher than minimum requirements. It's all quite painless after QuickTime 5.

For this reason alone, one should use QuickTime 5 as the minimum standard for your detection scheme. Once your audience has QuickTime 5 or better, updating is automatically prompted whether that be for an incremental improvement via component download as described above or the prompt to upgrade from version 5 to 6 that will come as soon as you encounter a movie that requires a core QuickTime 6 component such as the MPEG-4 codec. Of course, the audience will always have the option to be proactive and request the QuickTime Player to "Update Existing Software..." which will update without adding new components or run the QuickTime Updater to update existing components with the option to add new components, if available.

But what about CDs being played by people without Internet access? While Internet access is booming, not everyone with a computer has Internet access at the time they're experiencing your CD-based media. Fortunately, CD and DVD data disks are capacious enough to house complete standalone installers for both Mac OS and Windows so this issue is moot as far as providing the audience with access to a version of QuickTime that is adequate to your media. There are actually more ways to handle these detection chores on a CD than on the web.

Thus, our goal will be to detect the presence and version of QuickTime on the host system and then take appropriate steps to remedy any deficiencies by the most appropriate means available. The standard that we'll use is QuickTime 5 or better because that will provide us with component download as well as automatic, net-based updating. Alternatively, we'll be prepared to deal with those rare cases where immediately updating software isn't desirable.

Detecting the status of QuickTime on the host system: web

If your media is based partly or fully on the web, you'll be relying on the QuickTime plug-in because this is your gateway to QuickTime, the QuickTime Control Panel, and the QuickTime Player. A live Internet connection at some data rate is also assumed. The possibilities that we'll be testing for are:

1. QuickTime isn't present in any form

2. QuickTime is present but is pre-5.0

3. QuickTime is present and at version 5.0 or better.

Scripting solutions

To use a scripting approach, we have to assume that the browser is modern enough to support scripting and that scripting has been left to its default "on" status in the web browser preferences. Beyond that, we have to work around the fact that Internet Explorer doesn't support JavaScript access to Netscape-style plug-ins cross-platform and cross-browser as well as the fact that Netscape-style plug-ins aren't supported at all in recent Windows versions of Internet Explorer ((Win) 5.5 SP2 and newer). See the section on embedding QuickTime (below) for a more in-depth discussion of this factor.

Nonetheless, one can use a concoction of JavaScript, VBScript, and ActiveX to determine whether QuickTime is available or not. The scripts currently in use at: www.apple.com/quicktime/download/qtcheck/ do work most of the time. While this approach is serviceable for most occasions, it will fail if scripting isn't available for any reason.

QuickTime-based solutions

Using QuickTime to detect itself is actually the most reliable approach. But how can QuickTime know if it's not present? Well, it can't but there are ways around that little nattering detail. Simply develop an HTML page that uses a Meta-Refresh tag in the <HEAD> that looks like this:

```
<META HTTP-EQUIV="Refresh" CONTENT="30;URL=getQT5/dwnld_qt.html">
```

Essentially, this waits 30 seconds and then goes to another web page called, dwnld_qt.html. The page with the Meta-Refresh tag will also have an embedded movie. This will be a special kind of movie called a Reference Movie that will do our detective work for us if QuickTime 4 or better is present.

If QuickTime isn't present or too old to know what to do with reference and autoHREF movies (pre version 4), then the Meta-Refresh tag takes over after 30 seconds and redirects the audience to another web page that either encourages a download of QuickTime, making a strong argument for doing so, or provides alternate media such as a standard web page with JPEGs and GIFs instead of your more exciting media.

If QuickTime is present and is also new enough to know what to do with reference and autoHREF movies (QuickTime 4 or better), it will launch the movie before the Meta-Refresh tag can do anything and that reference movie will detect the exact version of QuickTime installed and launch one of several other movies. These other movies are a kind of movie, called an HREF Movie. At a minimum, there would be one HREF Movie for QuickTime 5 or better and one for less than QuickTime 5. The former would proceed with the intended media and the latter would prompt a QuickTime version update or show an alternate web page with JPEGs and GIFs instead of your more exciting media

Reference movies can be made with either Apple's free MakeRefMovie (http://developer.apple.com/quicktime/quicktimeintro/tools/) for MacOS and Windows or Peter Hoddie's XMLtoRefMovie (www.hoddie.net/xmltorefmovie). If you use XMLtoRefMovie, you may also be interested in Dave Egbert's helper application, QTRM Maker (http://homepage.mac.com/degbert/qtrm_maker.html).

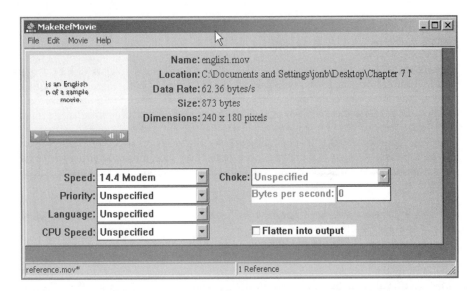

A reference movie (see: www.apple.com/quicktime/products/tutorials/refmovies.html and http://developer.apple.com/quicktime/quicktimeintro/tools/datarate.html) can detect network status, connection speed, language, CPU speed, and QuickTime version as well as set parameters such as choke speed and priority conditions. A minimum of QuickTime 3 is required for reference movies.

An HREF movie (see: www.apple.com/quicktime/products/tutorials/hreftracks.html for a tutorial on how to construct one using only a text editor and QuickTime Player Pro) is minimally a text track movie that passes an HREF tag to the web browser under certain conditions and at certain points on the timeline. Those conditions include mouse clicks and the end of a movie. An autoHREF does this automatically at a specific time in a movie. The HREF or autoHREF movie takes the form:

```
<URL> T<frame>
```

where the URL can be absolute or relative and the target can be a frame in an HTML frameset or the QuickTime Player. A minimum of QuickTime 4 is required for HREF movies.

Combination approaches

HTML Meta-Refresh tags can be combined with scripting and QuickTime self-detection to form a scheme that covers all possible contingencies and has few, if any, visual blemishes. Such a scheme has already been developed in such a way as to enable you to download a set of files that can be deployed throughout a QuickTime enhanced web site simply by dropping a folder into place and editing one HTML file. You can get in-depth information on this approach from: http://dopey.gcsu.edu/QTDR/. You can download the files from this site but they've also been provided with the attached CD, along with the site as it stood at the time of going to press – but please check for updates. Both are in the `Chapter12` folder, the HTML page is called `QuickTime Detection and Response (QTDR).htm` an expanded version of the archive is the `QTDR` folder which you should copy to your hard drive.

Elsewhere (CD, DVD, and local hard drive or kiosk)

If your media is based on removable media such as a CD or DVD data disk or is designed to be played from a local hard disk, you have additional options for the detection of QuickTime. Since these options are the same for all of these situations, we'll speak of CDs as a label for all forms of removable media and hard disks.

Another advantage of the CD environment over the web is that you're virtually assured that the audience has a stronger commitment to experiencing your media by virtue of the fact that they went to the trouble of acquiring the CD in the first place. This audience isn't as skittish as the web audience.

An easy and inexpensive way to develop a CD is to use HTML and a web browser. Think of this kind of CD as a web site that doesn't require an Internet connection. This approach allows the use of all the techniques that apply to the web that were described above so those need not be repeated here. To maximize the potential audience, this should be a Hybrid CD, one that can be used cross-platform (Macintosh and Windows, Roxio Toast is the premiere tool for creating Hybrid CDs). Put Mac specific files in the Mac partition (QuickTime installer for Mac, Web Browser, etc.) and Windows-specific and generic files in the other partition. A nice touch is to have a default HTML file in a prominent place on both partitions so the audience can get started with by double-clicking. Auto-starting a CD is something that you'll want to think twice about as this may be considered intrusive by many. Nonetheless, there are CD auto-start applications that will help you effect this (see: www.quicktimers.de).

Another, more elaborate, more expensive, and professional approach to developing a CD is to use applications such as Macromedia Director or iShell from Tribeworks. These high-end applications have built-in QuickTime detection capabilities. A QuickTime checker script written by Brennan Young for Director is included in Appendix C as an example. Here's how he uses it:

- Almost always I make a small ("stub") projector and keep the cross platform files separate from it, rather than wrapping them all up in the projector. This allows me to make best use of the space on a hybrid CD-ROM because the system-specific partitions only contain the Projector and Xtras. All other files are shared. In this way, the projector becomes more like a 'player', but of course, as author, you have control over which files it plays.

Responding to deficiencies in QuickTime

Now that we can figure out whether an appropriate version of QuickTime is present on the host system, it's time to think about what our responses will be to whatever those findings are. The positive result is easy: on with the show. A negative result requires some decision-making. There are two basic responses to determining that the status of QuickTime on audience computers is inadequate: redirection and remediation.

Redirection

The redirection strategy simply presents alternate media that isn't QuickTime dependent and preferably not dependent upon any other technology that might not be available by default. This alternate media might include a small notice that looks like, "You're not seeing the whole show. Download and install QuickTime (www.apple.com/quicktime/download) for a richer experience." A redirection strategy is usually reserved for those occasions where prompting the audience to download and install a substantial bit of software isn't a good idea, the home page of a web site for example. Redirection almost never refers to a CD because the audience has already committed to the CD by purchase or other means whereas a web site has no such upfront commitment to continue. Moreover, remediation in the case of a web site has many more barriers to completion than is the case with a CD or DVD data disk where a standalone QuickTime installer should be available. A free distribution license is available from Apple and details on that procedure may be found at: http://developer.apple.com/mkt/swl/agreements.html#QuickTime.

Remediation on the Web

Since bandwidth is a scarcer commodity on the Web than with a CD, the time it will take to download and install QuickTime becomes an important factor to consider in shaping a response strategy for the Web. Thus, we want to prompt an update over a full install whenever we can. Since our detection scheme can differentiate between QuickTime 5 or better on the one hand and no QuickTime or pre version 5 QuickTime on the other, we have only to decide how to handle these circumstances.

In the case of a version of QuickTime prior to 5, the most reliable approach is to prompt downloading the installer "stub," a small file that will enable the audience to do a full reinstall, minimum, or selective download of the latest version of QuickTime. The web page used to prompt this action needs to be as persuasive as you can make it. Reasons to cite include: free, easy, necessary to experience this really cool multimedia we've prepared for you.

In the case of QuickTime 5 or better, the best approach is to prompt an upgrade using the QuickTime Player. This will "Update Existing Software..." to the current version, which may require much less download time than a reinstall as described above. More than likely, this will be unnecessary as QuickTime will have prompted this upgrade on its own but there is the small chance that the QuickTime preference for auto-update has been changed from its default value (check for updates automatically) on audience systems. One clever way to do this is to have your reference movie invoke an autoHREF movie that targets and thereby launches the QuickTime Player showing a single graphic screen shot of how to select "Update Existing Software..." from the Player's Help menu. In that same graphic, include a text explanation of what to do.

As time goes on and there are fewer instances of QuickTime versions older than 5, this process can be reduced to even fewer steps.

Remediation on CD

A CD is so much faster than most Internet connections that doing a full install isn't a problem. So, test for QuickTime and be prepared to ask the audience to do a full install of QuickTime. It may also be a good idea to make sure that they note their QuickTime Pro license, if any, somewhere if they have version 4. If you're using HTML, an HTML hyperlink using a relative path can be used to provide the audience with a convenient way to launch the appropriate QuickTime installer (Mac OS or

WinOS). If you're using Director or iShell, use that environment to launch the appropriate QuickTime standalone installer as well as to play the media which includes QuickTime assets.

The installer can be customized to skip over most dialogs (except the license) making the installation faster and smoother than otherwise. Directions on how to engineer this are provided by Apple with the granting of the free license to distribute QuickTime on a CD (see: http://developer.apple.com/mkt/swl/agreements.html#QuickTime for details).

The QuickTime Pro 'nag' screen

One thing that you'll need to prepare your users for is the universally despised QuickTime Pro "Nag" Screen that pops up weekly with the QuickTime Plug-in and daily with the QuickTime Player. Comments about this and other input for QuickTime are received at quicktime@apple.com.

The nag will prompt your audience to upgrade to the "Pro" version, which may confuse some of your more naive users. Just tell them to ignore this and that they don't need it to experience your presentation.

Delivering the right version of a presentation

Maximizing the quality of the audience experience is often a matter of developing several versions of your media, each one optimized for a particular, definable segment of the audience. For example, your audience may be divided by the amount of bandwidth available to them, which is important to progressive download media and critical to real-time streaming. Some may be limited to analog modem delivery (28.8kbps to 56kbps), some may have ISDN, Cable Modems, or ADSL (128kbs to circa 8Mbs), others may have T1 or better connections (1.5 to 45Mbs) while still others are accessing your media via 100Mbs Local Area Networks or better. This is an enormous range.

You could simply create a lowest common denominator movie but that would subject the broadband audience to unnecessarily low levels of quality and performance. You could produce for the very high bandwidth movie but that would result in a much smaller audience and others would be either shut out entirely (real time streaming) or subjected to a long download before the media starts to play (progressive download).

Reference movies can pick up on the audience's connection speed and deliver a movie optimized for that level of bandwidth. Applications such as Cleaner 5 will do batch production of multi-data rate movies and even create the appropriate reference movie and associated HTML code for embedding your multi-data rate media in a web page.

Other factors that your reference movies can consider and respond to include CPU power (some codecs are so CPU-intensive that it may be wise to have different versions for high and low power CPUs), preferred language, and other variables. Perhaps the easiest way to get a good overall impression of what is possible is to launch the latest version of Apple's free MakeRefMovie and explore the interface.

Embedding media on a web page

Whether on an Internet web site or on a CD that uses HTML as the presentation vehicle, knowing how to embed QuickTime media in HTML is an essential skill set. There are about 40 embed tags listed at www.apple.com/quicktime/authoring/embed.html and described and exemplified through links from this page. Many of these have been described elsewhere in this book as well.

For those who rely upon HTML, it will be important to be conversant with embed tags and their use. It will also be important to be aware of the fact that there are other methods of including media in web pages and that those other methods are at odds with the embed approach.

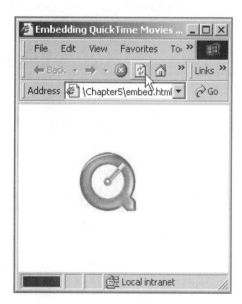

As mentioned previously, later versions of Microsoft Internet Explorer (IE 5.5 SP2 and IE 6) do not support Netscape style plug-ins. Instead, they require an Active X object and most of those objects do not support the embed tag. Instead, Active X objects require object tags. This requires a mixture of object and embed tags in order to assure that all web browsers can play your media.

Here is an example of how these tags can be mixed to cover the situation described:

```
<OBJECT CLASSID="clsid:02BF25D5-8C17-4B23-BC80-D3488ABDDC6B"
➥WIDTH="160" HEIGHT="144"
➥CODEBASE="http://www.apple.com/qtactivex/qtplugin.cab">
        <PARAM name="SRC" VALUE="sample.mov">
        <PARAM name="AUTOPLAY" VALUE="true">
        <PARAM name="CONTROLLER" VALUE="false">
        <EMBED SRC="sample.mov" WIDTH="160" HEIGHT="144"
➥AUTOPLAY="true" CONTROLLER="false" PLUGINSPAGE=
➥"http://www.apple.com/quicktime/download/">
        </EMBED>
        </OBJECT>
```

As you can see by comparing the object parameters with the embed parameters, they're nearly identical. The most significant part of the example above is where the path to the QuickTime Active X object is specified. With this, Windows versions of IE 5.5. SP2 and higher will download the QuickTime Active X object if it isn't already present or use it if it is present.

> This is very similar to what has to be done in JavaScript in order to get around Microsoft's implementation of that scripting environment. You've also seen this strategy in the QuickTime detection script where JavaScript and VBScript have to be used together to be able to communicate with Netscape style plug-ins.

The QuickTime Active X object, once installed, will work with both object and embed tags. In fact, it will work on Windows versions of IE 5.5 SP2 and higher even where there are no object tags. So, once you are assured that the audience has the QuickTime Active X object, you can rely exclusively on embed tags to invoke your media cross-platform and cross-browser but the safest strategy, especially with new material, is to use both object and embed tags redundantly.

Eventually, all browsers may support the object tag convention due to the fact that the World Wide Web Consortium (www.w3c.org) has endorsed the object tag as the preferred method (www.w3.org/TR/REC-html40/struct/objects.html) but that event will require the cooperation of all major web browser vendors and, as history shows, this doesn't happen often or quickly. This issue is addressed in detail for QuickTime authors at: http://developer.apple.com/quicktime/compatibility.html.

Summary

Workflow engineering involves shepherding resources and insuring delivery. As you choose those areas of QuickTime to focus most heavily upon, you'll find and develop more specific information but the principles enunciated here will serve you throughout.

Attending to project management principles, being diligent, staying abreast of what others like you are doing, and investigating how new tools and techniques fit or fail to fit your environment is an ongoing investment that will pay consistent dividends. Those hours won't be billable but they'll provide a return on your investment if done reflectively.

Delivering your media to the audience is the "last mile" and it's a critical mile. If the audience doesn't see your work, you may not be able to justify the effort you put into it. Surely, there will be additional challenges as competition for the eyes and ears of an increasingly demanding audience builds. QuickTime's architecture, being extensible as it is, will assure relevance well into the future. Investing in QuickTime as described here and elsewhere in this book will pay substantial dividends now and well into the future.

So, let's make movies!

A Appendix A: Web Links to QuickTime Compatible Products

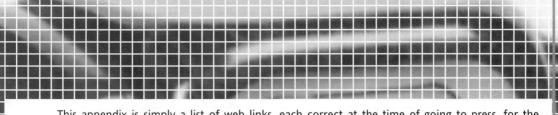

This appendix is simply a list of web links, each correct at the time of going to press, for the reader who wishes to find out more information on some of the many products that may be of use to the QuickTime developer. Many of these web sites are listed elsewhere in the book, but are repeated here in alphabetical order for ease of use.

Authoring applications

- Adobe After Effects www.adobe.com/products/aftereffects/main.html

- Adobe GoLive (Mac/Win) www.adobe.com/products/golive/main.html

- Adobe Premiere www.adobe.com/products/premiere/main.html

- Backbone Radio www.backbone.com

- cast: stream www.21stcenturymedia.com/products/overview.html

- Commotion Pro www.commotionpro.com

- Discrete Cleaner 5 www.discreet.com/products/cleaner

- Eline Technologies' VideoClix (Mac/Win) www.VideoClix.com

- EZediaMX www.ezedia.com

- Final Cut Pro 3 www.apple.com/finalcutpro/

- iMovie 2 www.apple.com/imovie/

- India Special Effects Titler www.dvfonts.com

- Live Channel www.channelstorm.com

- Macromedia Authorware (Mac/Win) www.macromedia.com/software/authorware

- Macromedia Director (Mac/Win) www.macromedia.com/software/director/

- Macromedia Flash (Mac/Win) www.macromedia.com/software/flash/

- Media 100 Cinestream www.discreet.com/products/cinestream/

- Media 100i www.media100.com

- MegaSeg www.megaseg.com

- MovieWorks DeLuxe www.movieworks.com

- QuickTime VR Authoring Studio http://guide.apple.com/action.lasso?database=macos guide&-layout=cgi_detail&-response=/ussearch/detail.html&prodkey=33499&-search

- REALVIZ Stitcher www.realviz.com/products/st/

- Sorenson Squeeze (Mac) www.sorenson.com/products/squeeze.asp

- Totally Hip HipFlicks (Mac/Win) www.totallyhip.com/lo/products/hfp/

- Totally Hip LiveSlideShow (Mac/Win) www.liveslideshow.com

- Totally Hip LiveStage Pro (Mac/Win) www.totallyhip.com/lo/products/lsp/

- Tribeworks' iShell www.tribeworks.com

- UPresent (Mac/Win) www.codeblazer.com

- VR Worx www.vrtoolbox.com

- Zoomifyer www.zoomify.com/zoomifyer/zoomifyer.asp

Free Authoring Tools http://developer.apple.com/quicktime/quicktimeintro/tools/

See: http://qtbridge.com/Tools.html for a very comprehensive listing. Much of this is in French, unfortunately.

Components

- Be Here: provides 360° live streaming Internet video www.behere.com

- Pulse: for creating and experiencing interactive, 3D animation www.pulse3d.com/about/quicktime.asp

- Streambox ACT-L2 Codec: delivers full-screen, full-motion video of VHS/DVD quality at 200 - 1200 Kbps www.streambox.com/products/act-l2_codec.htm

- Zoomify: A QuickTime Component that makes web images stream for fast initial display and on-demand viewing of fine details. Interactively zoom-in and explore gigabyte images, object movies, and even QTVR www.zoomify.com

- ZyGoVideo: provides high-quality video at prevalent modem rates (28.8 and 56 kbps) www.Zygovideo.com

B Appendix B: Embedding QuickTime with ActiveX

You can use an ActiveX control to embed your QuickTime movies in applications that support ActiveX controls on Windows like those of the Office suite. The detail is that the ActiveX control needs to be installed prior to both the authoring and the playback, so if you use an ActiveX control to deploy your content you'll need to include the installer for such ActiveX control you use. Here I'll use the QTVRControlX which allows you to embed QuickTime VR and just about any other type of QuickTime movie in any application that has support for the ActiveX control. Here I'm using such an ActiveX control to embed a QuickTime movie in MS Excel for Windows First download and install the ActiveX control which can be found at: http://members.fortunecity.com/birbilis/QT4Delphi/downloads/index.html

You can use the ActiveX control for free if you don't mind an alert box that says Unregistered every time you use it.

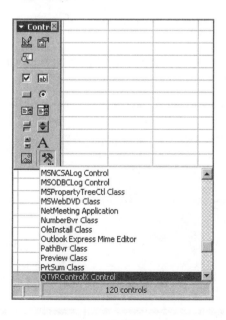

1.   Once the ActiveX control is installed, open MS Excel and from the View menu select Toolbars > Control Toolbox. This will bring up the Control Toolbox palette.

2.   From the Control Toolbox, click on the bottom right button that looks like two tools. A pop-up list will come up. Scroll down and select the QTVRControlX Control from the list.

3. The cursor turns in to a cross hair. With the cross hair drag out the area where you want the movie to appear.

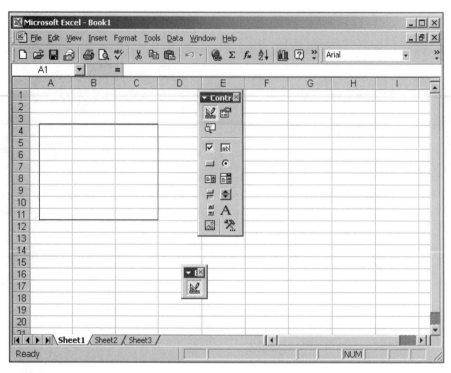

4. Right-click on the area you just drew and from the pop-up menu select QTVRControlX Control Object > Properties.

5. The QTVRControlX Properties window comes up. In the File name: field enter the name of the movie to add or browse until you find it with the ... button.

6. From the dialog box select the movie you want to embed in your Excel document. In this example we used the Chapter5\Coquitlam_video.mov file that we had previously copied to the Desktop.

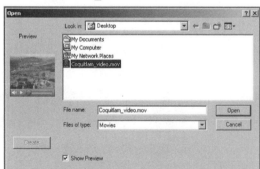

At this moment you may hear the audio of the movie playing.

7.   From the Control Toolbox palette click on the top left icon to exit the design mode.

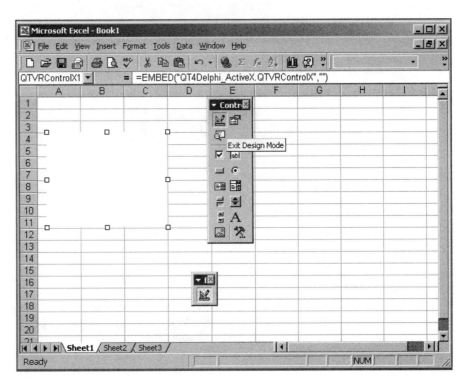

This will show the video for the movie but with no controller. If you click on the movie it stops; if you click twice it plays.

8.   To get the controller we need to set the properties for the object again. To do so click on the top left button for the Control Toolbox palette.

9.   Right click on the movie and from the pull-down menu select the QTVRControlX Control Object > Properties option.

10.   From the dialog box make sure that the controller visible option is checked.

11.   From the Control Toolbox palette click on the Exit Design Mode button, top left in the palette.

The movie should show up again but this time the controller should be visible and active, so you can control the playback of the movie from within.

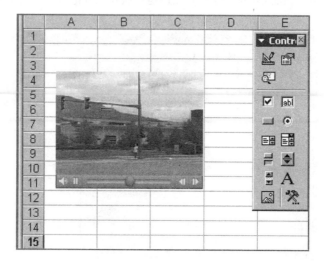

As you've seen QuickTime can be embedded within any application that supports the ActiveX control. On the other hand, we embedded a linear video movie using the QTVRControlX. QuickTime is flexible enough that this same process can be used for any other type of QuickTime movie including QuickTime VR (as the name of the ActiveX control implies), streaming QuickTime movies, audio files, and even MPEG-4 tracks if they're wrapped around a QuickTime movie, giving you the flexibility of adding rich media to applications that otherwise wouldn't be able to play these kinds of files. Remember, a QuickTime movie is more than just a linear movie!

C Appendix C: Lingo for Detecting QuickTime

This appendix contains a script example for a method of detecting the version of QuickTime installed, or lack of, on your users computer system. The in depth explanation of it is somewhat beyond the scope of the book, necessitating as it would a full explanation of the scripting language. There are pointers to web resources for further investigation throughout the book, of course if you intend using QuickTime with Macromedia Director in a complex manner the, friends of ED book, *Director Studio 8.5 (ISBN: 1903450691)* would be worthy of investigation.

You can use Lingo in Director to check for the existence (and version) of QT when your Director presentation is first launched. Then it's just a matter of telling Director where the QT installers are on the CD and dropping in an 'install' button.

See www.director-online.com/buildArticle.cfm?id=931.

This is an example of a code listing that would be coded as a Lingo behavior and attached to the first frame of a stub projector.

```
-- start Director code to detect QT & respond if deficient --

-- QT checker launcher
-- by Brennan Young
-- Based on code by George Langley
--
-- Check behavior inspector for documentation

property qtVersionRequired
property mainMovie
property installerLaunchQuitDelay
property MacinstallerPath
property WininstallerPath

on beginsprite me

  if checkForQT() then
```

```
    go to movie mainMovie
  else
   str = ""
   str = str & "No version, or an older version, of QuickTime has
been detected, "
   str = str & "and is required to view this presentation. The
installer will now be launched." & return
   str = str & "Please follow the directions as given, play the
demo file, then re-launch this presentation. Thank-you."
   alert str
   installerLaunchQuitDelay = 10 -- 10 frames to launch the
installer and then quit afterwards
  end if
end


-- we need a little delay to get the QT installer launched...
on exitFrame
 if installerLaunchQuitDelay > 0 then
  installerLaunchQuitDelay = installerLaunchQuitDelay - 1
 else if installerLaunchQuitDelay = 1 then
  halt -- we'll assume the installer has been launched
successfully, and we quit
 end if
 go the frame
end

on checkForQT
 qtversionRequired = float(qtversionRequired)
 if quickTimeVersion() < qtversionRequired then
  if the platform contains "Mac" then
  open MacinstallerPath
 else -- Windows
  open WininstallerPath
 end if
 else
  return true
 end if
end

on getPropertyDescriptionList me
 set pdlist to [:]
 addprop pdlist, #qtVersionRequired, [#comment:"Quicktime version
required", #format:#string, #default:"5.02"]
 addprop pdlist, #mainMovie, [#comment:"Relative path to main
movie", #format:#string, #default:"Main.dir"]
 addprop pdlist, #MacinstallerPath, [#comment:"Path to Quicktime
```

```
Installer (Mac)", #format:#string, #default:"@/Quicktime/quickTime
Installer"]
 addprop pdlist, #WininstallerPath, [#comment:"Path to Quicktime
Installer (Windows)", #format:#string,
#default:"@/Quicktime/quickTimeInstaller.exe"]
 return pdlist
end getPropertyDescriptionList


on getBehaviorDescription
 set str to ""
 set str to str&" QT checker launcher"&return
 set str to str&" by Brennan Young"&return
 set str to str&" Based on code by George Langley"&return
 set str to str&""&return
 set str to str&" Put this behavior in the framescript channel of
frame 1 of your stub projector movie"&return
 set str to str&" Be sure to adjust the path to the Quicktime
installer for both platforms before creating the projector"&return
 set str to str&" For more information about 'stub projectors' see
technote 14431 at the following URL:"&return
 set str to str&""&return
 set str to str&"
http://www.macromedia.com/support/director/ts/documents/d8_fast-
start_stub_proj.htm"&return
 set str to str&""&return
 set str to str&" This behavior will check for the latest versions
of QuickTime"&return
 set str to str&" on both Macintosh and Windows"&return
 set str to str&""&return
 set str to str&" Ensure that the QuickTime Asset Xtra is loaded
in the movie"&return
 set str to str&" or (preferably) in an "&quote&"Xtras"&quote&"
subfolder alongside your projector."&return
 set str to str&""&return
 set str to str&" Also ensure that a Quicktime installer is
included alongside your projector (or in a subfolder)"&return
 set str to str&" The default location for the installer expected
by this behavior is in a subfolder called 'Quicktime'"&return
 set str to str&" Note that "&quote&"@/"&quote&" indicates 'the
current folder', i.e. the location of the projector"&return
 set str to str&""&return
 set str to str&" Both the Mac and Windows self-contained"&return
 set str to str&" QT installers can be found at:"&return
 set str to str&"
http://www.apple.com/quicktime/download/standalone/"&return
 set str to str&""&return
 set str to str&" Be SURE to sign and send in the Quicktime
```

```
license agreement before distribution"&return
 set str to str&"
http://developer.apple.com/mkt/swl/agreements.html#QuickTime"&return
 set str to str&""&return
 set str to str&" TESTING:"&return
 set str to str&" to remove QuickTime from your computer to
test:"&return
 set str to str&" on Mac, launch the installer, click on
"&quote&"Custom"&quote&" install"&return
 set str to str&" and select "&quote&"Uninstall"&quote&" from the
pop-up menu."&return
 set str to str&""&return
 set str to str&" on Windows, use the De-install in your QuickTime
folder"&return
 set str to str&" in your Start Menu, and"&return
 set str to str&" be SURE to click "&quote&"Uninstall
Everything"&quote&"."&return
 return str
end
```

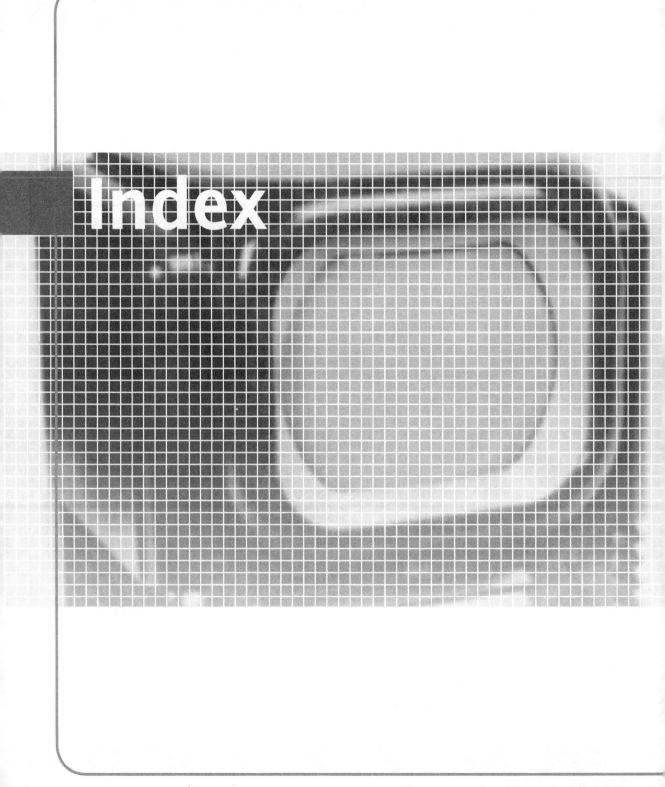

Index

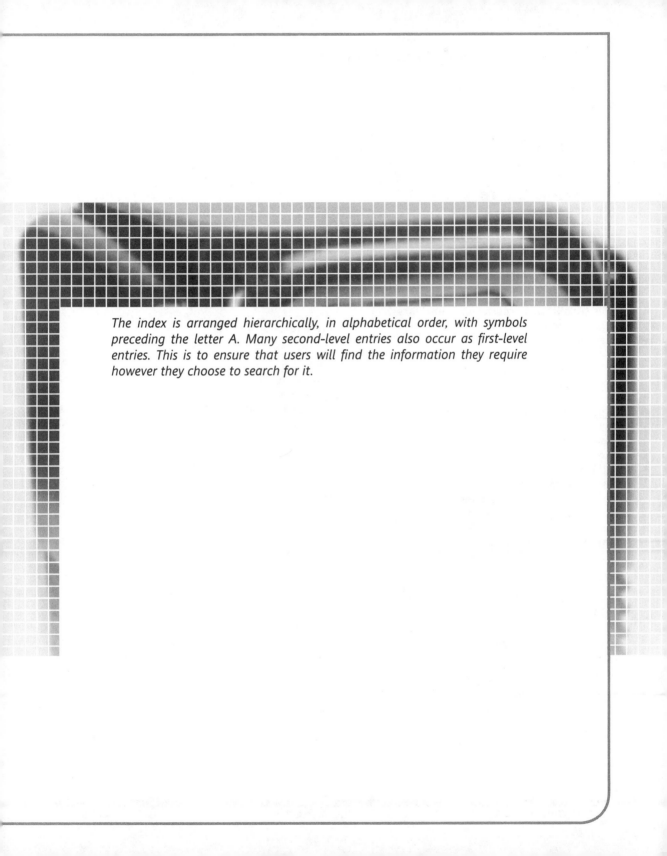

The index is arranged hierarchically, in alphabetical order, with symbols preceding the letter A. Many second-level entries also occur as first-level entries. This is to ensure that users will find the information they require however they choose to search for it.

Who this book is for

- Independent and aspiring filmmakers who need to gain professional competence in Final Cut Pro 2 – this book takes you from first look to intermediate level fast.
- Anyone wanting to learn FCP2 as an integral part of the digital filmmaking process

Praise for Revolutionary Final Cut Pro 2

Want to direct? Want to edit?, January 24, 2002

"Then this is the book for you. I've made 8 shorts now...and I wish I had this book 2 years ago! I've bought dozens of books over the last 3 years but this is the first one that's been wrote by real filmakers. How do I know? There are REAL tips in it. I mean those ones that come from really making a film...not the same moron advice that everyone gives. Buy this book if you're an editor or a director. Definitely if you're a director!"

clapperboard1998 from San Diego

The Brits do it again, February 14, 2002

"For some reason the British have the best graphics magazines...always the best reviews and tutorials. Thus it is no surprise that the book, Revolutionary – Final Cut Pro 2 by Blissett et al, is such a fine book. This book gives an excellent introduction to video production, in general, and FCP2 in particular."

Allen S. Melser from Rockville, MD United States

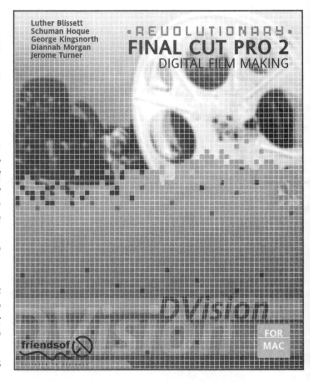

What this book covers

Whether you're putting together a wedding video, or making a production which will set you on your way to gaining your own star on the Hollywood Walk of Fame, this book will take you from a first look at Premiere 6 to professional competence, giving practical tuition at each step on all you need to know to fully master the skillset, including:

- Capturing and importing footage
- Performing edits, transitions, and composites
- Applying effects and animating clips
- Adding titles and exporting your finished movie

What this book covers

This book is for you if you're:

- New to Premiere 6 and value a thorough, practical and fast approach to learning
- A budding filmmaker looking to gain the skills that will lead to a career in the moving arts

This is a great book, February 28, 2002

"I can't quite put my finger on why I like this book so much. I think it has something to do with the fact it's a very 'warm' book... My editing has really improved in the last few weeks."

John Williamson from New York, NY

What this book covers

Whatever your level, DVision books deliver the core skills, advanced techniques and real-world case studies to send your digital video projects sky-high. Revolutionary After Effects 5.5 covers all you need to know, before you need to know it, backing up every piece of theory with solid practical tutorials:

- Setting up your hardware and importing material from a wide range of sources
- Compositing and building layers
- Animation and Effects
- Rendering your composite for DV or the Web
- Three full case studies – compositing a CGI animation, creating a web site banner, and enhancing a music promo – to put it all into practice

Who this book is for

Revolutionary After Effects 5.5 will radically improve your output if you are:

- A digital editor looking to advance your skills and polish your productions
- A digital artist wishing to enhance your skillset and quickly master a complex package

What this book covers

Final Cut Pro 3 is full of exciting new features, and this book covers them all, including:

- Real-time effects
- Color correction
- Adding voice-overs to your films
- The new media management tools

Plus an interview with Emmy nominated (*The West Wing*) Tina Hirsch, President A.C.E. (American Cinema Editors).

Who this book is for

This book is for you if you're already familiar with Final Cut Pro and need to get going with the sophisticated new features in Final Cut Pro 3. It focuses on what's new and doesn't go over old ground. So no more wasting time on books where only a fraction of the content is for you.

*Please note: If you're completely new to Final Cut Pro then you need a different book. **Revolutionary Final Cut Pro 3** from friends of ED DVision is the book you need. Not just an introduction to the software, it's a comprehensive primer in the fundamental techniques of digital video production.*

Who this book is for

- Anyone wishing to use Final Cut Pro 3 to edit digital video material to a professional competence
- Aspiring and independent filmmakers
- All who require expertize in post production in the filmmaking process

What this book covers

Revolutionary Final Cut Pro 3 Digital Post Production takes readers from the digitizing of footage through to the outputting of enhanced digital video. Focussing on how Final Cut Pro 3 can be utilized with other technologies to add SFX and titling, this book imparts knowledge acquired over many years from real-world filmmakers and editors and how that applies to the color correction, real-time, and other groundbreaking functionality that Apple have included in the latest release. There is an equal emphasis on output with serious consideration given to how choice of output – broadcast, DVD, Web, film – affect workflow decisions in the edit bay.

If you're serious about making movies, for whatever reason, then you need this book.

"I would like to thank you for doing this book because of the light it will shed on the editorial process."
Tina Hirsch A.C.E., President of American Cinema Editors

These words sum up much of what Transitions is about. It's a shedding of light; it's an empowerment of digital editors with the lessons and wisdom of the old ways. It speaks of the art of editing and the experience and even lifestyle of editing – showing digital editors that however shrouded in (and often obscured by) tradition and convention, this art is theirs. And it's now on the desktop – the technology has strengthened not diluted the art.

There is a great deal to being an editor. From the tricky decision of which cut to make first and the intricacies of building narrative, to the specifics of editing in genres, Transitions aims to capture the life and art of the editor, showing their overlap, indulging their differences, engaging in every author's unique experience and tapping into their hard-gotten wisdom.

Transitions is the ultimate resource for anyone who has learned the tool and wants to learn the technique, the art and the craft from the best.

Featuring an interview with Paul Hirsch – Oscar-winner for Star Wars!

www.DVisionaries.com

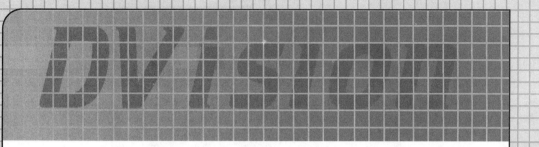

DVISION FROM FRIENDS OF ED DELIVER YOU TO THE
CREED PHILOSOPHY OF DIGITAL FILMAKING:

CREATE, **R**EALIZE, **E**DIT, **E**NHANCE, **D**ELIVER.

DVISION WILL GUIDE YOU ALL THE WAY
FROM THE GERM OF AN IDEA
TO OUTPUTTING YOUR CREATION TO DVD,
THE WEB, OR THE FORMAT OF YOUR CHOICE.

WWW.DVISION.INFO

Foundation Flash MX

What's Covered?

This book focuses relentlessly on the core skills that you need to get you started on your journey: understanding the interface; familiarizing yourself with the creative tools and their capabilities; grasping the relationships between a Flash movie's graphical, multimedia, text, and code ingredients; gaining insight into how to put all the pieces together and hook them up with ActionScript; and using ActionScript to articulate your movies and make them truly dynamic and interactive. All these aspects (and much more) are covered in detailed tutorials and exercises, reinforced with a case study that runs throughout the book and builds into a fully functional personal web site.

Who's it for?
Anybody who has never used any version of Flash before.

Flash MX Video

Go to Macromedia's web site, take a look at the list of the top ten features in the exciting new Flash MX release, and you'll find that the number one new feature is the ability to include genuine video material in Flash for the first time.

Hard work, some third-party software companies, and some work-arounds offered a tantalising glimpse of the potential for Flash presentations incorporating video for a select few Flash 5 designers. Now, Flash MX gives everyone the opportunity to use the dramatic impact of video in their site design, sure in the knowledge that the ubiquitous Flash player will allow their audience to view the results of their work.

friends of ED were the only publisher to take the increase of video use with Flash 5 seriously, and have substantial experience of publishing on Digital Video technologies with their DVision imprint. With Flash MX Video, they use this knowledge to take a reader from their first encounter with video to creating a dynamic Flash site with video and sound. The book includes:

- How to edit and prepare digital video before bringing it into Flash
- How to effectively load and use video in Flash
- A fully worked, real-world case study using digital video and sound
- The options for scripting with video

This book is not intended for those with substantial digital video experience and, as such, will not assume that the reader has access to any software apart from Flash MX.

For purchasing Revolutionary QuickTime Pro, Totally Hip is offering you a $100 USD special discount off the full purchase of our award-winning LiveStage professional QuickTime Authoring Tool.

LiveStage Pro is a QuickTime 5 Authoring Environment — LiveStage professional is recognized as the leading interactive digital video and interactive authoring solution. It integrates content from over 60 industry standard formats for video, audio, photographs, images, Flash, and VR into a single project and delivery solution. It works in a seamless cross-platform authoring, collaboration, and delivery environment. The tool to have for anyone wanting to create, produce, and deliver interactive QuickTime content.

LIVESTAGE PROFESSIONAL
LiveStage™ Professional
QuickTime 5 Authoring
Environment
www.totallyhip.com

To order the most recent version of LiveStage Professional at the special discount price, send us an email today!

Send email to: sales@totallyhip.com
Enter in Subject: QuickTime for the DVision special offer

totallyhip.com

Address:	Totally Hip Software, Inc.
	Suite 201-1040 Hamilton Street
	Vancouver, BC V6B 2R9
Phone:	1-604-685-6226
Fax:	1-604-685-4057

Not valid with any other offer. Applies to purchases of single units only.

Thank you for buying this DVision book. In order to help us produce the books that you would like to see in the future, please help us by filling out and returning this questionnaire to the address shown on the reply card at the back of this book:

Have you previously purchased other books from friends of ED?
- ☐ No
- ☐ Yes, but not DVision
- ☐ Yes, a different DVision title
- ☐ Yes, more than one DVision title

If you have already purchased a DVision book, which titles do you own?
....
....

How old are you?
- ☐ <21
- ☐ 21-35
- ☐ 36-55

Roughly how much do you spend each year on digital video products?
- ☐ $1000 or less
- ☐ $1000-5000
- ☐ $5000-10,000
- ☐ $10,000+

On average how much time do you spend using digital video products each week?
- ☐ 5 hours or less
- ☐ 5-20 hours
- ☐ 20-40 hours
- ☐ 40+ hours

How seriously do you take Digital Video?
- ☐ I'm just learning
- ☐ I do it for fun
- ☐ I want to do it for a living
- ☐ It's my job

What role(s) do you consider you play best in the production process:
....
....
....

Do you own or rent your digital video hardware?
- ☐ Own
- ☐ Rent
- ☐ Both

If both, please expand :
....
....

Where do you first look for information on digital video?
- ☐ Magazines/books
- ☐ Film groups
- ☐ Web sites

If web sites please tell us which ones:
....
....
....

If magazines please tell us which publications:
....
....
....

What do you need information on?
....
....
....

What other production processes, or digital video production skills would you like information on?
....
....
....

Where are you now with regards to digital video production, and where do you want to be?
....
....
....

Where do you buy usually books on Digital Video from?
- ☐ Online
- ☐ In major bookstores
- ☐ In independent/specialist bookstores

How would you like to access information on forthcoming DVision titles?
- ☐ Online
- ☐ Mailing lists
- ☐ Other, please specify
....

On average how much time do you spend online each week?
- ☐ 5 hours or less
- ☐ 5-20 hours
- ☐ 20-40 hours
- ☐ 40+ hours

friendsof

DESIGNER TO DESIGNER™

friends of ED writes books for you. Any suggestions, or ideas about how you want information given in your ideal book will be studied by our team.

Your comments are valued by friends of ED.

For technical support please contact support@friendsofed.com.

Freephone in USA	800.873.9769
Fax	312.893.8001
UK contact: Tel:	0121.258.8858
Fax:	0121.258.8868

Registration Code: 0527RC4849MIMU01

Revolutionary QuickTime Pro - Registration Card

Name ....

Address ....

City ....State/Region ....

Country ....Postcode/Zip ....

E-mail ....

Profession: film student ☐   freelance filmmaker ☐
part of an agency ☐   inhouse editor ☐
other (please specify) ....

Age: Under 20 ☐ 20-25 ☐ 25-30 ☐ 30-40 ☐ over 40 ☐

Do you use: mac ☐ pc ☐ both ☐

How did you hear about this book?...

Book review (name)..

Advertisement (name) ....

Recommendation ....

Catalog ....

Other ....

Where did you buy this book? ....

Bookstore (name) ....City..............................

Computer Store (name)...

Mail Order..

Other..

How did you rate the overall content of this book?
Excellent ☐   Good ☐
Average ☐   Poor ☐

What applications/technologies do you intend to learn in the near future?...

....

What did you find most useful about this book? ....

....

What did you find the least useful about this book? ....

....

Please add any additional comments ....

....

What other subjects will you buy a computer book on soon?

....

....

What is the best computer book you have used this year?

....

....

Note: This information will only be used to keep you updated about new friends of ED titles and will not be used for any other purpose or passed to any other third party.

friendsof

D E S I G N E R   T O   D E S I G N E R ™

NB. If you post the bounce back card below in the UK, please send it to:

friends of ED Ltd.,
30 Lincoln Road,
Olton,
Birmingham.
B27 6PA

BUSINESS REPLY MAIL
FIRST CLASS   PERMIT #64   CHICAGO, IL

POSTAGE WILL BE PAID BY ADDRESSEE

**friends of ED,
29 S. La Salle St.
Suite 520
Chicago Il 60603-USA**